Software
Requirements
& Specifications

ACM Press Books

This book is published as part of ACM Press Books – a collaboration between the Association for Computing Machinery and Addison-Wesley Publishing Company. ACM is the oldest and largest educational and scientific society in the information technology field. Through its high-quality publications and services, ACM is a major force in advancing the skills and knowledge of IT professionals throughout the world. For further information about ACM, contact:

ACM Member Services
1515 Broadway, 17th Floor
New York, NY 10036-5701
Phone: +1-212-626-0500
Fax: +1-212-944-1318
E-mail: ACMHELP@ACM.org

ACM European Service Center
Avenue Marcel Thiry 204
1200 Brussels, Belgium
Phone: +32-2-774-9602
Fax: +32-2-774-9690
E-mail: ACM_Europe@ACM.org

OTHER TITLES IN THE SERIES

Software
Requirements
& Specifications

a lexicon of practice, principles and prejudices

MICHAEL JACKSON

ADDISON-WESLEY PUBLISHING COMPANY

Wokingham, England • Reading, Massachusetts • Menlo Park, California
New York • Don Mills, Ontario • Amsterdam • Bonn • Sydney • Singapore
Tokyo • Madrid • San Juan • Milan • Paris • Mexico City • Seoul • Taipei

The programs in this book have been included for their instructional value. They have been tested with care but are not guaranteed for any particular purpose. The publisher does not offer any warranties or representations nor does it accept any liabilities with respect to the programs.

Many of the designations used by manufacturers and sellers to distinguish their products are claimed as trademarks. Addison-Wesley has made every attempt to supply trademark information about manufacturers and their products mentioned in this book. A list of trademarks and their owners are mentioned below.

Cover designed by Arthur op den Brouw
and printed by Oxted Press Ltd, Oxted, Surrey.
Typeset by Pantek Arts, Maidstone, Kent
Printed and bound in Great Britain by the University Press, Cambridge

First printed 1995.

ISBN 0-201-87712-0

British Library Cataloguing-in-Publication Data
A catalogue record for this book is available from the British Library.

Library of Congress Cataloging-in-Publication Data applied for.

Trademark notice
Eiffel™ is a trademark of Interactive Software Engineering Incorporated.
Kodak™ is a trademark of Eastman Kodak Company.
Simula 67™ is a trademark of Simula AS.
Smalltalk™ is a trademark of Xerox Corporation.

Addison-Wesley Publishers would appreciate any comments you have about this book. Please send any correspondence to the follwing email address:
ipc@awpub.add-wes.co.uk

FOR JUDY

Permissions

The publisher wishes to thank the following for permission to reproduce material in this book.

Quotations from: S. Schlaer and S.J. Mellor (1992) *Object Lifecycles: Modelling the World in States*; B. Meyer (1988) *Object-oriented Software Construction*; Poinsot quoted in M. Minsky (1972) *Computation: Finite and Infinite Machines*; E. Yourdon and L. L. Constantine (1979) *Structured Design*; C. Morgan (1990) *Programming from Specifications*; and T. DeMarco (1982) *Controlling Software Projects*. Reprinted by permission of Prentice-Hall, Englewood Cliffs, NJ. Alan M. Davis, *Software Requirements: Analysis and Specifications*, © 1990, p. 66. Reprinted by permission of Prentice-Hall, Englewood Cliffs, NJ.

H. Abelson and G.J. Sussman (1985) *Structure and Interpretation of Computer Programs*. Reproduced by permission of MIT Press. I. Jacobson (1992) *Object-oriented Software Engineering: A Use Case Driven Approach*, © 1992 ACM Press. A division of the Association for Computing Machinery Inc (ACM). With permission from the publishers, Addison-Wesley Publishers Ltd, Wokingham, England. W.P. Stevens, G.J. Myers and L.L. Constantine (1974) Structured design, *IBM Systems Journal*, **13**(2) 155–39, © International Business Machines Corporation. A.J. Ayer (1936) *Language, Truth and Logic*. Reproduced by permission of the publishers, Victor Gollancz Ltd, London. D. Ross (1977) Structured analysis (SA), *IEEE Software Engineering Transactions*, **3**(1) 16–37, © 1977 IEEE. Reproduced by permission. C. Babbage (unpublished manuscript, December 1837) *On the Mathematical Powers of the Calculating Engine Oxford*, Buxton MS7 Museum of Science. Reprinted by permission of Miss Elizabeth Buxton.

W. Swartout and Balzer R. (1982) On the inevitable intertwining of specification and implementation, *Communications of the ACM*, **25**(7) 438–40; and R.E. Johnson (1992) Documenting frameworks using patterns, *OOPSLA '92 Proceedings, ACM SIGPLAN Notices*, 27(10) 63–76, © ACM Press. A division of the Association for Computing Machinery Inc (ACM). Quotation from Punch cartoon, March 1869, © Punch Publications Ltd. Reproduced by permission of Punch.

P. Naur and B. Randell (eds), (1969) *Software Engineering Report on a Conference Sponsored by the NATO Science Committee* Garmisch, Germany 7–11 October 1968. E.W. Dijkstra (1965) Programming considered as a human activity, *Proceedings of the IFIP Congress* 213–17. © 1965 Elsevier Science B.V. B.W. Kent (1974) *Data and Reality* Reprinted with kind permission from Elsevier Science B.V., Amsterdam, The Netherlands. © 1974 Elsevier Science B.V. Quotation from De Marneffe in E. Knuth (1974) Structured programming with go to statements, *ACM Computing Surveys*, **6**(4) 261–301. Lewis Carroll (1871) *Through the Looking Glass* Macmillan. P. Kraft (1977) *Programmmers and Managers: The Routinization of Computer Programming in the US*, © 1977 Springer-Verlag GmbH.

Diagram on p. 91 from D.J. Hatley and I.A. Prihbhai (1988) *Strategies for Real-Time System Specification* Dorset House Publishing Co.

CONTENTS

FOREWORD

I first met Michael Jackson in 1975, in Chapel Hill. He delivered a lecture at the University of North Carolina on his recent book. That hour gave me a deep understanding of years I had spent as a COBOL programmer. The scales fell from my eyes, and I saw in his JSP FRAME a systematic way of deriving programs that I had previously generated by guesswork, intuition and rote. I went on to study his classic Principles of Program Development. I immediately had great respect for the book and its author, and that respect has deepened over the years.

When I read this wonderful new book, it reminded me of a popular saying in Chapel Hill: 'If you don't like the weather, just wait a while.' It is guaranteed to change, from one pleasant climate to another. This book is the same, an unordered collection of pieces, each delightful in a different way.

Some pieces present formal methods, precise and elegant and beautiful. Michael's treatment of The Bridges of Königsberg, for instance, rephrases Euler's seminal problem of graph theory as an exercise in specification. The subtle answer jumps out to any programmer, and a powerful technique is taught well and gently. Such passages are expected from a leader in the software development field.

But if that doesn't tickle your fancy, just wait a short while. The very next piece is an insightful war story that could be collected and told only by a veteran software engineer. Michael's time in the trenches allows him to see that true BRILLIANCE manifests itself in simplicity. Michael knows programs and people.

And so the pieces of this book will flow past you, in whatever order you choose to read them. You will move from principles to examples, from theory to practice, and from tiny toy problems to insightful glimpses of huge systems. Along the way you'll survey a variety of useful problems and problem domains.

Although the form of the book varies, its deep message is clear in every piece. If software is to become an engineering discipline, we must deal with precise and useful requirements and specifications. When you finish this book, you will agree with Michael that 'Description is at the heart of software development.'

If this book has a flaw, it is a flaw it shares with Fred Brooks's *Mythical Man Month*, which also came from Chapel Hill in 1975. This book is so delightful to read, you may forget that you're learning something. But don't be fooled by the book's grace and charm – there is real substance here. After you skim a piece, go back later and re-read it in detail. You'll see more the second time around, and you will become a better software engineer.

Jon Bentley
May 1995

PREFACE

The *practice* of the book's title is the practice of software development, especially of the requirement and specification activities that often precede programming. The *principles* are those that I believe should govern software development and the methods by which we try to make it easier and more effective. And the *prejudices* are the settled personal opinions that I have formed over some years of thinking about these things.

The central theme of the book is the relationship of method to problem structure on one side and to description on the other. To deal with a significant problem you have to analyse and structure it. That means analysing and structuring the problem itself, not the system that will solve it. Too often we push the problem into the background because we are in a hurry to proceed to a solution. If you read most software development texts thoughtfully, you will see that almost everything in them is about the solution; almost nothing is about the problem.

On the other side, description is important because it is the clay in which software developers fashion their works. Methods are, above all, about what to describe; about tools and materials and techniques for descriptions; and about imposing a coherent structure on a large description task.

This book does not explain or advocate one particular development method. Nor is it a survey of methods, or an encyclopaedia of techniques and notations. It explains what I hope and believe are useful ideas and insights – both my own and other people's. It is arranged as an alphabetically ordered set of short pieces forming a *lexicon*, or a kind of specialized dictionary. Because many of the ideas are neglected or simply unfamiliar, the selection of topics, the content and some of the terminology are unconventional. This is not in any way meant to be a standard reference work.

I chose the dictionary form for two reasons. First, because a more structured arrangement would have seemed to promise a unity and a completeness that I cannot attain. This is a collection of ideas and insights, not a new method. Second, putting the same point more positively, because I believe that many of the ideas in the book can be applied piecemeal in many different development contexts. They can be used to make local improvements in established methods, and to shed light on some of the local difficulties and problems that are met in any development.

Software development should be a thoughtful activity. You should think not only about the problem and its solution, but also about the way you're tackling it. Some software developers and method users behave as if they were bicycle riders. When you are riding a bike you shouldn't think about what you're doing. If you do think about it you'll probably fall off. But software development isn't like bike riding. You'll be a much better developer if you think consciously about what you're doing, and why. This book is intended to help you.

When you encounter a difficulty in software development, what you need above all is a set of appropriate conceptual tools. Perhaps you're trying to describe something that stubbornly refuses to fit cleanly into your description; or to disentangle the simple problems that you feel sure must lie beneath the intractable complex problem that is holding you up. The right conceptual tools help you to think consciously about what you're doing, often just by providing names for concepts that you already had but never articulated. So when you're struggling to get a description right it's helpful to be able to ask yourself: Have we got the right description *span* here? Are we sure we understand the *designations* well enough? Have we made a spurious *classification*? And when you're dealing with a problem complexity it's helpful to be able to ask yourself: Is this a *multi-frame* problem? Is there a *problem frame misfit* here? Are we trying to look at *shared phenomena* from the point of view of only one *domain*?

I hope that the lexicon form of the book will work to underline its nature. It is offered as a resource from which you can take what you want, not as another orthodoxy that demands acceptance or rejection as a whole. The arrangement of the book, I hope, will encourage you to browse and skip from piece to piece, and I don't expect it to be read straight through. Inevitably, this has led to some repetition, but not enough, I hope, to seem tedious. I have tried to make each piece self-contained but, of course, that is not always possible, especially for some of the pieces about less familiar ideas – such as problem frames. So there is a full index, and cross-references, capitalized in the text, from each piece to other relevant pieces. If you're feeling puzzled by a piece it may be a good idea to follow some of the cross-references in its earlier paragraphs before reading on.

If you prefer to read more systematically, you could start with the Introduction, which comes, out of alphabetical order, at the beginning. The Introduction lays out some of the main ideas, and puts them in context. Then you can follow the cross-references from the Introduction to anything that catches your interest, and so onwards from one piece to another. There is a bibliography that expands the short and informal references – both to books and to their authors – appearing in the text and adds a few bibliographical notes.

Another way of using the book is by taking a tour around one theme or topic at a time. I've prepared some itineraries of tours you might take. Most of them are quite short and don't try to include everything about their themes. You can take them in any order. As with most tours, the time needed will depend on how long you spend on the places of interest. Some places of interest appear in more than one tour. If you visited a place on a previous tour, you could stay on the bus. On the other hand, you might see something you hadn't noticed on your first visit.

An Overview
    Introduction → Descriptions → What and How → The Problem Context → Problem Frames → Method

The Nature of Software Development
    Software → Aspects of Software Development → Software Engineering → Deskilling → Mathematics

The System and the World
    Machines → What and How → The Application Domain → Implementation Bias → Domains → Context Diagrams → Domain Interactions → Shared Phenomena → Connection Domains

Some Aspects of Method
    Brilliance → Method → Deskilling → Problem Sensitivity → Polya → Frame Diagrams → The JSP Frame → Procrustes → The Fudge Factor

Different Kinds of Description
    Descriptions → Designations → Refutable Descriptions → Logical Positivism → Definitions → Rough Sketches

Describing the World
    What and How → Domain Characteristics → Phenomena → Individuals → Predicate Logic → Ambiguity → Informal Domains → Object-Oriented Analysis → Hierarchical Structure

Phenomenology
    Phenomena → Individuals → Identity → Existence → Is → The Narrow Bridge → Reification → Events and Intervals

The Technology of Description
Designations → Classification → Scope of Description → Span of
Description → Arboricide → The Bridges of Königsberg → Entity–
Relation Span

Being Precise
Dekker → Mathematics → Critical Reading → Designations → Top–
Down → Dataflow Diagrams → Rough Sketches → Restaurants →
Specifications

Analysing Problems
Problem Sensitivity → The Problem Context → Problem Frames →
Frame Diagrams → The JSP Frame → The Calendar → Problem
Complexity

Problem Complexity
Problem Complexity → The Calendar → Problem Frames → The
Package Router Problem → A Multi-Frame Problem → Hierarchical
Structure

Structures of Descriptions
Trip-lets → Partial Descriptions → Models → Moods → Requirements
→ Implementation Bias → Composition → A Multi-Frame Problem

Languages and Notations
Raw Materials → Poetry → Graphic Notations → Tree Diagrams →
Designations → Predicate Logic → Entity–Relation Span

Problem Frames
The Problem Context → Polya → Problem Frames → Simple IS Frame
→ Simple Control Frame → Connection Frames → Workpieces Frame
→ The JSP Frame → Misfits

Whatever your approach to this book I hope it will be useful to you: that
you will find something in it to help you in your work, to illuminate a difficulty you have struggled with, to offer amusement or insight, to provoke
you to thought, or in any other way to repay you for having opened it.

Michael Jackson
May 1995

ACKNOWLEDGEMENTS

Much of my working life so far has been occupied with devising, teaching, and using software development methods. In the 1970s and early 1980s I was deeply involved in the JSP method of program design and the JSD method of system development. Some of the themes and ideas of this book emerge indirectly from the successes of that work; some from its failures. I learned a lot from the many people I worked with during those years – especially from John Cameron.

I also learned a lot, although I did not always realize it at the time, from some people whose ideas about method were diametrically opposed to my own. As Mark Twain said: 'When I was a boy of fourteen, my father was so ignorant I could hardly stand to have the old man around. But when I got to twenty-one I was astonished at how much the old man had learned in seven years'.

Many of the ideas in this book have been formed and sharpened during several years of cooperation with Pamela Zave. Particularly, they have been influenced by her approach to multiparadigm specification, and have benefited from the insightful work that she has done in cooperation with Peter Mataga on specifying telephone switching systems.

Daniel Jackson has helped me in more ways than I can count. He read the whole book in at least two of its versions and commented in detail on every part of it. He explained many things I had not known or had misunderstood. He discussed many of the topics with me at length. And he has always been ready to offer advice, encouragement, and constructive criticism at just the right moments. As a small recompense I have stolen a quotation by Niels Bohr from his PhD thesis.

Some of the ideas in the book have been aired at meetings of the Software Development Research Group of the University of the West of England, Bristol. I am grateful to the other members of the group – Barry Cawthorne, Ian Beeson, Richard McClatchey, Steve Probert, Tony Solomonides, and Chris Wallace – for their interest and help. Chris Wallace introduced me to the work on patterns in object-oriented design.

Tom DeMarco helped me generously with many acute and sensitive comments. His suggestions have removed many stumbling blocks from the reader's path.

Much of the treatment of Dekker's algorithm follows the presentation in Dick Whiddett's book *Concurrent Programming for Software Engineers*.

Andy Ware of Addison-Wesley has been unfailingly tolerant and courteous to an unreasonable and curmudgeonly author. And Susan Keany has been an agreeable and efficient production editor. It has been a pleasure to work with them both.

To all these people, and to everyone else who has helped me, I am very grateful.

INTRODUCTION

Software development has many aspects. David Gries sees it as logic and mathematics. Enid Mumford sees it as a socio-ethical challenge. Kristen Nygaard sees it as a field of labour employment relations. Watts Humphrey sees it as a problem in manufacturing process control. Other people see it as a kind of engineering – an activity of building useful things to serve recognizable purposes. I'm one of those people. The engineering aspects interest me most. So of course I claim that they are the most important.

The Machine and the World

To develop software is to build a MACHINE, simply by describing it. This is one good reason for regarding software development as engineering. At a general level, the relationship between a software system and its environment is clear. The system is a machine introduced into the world to have some effect there. The parts of the world that will affect the machine and will be affected by it are its APPLICATION DOMAIN. That's where your customers will look to see whether the development has fulfilled its intended purpose. You don't gauge the success of a theatre reservations system by looking at its computers. You look at the world outside. Can people book seats easily? Are the theatres full? How long does it take to pick up a ticket? Are all the credit card payments properly accounted for? Are cancellations handled smoothly?

This distinction between the machine and the application domain is the key to the much-cited (but little understood) distinction between WHAT AND HOW: *what* the system does is to be sought in the application domain, while *how* it does it is to be sought in the machine itself. The problem is in the application domain. The machine is the solution.

Focusing on Problems

An inability to discuss problems explicitly has been one of the most glaring deficiencies of software practice and theory. Again and again writers on development method claim to offer an analysis of a problem when in fact they offer only an outline of a solution, leaving the problem unexplored and unexplained. Their readers must work out their own answers to the question: If this is the solution, what was the problem? Ralph Johnson, a leading advocate of design patterns in object-oriented development, has this to say:

> 'We have a tendency to focus on the solution, in large part because it is easier to notice a pattern in the systems that we build than it is to see the pattern in the problems we are solving that lead to the patterns in our solutions to them.'

That's unfortunately true. And this tendency to focus on the solution has been harmful both to individual development projects and to the evolution of methods. Many projects have failed because their REQUIREMENTS were inadequately explored and described. The requirements are located in the application domain, where the problem is; but in most developments all the serious documentation and discussion focuses on the machine which is offered as a solution to the problem. At best there will be a careful description of the coastline where the machine meets the application domain. But the hinterland of the application domain is too often left unexplored and unmapped.

Domain Descriptions

Paying serious attention to the application domain means writing serious, explicit and precise DESCRIPTIONS. Don't think it's good enough to interview a few people and make a few rough notes. Don't say: 'Everyone knows what you do when you book a theatre seat', or 'Everyone knows that the seats become available when the show is scheduled'. What everyone knows is often wrong, and always very far from complete.

Above all, don't think it's good enough to describe the processing that your system will do. If you think of your system as processing input and output flows of data, then the application domain you must describe is what's at the other end of those flows. If you think of your system as processing transactions, or operations, or use-cases, then the application domain you have to describe is the world where the transactions or operations or use-cases are initiated. The processing of the data flows, or transactions, or operations, or use-cases is what the machine does. It's part of the solution, not part of the problem. Leave it till later.

Modelling

There's a big temptation to believe that you can describe the application domain and the machine all together, in one combined description. The justification for this belief is that some part of the machine is often a MODEL of some part of the application domain. That means that there's some description that's true both of the machine and of the application domain. So why not just write that description and save some duplication of effort?

Here's why. A description of a modelling relationship is always incomplete: there's more to say about the application domain, and more to say about the machine too. You need to say those things somewhere. You ought not to say them in the common description, because they're not common. In principle you really need three descriptions: the common description; the description that's true only of the machine; and the description that's true only of the application domain. If you make all of those descriptions, and separate them carefully, you'll be all right.

But if you make only one description, you will surely be tempted to put things into it that describe only the machine, and to leave out things that describe only the application domain. After all, you have to describe the machine sooner or later, don't you?

You can see the results clearly in many object-oriented modelling descriptions. Often they are accompanied by fine words about modelling the real world. But when you look closely you see that they are really descriptions of programming objects, pure and simple. Any similarity to real-world objects, living or dead, is purely coincidental.

Description Technique

Description is at the heart of software development. It is not an exaggeration to say that the whole business of software development is making descriptions. Programs are descriptions of machines; requirements are descriptions of the application domain and the problems to be solved there; and specifications are descriptions of the interface between the machine and the application domain. Every product of development is a description of some part or aspect or property of the problem or of the machine or of the application domain.

That's why the techniques of description are of prime importance for developers. The importance of some issues of descriptive technique is well recognized: language is obviously important, because language is the RAW MATERIAL of description. But some other aspects have not been given their due prominence:

- DEFINITION. You must distinguish between defining new terms and using existing terms to make statements. Without this distinction it's impossible to know whether you're talking about the world or talking about the terminology for talking about the world. Yet it's a distinction that's often ignored or blurred.

- Description SCOPE and SPAN. The scope of a description restricts the *classes of phenomena* it can talk about. The scope of a world rainfall map is different from the scope of a world population map. The span restricts the *area of the world* it can talk about. The span of a rainfall map of France is different from the span of a rainfall map of Italy. If you choose the wrong scope or span for a description you've shot yourself in the foot. You'll find your work can only limp along.

- REFUTABLE DESCRIPTIONS. Most – perhaps all – of your descriptions should be refutable. A refutable description says something precise about the world that could be refuted by a counter-example – for example: 'No company employee works on more than one project at any one time'. Find an employee working on two projects at one time and you have shown conclusively that the description is not true. Descriptions that can't be refuted don't say much.

- PARTIAL DESCRIPTION. Because the application domain is usually large and complex, you need ways of *separating concerns*. That just means not thinking about everything at once, but structuring a complex topic as a number of simpler topics that you can consider separately. Structure is even more important in analysis than in program design.

- HIERARCHICAL STRUCTURE is one way of separating concerns. Usually it doesn't work well and some kind of parallel structure is better. The separation of a coloured picture into cyan, magenta, yellow, and black overlays is a better metaphor for description structuring than the hierarchical assembly structure of parts in manufacturing. Hierarchical structure is the sand on which TOP-DOWN methods are built.

- It's important to separate descriptions of different MOODS. A description in the *optative* mood says what you want the system to achieve: 'Better seats should be allocated before worse seats at the same price'. A description in *indicative* mood says how things are regardless of the system's behaviour: 'Each seat is located in one, and only one, theatre'.

Methods and Problem Frames

Failure to focus on problems has harmed many projects. But it has caused even more harm to the evolution of development METHOD. Because we don't talk about problems we don't analyse them or classify them. So we slip into the childish belief that there can be universal development methods, suitable for solving all development problems. We expect methods to be panaceas – medicines that cure all diseases. This cannot be. It's a good rule of thumb that the value of a method is inversely proportional to its generality. A method for solving all problems can give you very little help with any particular problem.

But have you ever read a book on a development method that said: 'This method is only good for problems of *class X*'? Probably not. It's not surprising, because without an established discipline of analysing and classifying problems there can't be a usable vocabulary of *problem classes* X, and Y, and Z.

Classifying problems and relating them to methods is a central theme of this book. The crucial idea here is the idea of a PROBLEM FRAME, derived from the work of POLYA. A problem frame defines a problem class, by providing a ready-made structure of *principal parts* into which all problems of the class must fit. Whether a particular problem fits a particular frame depends on the structure and characteristics of the application domain, and the structure and characteristics of the requirement.

A good method addresses only those problems that fit into a particular problem frame. It exploits the properties of the frame and its principal parts to give systematic and sharply focused help in reaching a solution. This means that the power of a method depends on the quality and precision of the frame. There's a principle here:

- *The Principle of Close-Fitting Frames*
  The purpose of a problem frame is to give you a good grip on the problem. So the frame must define and constrain the problem very closely indeed.

You can't work effectively on a problem that's wobbling around in a sloppy, loose-fitting frame.

Problem Complexity

The largest description structures in software development are the structures that arise from PROBLEM COMPLEXITY. A complex problem is a problem that cannot be completely accommodated by any available frame and completely solved by any available method. You need more than one view of the same problem. That's not just taking more than one view of the machine – for instance, data, function, and state transition, or class hierarchy, object aggregation, and object interaction. It's more like recognizing that the same problem is simultaneously a control system problem, an information system problem, and a message switching problem. It's a MULTI-FRAME PROBLEM.

The task, then, is to separate out the different problem frames in their parallel structure. Identify the principal parts of each frame; and identify the overlapping parts and aspects of the application domain and requirement that they cover. This is the essence of problem decomposition. When you separate a problem by problem frames, you're separating it into simpler sub-problems *that you know how to solve*. Then you have a real chance of mastering the complexity that is found in every realistic software development.

THE LEXICON

Ambiguity

Everyone has a favourite example of ambiguity in natural language. My own favourite is the pair of signs I saw displayed at the foot of an escalator in an airport:

What do they mean? If I want to travel on the escalator I must be wearing shoes. So, by the same token, if I want to travel on the escalator I must be carrying a dog. No, surely that's not right – let's try again. If I want to travel on the escalator and I have a dog with me, then I must carry the dog. So, by the same token, if I want to travel on the escalator and I have some shoes with me I must wear the shoes. That seems reasonable. But unfortunately, I had just been shopping, and was carrying a bag containing two pairs of new shoes in addition to the pair already on my feet. I can't wear three pairs of shoes at once.

You can dispel this kind of ambiguity by a little thought and common sense. And when you've dispelled it you can stop it coming back by a little formalization. In PREDICATE LOGIC the sign on the left must mean something like this:

$$\forall x \bullet (\text{OnEscalator}(x) \rightarrow$$
$$\exists y \bullet (\text{PairOfShoes}(y) \wedge \text{IsWearing}(x,y))$$

For each individual x that is on the escalator, there is at least one y such that y is a pair of shoes and x is wearing y. And the sign on the right must mean:

$$\forall x \bullet ((\text{OnEscalator}(x) \wedge \text{IsDog}(x)) \rightarrow \text{IsCarried}(x))$$

For each individual x that is on the escalator and is a dog, that individual x is being carried.

I hope you're not satisfied that we've dispelled the ambiguity altogether. Because the world of people and dogs and escalators in airports is an INFORMAL DOMAIN; just formalizing it leaves many questions unanswered. Do dogs really have to wear shoes – or was that an error in the formalization? What counts as a pair of shoes? What counts as wearing them? And what, exactly, is a dog? You need a set of DESIGNATIONS to answer these questions.

Did you also wonder why the formalizations say that dogs *are* carried and shoes *are* worn, but the notices say that dogs *must be* carried and shoes *must be* worn? I hope you did. It's an important difference in meaning: the formalizations are in the *indicative* MOOD, while the notices are in the *optative* mood. Being very precise isn't easy.

The Application Domain

You can think of a software development problem as a problem of constructing a machine. A word-processing system is a machine, just like a typewriter. A telephone switching system is a machine, just like an old-fashioned exchange with clattering relays and rotary switches. An information system is a machine, just like those mechanical address book gadgets that open to the page you want when you press the button with the right initial letter. Of course, in every case the machine implemented in computer software is vastly more versatile and powerful; but it's still a machine.

The purpose of the machine is to be installed in the world and to interact with it. The part of the world in which your machine's effects will be felt, evaluated, and – if you are successful – approved by your customer, is the application domain. I'm using the term *application domain* to mean something entirely specific to the problem in hand. Not a generic domain, denoting a class of applications, as in the phrases *the banking domain*, or *the telephone switching domain*, or *the command and control domain*; but this particular company's employees, this particular aeroplane's control surfaces, these particular suppliers and products and orders. The application domain is where your particular customer's requirements are to be found. If you don't identify the application domain correctly, you won't be able to focus on your customer's requirements.

I use the term application domain rather than *environment*, because environment, to me, suggests something that physically surrounds the machine. But the application domain can include intangible things like the graphic images for a drawing package, or pay scales and labour agreements and employment legislation for a payroll system, or the fonts for a word-processing package, or the rules of safe aviation for an air traffic control system, or the source programs to be compiled by a compiler. These things don't surround the machine: on the contrary, in some cases it makes much more sense to think of them as residing inside it.

It is always right to pay serious attention to the application domain. If you are developing a system to control a complex device – say, a large laboratory or medical instrument – you obviously need to understand the device, and how it works, and how it can be controlled. That may mean studying the device manufacturer's manual and making it an integral part of your system documentation; or it may mean making your own careful investigation and description of the device. But in either case it's absolutely essential to achieve an understanding of the device, and to capture your understanding in an explicit description.

The same is true of any application domain. Compiler writers don't imagine that they can go ahead with their development without an explicit description of the source language to be compiled and the target language of the compiled programs. Developers of sales order processing systems, equally, should not imagine that they can go ahead with their development without an explicit description of the customers and products and suppliers and orders and accounts and everything else that the system is about.

A second, and crucially important, reason for achieving an understanding of the application domain is to allow you to begin to recognize the shape of the problem. A problem is characterized less by the nature of the machine you will build than by the structure and properties of the application domain, and of your customer's REQUIREMENT in the application domain. The application domain is, in an important sense, the material you have been given to deal with; the requirement is what you have to do with it. Understanding it gives you a basis for choosing the right PROBLEM FRAMES and METHODS for solution.

Identifying the application domain isn't always completely straightforward. There may be an existing system – perhaps purely clerical, perhaps partly mechanized – that must be modified, extended, or replaced. In the standard data processing and administrative applications, such as payroll and purchasing and sales order processing, there will always be such an existing system unless the whole organization is new. It may seem natural to start investigating the requirements for the new system by looking at the old system first: this is the first step in the early versions of Structured Analysis of the DeMarco and Gane and Sarson school. But there's a danger here. If you're developing a payroll system, you can easily slip into thinking that the application domain for your system is the payroll department itself. That would mean that the requirements are all about the documents that are passed from clerk to clerk there. Well, they may be. It's not impossible. But then it wouldn't be a payroll system: it would be a clerical support system. Your customer's requirements are much more likely to be about the employees and their pay scales and their work and their overtime hours, and their absences and holidays, and promotions and retirements and pensions. They are what you must describe.

Sometimes it's hard to separate the application domain from the machine. Which is the application domain, and which is the machine, if you're developing an operating system? After all, they're both inside the same physical computer. But they're still quite distinct. If you're the operating system developer, your application domain is the world of the programs that will use your operating system, or 'run under' it. The machine you are constructing is the machine to be provided by the operating system itself. As always, you will construct it by specializing a general-purpose computer. But the specialized machine will occupy only a part of the physical computer's resources, leaving the remainder for the application domain – that is, for the user programs.

There are other ways in which all or part of a physical computer can form the application domain in a problem context. For example, suppose that your problem is to report on computer usage for enquiries made by users of an information system. Then the computer, and the enquiries run on it, and perhaps the users themselves, form your application domain. The machine you are building for this reporting problem will, no doubt, be implemented on another part of the same physical computer that runs the information system.

The essential point, of course, is that the identification of the application domain, and its separation from the machine, are not absolute but relative: they are relative to the problem to be solved. Determining which is the machine and which is the application domain is the crucial first step for understanding and framing a problem.

Arboricide

Arboricide is the murder of trees. The word is formed on the analogy of fratricide and matricide, and, like them, it denotes an offence. Not an offence against the environment – we are not talking here of the destruction of the rain forests – but an intellectual offence. The victims of arboricide are the descriptive tree structures that are so often found in software, holding together many individual elements in one coherent and immediately understandable harmony. Arboricide is the wilful refusal to understand and harmonize, insisting instead on cruelly dissecting the tree into its constituent individuals, discordantly focusing on the severed stumps that are all that remains of their once transparently obvious relationship.

People whose trade is the construction of difficulty from simplicity often exploit the obfuscating effects of arboricide. At one time there was a great fashion in the English Sunday newspapers for puzzles of this kind. 'Alan, Bill, Charlie, Dave, Eddy, Fred, Geoff, Harry, Ian, Joe and Keith are all related', we are told. 'Geoff's uncle's brother is Harry's cousin. Eddy's grandfather is Ian's uncle. Alan is not Fred's nephew. Harry's father is Keith's brother'. And 12 other pieces of information of the same kind. The puzzle is: 'Who is Geoff's cousin?' Solving a puzzle like this could take you the whole of Sunday afternoon, and the whole of the rest of the week too. The following Sunday the solution would appear:

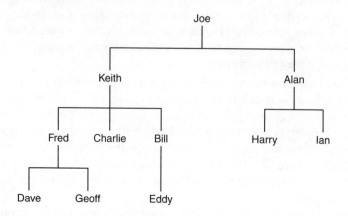

Obviously, Geoff's cousin is Eddy. The family tree reveals at once the relationships that are so hard to piece together from its fragments.

Software development should not be a trade of constructing difficulty from simplicity. Quite the contrary. So where there are trees to be shown you should show them, and refrain from turning the relationships they describe into a puzzle. It is, essentially, a matter of the SPAN OF DESCRIPTION. To show the family relationships in their full clarity and simplicity you need one description whose span is the whole family: 16 descriptions, each spanning just one or two family members, are not a good substitute.

Arboricide, then, is using a smaller description span when a larger one would be better. How can you recognize when a larger one would be better? The clearest indication is that you find you need to use terms whose meanings could not possibly be defined within the span you have chosen. Here's an example from the design of a simple batch program.

Suppose that you are designing a program to update a customer database from a file of transactions. To optimize access to the database, the transaction file has been sorted into customer number order. For each customer in the database the batch may contain no transactions, one transaction, or many. A traditional recipe for such a program is to structure it as a main loop, reading and processing one transaction record in each iteration of the loop. In outline, the program structure looks like this:

Now you must fit the reading and writing of the customer database records into the span of the Process-1-Transaction component. This is not so simple. You have to write a customer database record after applying all the transactions for the customer; and you have to read a customer database record before applying all the transactions for the customer. But the span of the Process-1-Transaction component is just one transaction record. If your whole universe consists of one transaction record, there is no way in which you can define the terms *before all the transactions for a customer* and *after all the transactions for a customer*. These concepts make sense only in a span which contains at least the complete ordered collection of transaction records for one customer.

To avoid any danger of arboricide, and a wasted Sunday afternoon, your complete program structure must have components for all the necessary spans. When it's all spelled out explicitly it should look something like this:

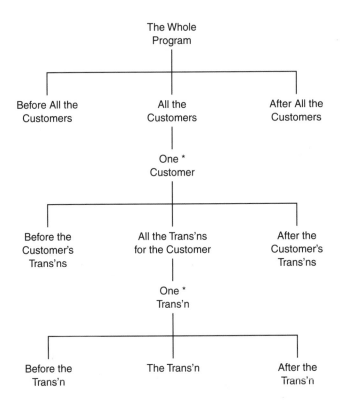

With this structure you won't need the familiar first-time switch, and the trick of initializing the *current-customer-identifier* variable to spaces. They are just devious ways of overcoming the problems that an inadequate span gives you. They let you import into the smaller span some distinctions that make sense only in the larger span, so that you can hide the basic inadequacy of your design. This is why the traditional main-loop-per-record recipe is so badly wrong. It recommends arboricide. If you follow its recommendation you must be prepared to swallow some nasty medicine.

(A final word on the exclusively male family tree, and an apology for any readers who may be inclined to accuse me of sexism. It's true that I might have made an exclusively female family tree. But if you include both male and female members of the family, what you get is not a family tree, but a family directed graph. I do not know a suitable word for the murder of directed graphs. Sorry.)

Aspects of Software Development

For a dinner table conversation, it was rather a serious subject. In 1993 the computer system project for the London Stock Exchange failed disastrously. £400 million spent and nothing to show for it. Who was to pay? What had gone wrong? Why do so many software developments end in disaster?

'Pure ignorance,' said the mathematician. 'Software development is essentially a branch of mathematics. That is why computer science departments in universities have so often been closely associated with mathematics departments. You must understand that a program is a mathematical object. Its development is therefore a mathematical activity, of a particularly challenging kind. Those who engage in it should, of course, be competent both in using the appropriate mathematical notations and in drawing on the appropriate body of mathematical knowledge – that is, on knowledge of the relevant theorems. While we continue to ignore these facts we will continue to perpetrate disasters.'

'That's all very well,' said the finance director, 'but in my company we build systems to improve our business performance. I imagine that the Stock Exchange does the same. Software isn't mathematics: it's business. I think of a software development project as a capital investment. The test of its success is simply the value of the return on that investment to the company. The return in this case seems to be negative. The essential tools in a software project are financial risk analysis and discounted cash flow calculation.'

'Of course you are right,' said the manager. 'But the key to achieving profitability and return on investment is to improve the development process, and with it the cost and quality of the end product. Software developers like to think they're doing something very special, but in fact it's an industrial process just like any other. The essence of software development is a quantitative approach to measuring and improving the performance of the software development process. What you don't measure you can't control.'

'But surely software development is done by people. And for people, isn't it?' said the sociologist. 'Software is situated. You talk as if the system and its development were something objective, but really it has to be continually renegotiated subjectively between the various stakeholders, who all have their own agendas and perspectives. The success of any system depends directly on facilitating the negotiation, and on the determinant individual and group relationships in the societal context. I suspect that the Stock Exchange members belong to an authoritarian culture in which the dominant behaviour is inimical to peer group negotation: perhaps that explains their failure.'

'Yes,' said the lawyer. 'That is as may be. But there is another aspect to be considered. Remember that software development is the process of creating a potentially valuable piece of intellectual property. The essential issues in many cases, therefore, are legal, the primary considerations arising under the law of contract. Clearly, the purchasers and providers of the Stock Exchange system failed to clarify the terms of their contract, and are therefore unable to settle their dispute satisfactorily. I have heard that the legal concept of a contract is becoming recognized as a sound basis for technical agreement between specifiers and implementers, as I believe computer people call them.

'There is a more general point also,' she continued. 'The property created must be protected, either by copyright or by patent or both. Its creators must avoid wittingly or unwittingly drawing on or embodying the intellectual property of other parties. That is the law. And,' she added, 'recent cases have shown clearly that the most successful software companies regard the law and the courts as vital tools in their activities.'

'This all seems ridiculous to me,' said the stockbroker. 'The plain fact is that the system was meant to serve the needs of the brokers and jobbers of the Stock Exchange, and it didn't. It usually takes a professional working member of the exchange at least five years to learn how the Stock Exchange works, and I don't see why the analysts and programmers who make computer systems should expect to pick it up much more quickly. A system for a particular business can only be built by people who are experts in that business. Domain knowledge, I think it's called. That's what matters.'

They are all right, aren't they? At least, up to a point. Each one of them is pointing out a factor that can sometimes make or break a software development project. You can find plenty of examples of software development projects that failed because a lack of mathematical rigour led to incorrect programs that were unusable or life-threatening. Many projects fail commercially because business factors are ignored in a flush of technical enthusiasm. Many fail because they produce systems that don't fit the organization or meet the human needs of the people who must operate them or use their results. Many fail because their developers simply don't know enough about the application area and don't take enough trouble to learn.

In a large project several of these factors may be crucially important: getting just one of them wrong can lead to failure. There's nothing new in this. The railway engineers of the middle decades of the nineteenth century would have understood perfectly. When Brunel and Robert Stephenson were building railways in the 1830s and 1840s, they were expected to involve themselves with raising capital, appearing before Parliamentary Committees, conciliating influential people who might oppose the necessary bill in Parliament, negotiating with landlords over whose land the tracks were to be laid, managing huge gangs of labourers, and dealing with subcontractors. Railway engineers had to be expert in finance, in politics, in real estate, in labour management, and in procurement. Why should we be surprised if software engineers may need to draw on expertise in mathematics, financial analysis, business, production quality control, sociology, and law, as well as in each application area they deal with?

We should not be surprised. But in most projects most of these factors are not very significant. Different considerations are important in different kinds of software development project. What matters in avionics software is different from what matters in building a word-processing package; the success of a compiler and the success of an on-line banking system depend on entirely different concerns. Developing an operating system doesn't involve much sociology. Financial analysis plays little part in the specification and design of switching software for a telephone exchange. Business concerns are largely irrelevant to compiler construction. Mathematical rigour is not always of decisive importance.

The question, then, is: What is common to all software development projects? When all the experts – the lawyers and sociologists and financiers and quality controllers and entrepreneurs and mathematicians – have claimed the substance of their different disciplines, is there anything left that belongs just to software development? Or are we left only with the grin of the Cheshire Cat when its body has vanished?

Software development does have a substance all of its own that gives it its special character and justifies its recognition as a subject in its own right. Software development is about building machines of a special kind, and building them in a certain kind of way. We build the kinds of MACHINE that can be physically embodied in a general-purpose computer, and can be built simply by describing them. The general-purpose computer accepts our programs – our description of the particular machine we want – and converts itself into that machine. It actually adopts the properties and behaviour of the machine we have described, and itself becomes that machine.

These machines we build are tangible things that interact with the world: otherwise they would be of no use. A word processor is as much a machine in the physical world as a typewriter is. A process-control system for a chemical manufacturing plant is a machine that will interact with the plant and open and close its valves. An avionics system is a machine that regulates the engines and control surfaces of the aeroplane in which it is installed. A management information system is a machine that fits into an organization and takes in data that it manipulates to produce useful information about the organization's activity. It is this relationship between our DESCRIPTIONS and the physical world that allows us, if anything does, to claim that software development is engineering.

That's why none of the people round the dinner table got to the heart of the matter. What they are talking about may be important on one project or another, but they have missed the central point. Our business is engineering – making machines to serve useful purposes in the world. And our technology is the technology of description.

The Bridges of Königsberg

In the early eighteenth century, the ladies and gentlemen of the city of Königsberg in East Prussia amused themselves with a fascinating question. Königsberg was divided into four areas by the River Pregel; the river was crossed by seven bridges:

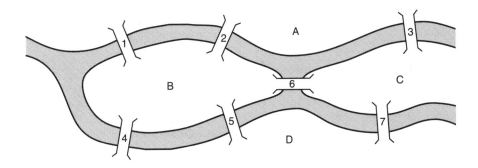

The question that fascinated the ladies and gentlemen was this: Was it possible to make a journey around the city that crossed each bridge exactly once, starting and finishing in the same area? The puzzle was much discussed in the drawing rooms of Königsberg, but no conclusion was reached until the great mathematician, Leonard Euler, answered the question in 1736. In arriving at his answer (which he published in a famous paper in the Communications of the Scientific Academy of St Petersburg), he laid the foundations of the branch of mathematics known as graph theory. A graph has a number of *vertices* connected by *edges* – or, if you prefer, *nodes* connected by *arcs*. The graph form of the Königsberg puzzle can be obtained by shrinking each area into a vertex and representing each bridge by an edge, giving a picture like this:

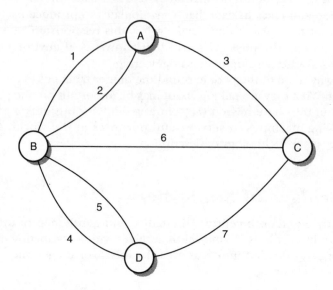

In graph theory the desired journey is called an Euler circuit: it goes along each edge exactly once, and finishes at the vertex where it began.

But you don't need graph theory to solve the puzzle. Euler's key idea is just this. Imagine a traveller making a successful journey, and imagine four observers stationed in the four areas. Then describe the traveller's behaviour from the point of view of each observer. From each observer's point of view, the significant events are:

● an Arrival of the traveller in the observer's area; and
● a Departure of the traveller from the area.

Of course an Arrival in one area is also a Departure from another area; but each observer sees at most one end of any crossing of a bridge – either an Arrival or a Departure, but never both.

The observer in the area in which the route starts and finishes sees the traveller make some number of Excursions from the observer's area: each Excursion consists of a Departure followed by an Arrival. An observer in any other area sees some number of Visits: each Visit consists of an Arrival followed by a Departure. They might make these descriptions:

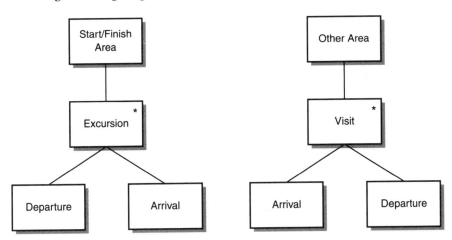

With these descriptions before you, you can see your way to a solution. The traveller makes a number of complete Excursions from the Start/Finish Area, and also a number of complete Visits to each Other Area. So in each area the number of Departure events must be equal to the number of Arrival events. Because a successful journey crosses each bridge exactly once, each area must have an even number of bridges: half are used for Departures, and half for Arrivals. But if you look at the map you see that each area has an odd number of bridges. Just one with an odd number would be enough to make a successful journey impossible. So the solution to the puzzle is that no journey can be made that meets the required conditions.

Once you've seen the solution, it's very obvious. But seeing it depends on looking at the problem in the right way. In this problem, as often, looking at it in the right way means making descriptions of the right SPAN: biting off the right amount of the world in each description. The ladies and gentlemen of Königsberg never solved the puzzle because they never chose the span of description that would yield the necessary insight. Several other description spans might have been chosen, but none of them would have led to a solution. For example:

- A description for each bridge. The span is all the crossings of the bridge (of which a successful journey would contain only one).

- A description for each pair of areas. The span is all the crossings, in either direction, between one area of the pair and the other.

- A description for each area's arrivals. The span is all the crossings into the area.

- A description for each area's departures. The span is all the crossings out of the area.

- A description for the whole journey. The span is all the crossings of all the bridges.

Most likely the good ladies and gentlemen of Könisgberg chose the last span, and just tried to think about the whole journey all at once. It's easy to make this kind of choice. But it's usually wrong.

Brilliance

Some years ago I spent a week giving an in-house program design course at a manufacturing company in the mid-west of the United States. On the Friday afternoon it was all over. The DP Manager, who had arranged the course and was paying for it out of his budget, asked me into his office.

'What do you think?' he asked. He was asking me to tell him my impressions of his operation and his staff. 'Pretty good,' I said. 'You've got some good people there.' Program design courses are hard work; I was very tired; and staff evaluation consultancy is charged extra. Anyway, I knew he really wanted to tell me his own thoughts.

'What did you think of Fred?' he asked. 'We all think Fred's brilliant.' 'He's very clever,' I said. 'He's not very enthusiastic about methods, but he knows a lot about programming.' 'Yes,' said the DP Manager. He swivelled round in his chair to face a huge flowchart stuck to the wall: about five large sheets of line printer paper, maybe two hundred symbols, hundreds of connecting lines. 'Fred did that. It's the build-up of gross pay for our weekly payroll. No one else except Fred understands it.' His voice dropped to a reverent hush. 'Fred tells me that he's not sure he understands it himself.'

'Terrific,' I mumbled respectfully. I got the picture clearly. Fred as Frankenstein, Fred the brilliant creator of the uncontrollable monster flowchart. That matched my own impression of Fred very well. 'But what about Jane?' I said. 'I thought Jane was very good. She picked up the program design ideas very fast.'

'Yes,' said the DP Manager. 'Jane came to us with a great reputation. We thought she was going to be as brilliant as Fred. But she hasn't really proved herself yet. We've given her a few problems that we thought were going to be really tough, but when she finished it turned out they weren't really difficult at all. Most of them turned out pretty simple. She hasn't really proved herself yet – if you see what I mean?'

I saw what he meant.

The Calendar

The calendar is not completely simple. I'm talking about the ordinary Gregorian calendar that we use in the West, and I'm talking about the kind of simplicity that lets you describe something in just one easy description. However hard you try, you can't fit the calendar into one regular structured description.

This kind of descriptive complexity is a junior form of PROBLEM COMPLEXITY. Problem complexity is what you have when you can't fit your problem into one PROBLEM FRAME for which you have a fully effective METHOD. Complexity in this sense is purely relative. If you had a more powerful method; and the method were effective for a more capacious problem frame; and the problem frame fitted your problem; then the problem would be simple. But as it is, you need more than one problem frame to handle it, so you've got to put more than one partial solution together to get your final result.

We are well equipped by nature and structured programming for describing things that come in regular structured cycles. For such cycles we have sequence, selection, and iteration – semi-colon, if-else, and do-while, if you prefer – out of which we can make the structures of structured programming. You might say that we have an effective method for describing problems that fit into one 'regular structured cycle' problem frame.

But the calendar doesn't fit into one regular structured cycle. In the notation of TREE DIAGRAMS, the calendar looks like this:

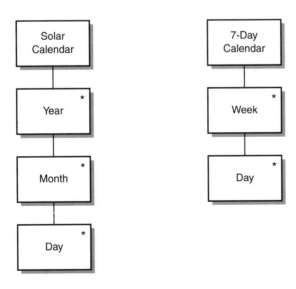

There are really two calendars, or two different views of the same calendar, if you prefer. The Solar Calendar is a regular structured cycle – well, regular enough – of days within months within years. Each day fits entirely into one month, and each month fits entirely into one year. The 7-Day Calendar is another regular cycle, this time of days within 7-day weeks. Each day fits entirely into one week. You can read about the 7-Day Calendar in the book of Genesis.

The two views fit together, because they are pinned together by the days. The days in the Solar Calendar are exactly the same days as the days in the 7-Day Calendar. The complexity consists in the fact that there is no way of composing these two views of the calendar into a single regular structured cycle. In particular, you can't just insert the weeks under the months, like this:

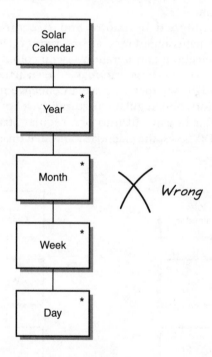

The weeks don't fit in because some weeks spill over from one month to another, and from one year to another. This is a *structure clash*, because the two structures of the calendar clash with one another. More exactly, it is a *boundary clash*, because the boundaries of the weeks clash with the boundaries of the years and months.

This complexity of the calendar is not an invention of a particular design method, or a consequence of the tree diagram notation. You can't make it go away by deciding to use a different structured method. The complexity is there, and it is a major benefit of a method if it forces you to recognize this kind of complexity when it is present in a problem. In software development, a complexity ignored is a disaster waiting to happen.

The structure clash between the two calendars is real enough to have caused a lot of expense and inconvenience for business and government. For that reason there have been many proposals for calendar reform. George Eastman, of Kodak fame, financed an energetic campaign for change. In 1923, the very year in which Greece became the last country in Europe to adopt the Gregorian calendar, the League of Nations created a Special Committee of Enquiry into the Reform of the Calendar. Their aim was to get rid of the structure clash.

The number of days in a solar year is astronomically determined and can't be altered if the seasons are to come at the same times in each year. So the Committee considered proposals for a 'fixed calendar', in which a week would continue to consist of seven days but the first day of the year would always be a Monday. To achieve this result it would have been necessary to have one 'blank' day at the end of the year (two in leap years), this blank day belonging to no week. This idea was fiercely resisted by representatives of the religions – Judaism, Christianity, and Islam – that observe a weekly Sabbath day. For them it would have meant that their Sabbath would be on a different day of the week each year: Sunday one year, Saturday the next, Friday the next, Wednesday the year after that. The ecumenical virtues of this arrangement seemed small compared with the extreme inconvenience for Sabbath observers working in secular organizations.

In the end the Committee received suggestions for nearly 200 different schemes of reform. But in 1931, after eight years of furious activity by proponents and opponents of change, it finally resolved to leave the calendar alone. Mr Eastman died a disappointed man.

Classification

In an illuminating paper on *Object-Oriented Classification*, Peter Wegner points out that Servius Tullius divided the Roman people into five classes according to their ability to pay taxes, and that Linnaeus divided animals and plants into genera and species according to their physical attributes. Smalltalk programmers divide computational objects into classes according to their local data structures and their responses to messages. Pupils in school are divided into classes to be taught together.

Classes, in this broad sense, are of central importance in software development. When you assign two individuals to the same class you decide that for some purposes you will treat them identically, paying attention to what they have in common rather than to their differences. This identical treatment is what makes generalization possible: one general rule can apply to all the individuals of a class.

Obviously, deciding which classes to recognize is an important early step in description. Z, for example, is a formal notation for software description. (You can read about Z in John Wordsworth's book *Software Development with Z*.) In Z, one of the first steps is to decide on the basic classes or given sets of the problem. Specifying a library, you might begin by declaring the given sets:

[*Book, Person*]

There are individuals that are Books, and individuals that are Persons. So far, so good. But, unfortunately, by the defined meaning of your chosen notation, you have also implied that:

- any individual that is ever a Book is always a Book: being a Book is a permanent property;

- any individual that is ever a Person is always a Person: being a Person is also a permanent property; and

- no individual can be both a Book and a Person: being a Book and being a Person are mutually exclusive.

That makes good sense for Books and Persons. But when you come to use Z for another application you may find yourself writing:

[*Customer, Employee*]

or:

[*Student, Teacher, Classroom, Subject*]

Are you sure that the same individual cannot be both an Employee and a Customer? Are you sure that individuals do not *become* Customers? *Cease to be* Employees? Do Students never become Teachers? The right answer to any of these questions may be Yes or No: it will depend on the problem you are solving. But you must allow yourself – or, better still, force yourself – to examine these questions carefully. Don't just passively accept the answers implicit in a notation.

Writing DESIGNATIONS is a positive encouragement to careful thought here, especially if you take an explicit view of time such as the EVENTS AND INTERVALS view. If you have just written:

c is a customer of the company	$\approx$ Customer(c)
e is an employee of the company	$\approx$ Employee(e)

you can hardly avoid wondering whether perhaps you have left out an interval argument. Perhaps you should have written:

c is a customer of the company in interval v	$\approx$ Customer(c,v)
e is an employee of the company in interval v	$\approx$ Employee(e,v)

Because designations never embody assertions, you are also led to wonder whether you should – or should not – write a separate explicit assertion that no one is both a Customer and an Employee *at the same time*:

$$\neg\exists\, v,x \bullet (\text{Customer}(x,v) \wedge \text{Employee}(x,v))$$

That is, you can't find a v and an x for which it's true that x is a Customer in interval v and x is also an Employee in the same interval v.

Or even, perhaps, that anyone who is *ever* a Customer can't *ever* be an Employee, and vice versa:

$$\neg\exists\, v,w,x \bullet (\text{Customer}(x,v) \wedge \text{Employee}(x,w))$$

That is, you can't find a v and a w and an x for which it's true that x is a Customer in interval v and x is also an Employee in interval w.

There is still another fundamental question to ask yourself about every designation you write: Should this be a *designated* phenomenon, or should it instead be a *defined* term? Suppose that you are describing a library. You write these designations:

m is a library member in interval v	$\approx$ Member(m,v)
Member m enrols in the library in event e	$\approx$ Enrol(m,e)
Member m resigns from the library in event e	$\approx$ Resign(m,e)

Later, perhaps, you find yourself describing the life history of a library member in a tree diagram:

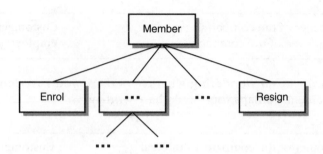

There's a little conundrum here. Do you continue to be a member *after* resigning? And do you have to be a member *before* you enrol? No doubt enrolment is restricted to some class of individuals: most libraries accept only human beings as members; some accept only adults; and some accept only children. But it doesn't make sense to accept only members as members. That sounds too much like Catch-22. You should introduce the predicate Member(m,v) in a DEFINITION, not in a designation. It is true of any individual who has enrolled and has not yet resigned. Surprisingly, most entity classifications are like this. They should be defined in terms of designated events.

Classification techniques in software development have been strongly influenced by programming notions like strong typing, and by analogies with biology. Neither influence has been an unmixed blessing. One effect has been to concentrate attention on the classification of entities – individuals that change over time. But it is at least as important, in many problems, to pay attention to the classification of events. An event, of course, can't be in different states in different intervals of time: it occurs just at one instant, between two intervals. But its classification may depend on the states and identities of its participants; or, more generally, on the state of the domain when it occurs.

Telephone switching is like that. In even the simplest telephone system the observable event of lifting the handset ('going off hook' in the jargon of telephony) can have two interpretations. If the phone is ringing, lifting the handset is answering an incoming call; but if the phone is silent, lifting the handset is initiating an outgoing call. You want to be able to talk about *answer* events in one description and *call-initiation* events in another.

In a Private Automatic Branch Exchange (a 'PABX'), the interpretation of directly observable events at a telephone is much more complex. You will need to make generous use of event classification by definition. The telephone has only one handset, but it can multiplex among several calls in progress on different lines. In effect, there are several 'virtual telephones', each with its own line but all sharing the one handset. Each virtual telephone has a button and a light to display the state of the call on its line. Pressing one of these buttons 'selects' a virtual telephone. This action, performed while the phone is off hook, can be interpreted in many ways. For example:

- If there is an incoming call ringing on the line, pressing the button answers the call; but if the line is idle, pressing the button initiates an outgoing call. In both cases, if a call is already in progress on another line and is not 'put on hold' before the button is pressed, pressing the button 'deselects' the other line and terminates the call already in progress.

- If a call between two other phones is in progress on the line, pressing the button 'bridges on to' the call, joining in as a third party to the conversation.

- If there is an incoming call that has been 'put on hold' on the line, pressing the button resumes that call.

- If there is a call that has been 'put on hold' on the line, and the phone is active in a call on another line, and the 'conference' button has been pressed, pressing the button joins both calls together in a 'conference call'.

Clearly, each event in which a button is pressed must be classified as an event of one or more virtual telephones. The classification is dynamic. It depends on the state of the line associated with the button, and the state of any other virtual telephone at which a call is already in progress.

You can do a lot with classification. Use it as much, and restrict it as little, as you can.

Composition

Divide and conquer. Separate your concerns. Yes. But sometimes the conquered tribes must be reunited under the conquering ruler, and the separated concerns must be combined to serve a single purpose. That is the role of composition. Composing descriptions is sometimes an indispensable operation in software development.

But only sometimes. When you make two descriptions of an existing, visible, tangible, APPLICATION DOMAIN, the domain itself embodies the result of composing them. It demonstrates the answer to the question: What do you get if you have something of which both this description is true *and* that description is true? Check each description separately against the domain, and if they are both true separately then their composition is a true description of the domain you can see.

It's not always so easy. If you are describing – that is, building – a MACHINE, you want the machine to behave like this, *and* like this, *and* like this. But the available general-purpose computer may not be equipped to accept all three of your descriptions and behave according to all of them at once. For example, if your descriptions specify three concurrent sequential processes, your computer may be unable to perform multiprocessing or multitasking. Then you must put your three descriptions together into one, composing the three sequential processes into one sequential process that your computer can execute. The same problem can arise in database implementation. Perhaps you would like to be able to describe several database views, and leave the machine to compose them. But you may well be forced to compose them yourself, to placate a computer that can accept only one schema for one database.

Even when the computer is able and willing to accept several descriptions, you may still want to compose them. You may just want to visualize in detail what you have described. Or you may want to convince yourself that it is not self-contradictory like an M C Escher drawing – that it won't cause some kind of deadlock when your computer tries to satisfy two contradictory descriptions at once.

Some composition is almost inevitable. Whenever you write a program in C or a method in Smalltalk that reads an input stream and writes an output stream you are composing one process that reads the input with another process that writes the output. The JSP program design method is based on doing this composition explicitly, deriving the program structure by composing the structures of the input data streams with the structures of the output data streams. Look at these TREE DIAGRAMS:

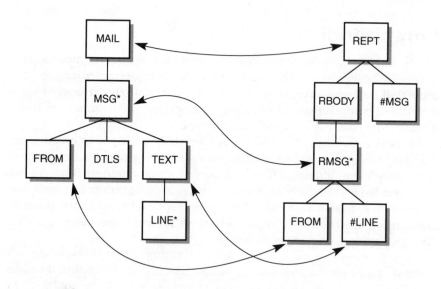

An input stream, MAIL, contains a number of messages, each with a FROM field, some details, and a TEXT consisting of a number of LINEs. A report is to be displayed, whose body has an entry RMSG for each message, containing the message's FROM field and a count of its LINEs. The report ends with a count of the messages. The arrows between the data structures show the correspondences between their parts. The program structure is composed from these structures and their correspondences. Here it is:

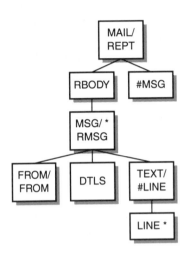

This kind of composition is an old idea, but often very useful. I wrote about it in my 1975 book *Principles of Program Design*.

Sometimes you need composition just for more efficient program execution. If a large and complex data structure must be traversed to produce two results, it may be much more efficient to combine both traversals into one. If the machine must perform a data manipulation in several successive phases, you can sometimes make large savings by combining two or more phases into one.

The principle of composition in the interests of efficiency is known as the 'Shanley Design Criterion'. The engineering design of a system should be integrated, so that each physical component achieves as many of the system's purposes as possible. A long time ago, Pierre de Marneffe expounded the Shanley Principle, and claimed that it applies to software. He illustrated it like this:

'If you make a cross-section of, for instance, the German V-2 [rocket], you find external skin, structural rods, tank wall, etc. If you cut across the Saturn-B moon rocket, you find only an external skin which is at the same time a structural component and the tank wall. Rocketry engineers have used the 'Shanley Principle' thoroughly when they use the fuel pressure inside the tank to improve the rigidity of the external skin!'

De Marneffe's observations were quoted with approval by Donald Knuth in his 1974 paper *Structured Programming with go to Statements*. But don't be too enthusiastic and too quick to apply the Shanley Principle. Unnecessary composition exacts a price. When I mentioned the Shanley Principle in a conference talk, Barry Boehm pointed out that the product of composition is often more fragile than its parts. It is certainly more complex; and it may have a single point of failure where a less highly optimized product would be more robust. That's why so much of the effort that goes into programming and operating systems is devoted to reducing the need for composition.

So your motto should be: 'Separate where you can, and compose where you must'.

Connection Domains

When you turn on a light, you probably think of your movement of the control button and the illumination of the light as a single event. In fact, of course, something more complex is going on. If the switch is of the old-fashioned tumbler design, moving the button compresses a spring; then, when the button reaches the end of its travel, the spring expands, and the electrical contact snaps into place; only then can the current start to flow. And it still takes some time to heat the lamp filament. But it doesn't matter. For all practical everyday purposes there is only one event. The event is a SHARED PHENOMENON, shared between you and the light. In the same way, when you and I are in conversation, I hear each word as you speak it, although the sound waves take some time to travel from you to me. In practice, we think of the speaking and the hearing of each word as a single event, shared by the two of us.

Shared phenomena, viewed from different perspectives in different domains, are the essence of domain interaction and communication of any kind. The arrival of a lift at a point six inches from its home position at a floor *is* the closing of the electro-mechanical sensor, which in turn *is* the setting of a bit in the memory of the controlling computer. The emission of a signal on a certain line by the computer *is* the switching on of the lift winding motor. You can think of the domains as seeing the same event from different points of view.

This treatment of what you can observe in two domains as a single phenomenon makes sense only if certain preconditions are met. First, the correspondence between the observations in the two domains must be reliable enough: it must be virtually impossible for the sensor not to close when the lift arrives, or for the motor not to start when the computer sends a signal. If the observation can be true in one domain while the corresponding observation is false in the other domain, you can hardly treat them as observations of the same phenomenon. Second, if the shared phenomenon is an event, it must be well enough synchronized between the domains: there must be no significant delay.

What is to count as sufficient reliability, or as good enough synchronization, depends, of course, on your purpose. When you turn on the reading light in some aeroplanes, there is a noticeable delay before the light comes on. The button you pressed sent a signal to a computer system which is taking a little time to respond. For some purposes the delay is significant. If you're unfamiliar with the way the lights work, and your reactions are very quick, you might press the button again, thinking that it didn't work the first time. But in other circumstances the delay is probably not significant: in the timescale of reading even a few words of a book or magazine it's negligible. Certainly you don't have time to do anything else while you're waiting. Yet the same delay in voice transmission in an international telephone call can make conversation impossible.

When the preconditions of speed and reliability are not met, you have to recognize the presence of another domain: the connection is a domain in its own right. Think about sending and receiving letters. If the postal service were as quick as lightning and as reliable as the sunrise, then sending and receiving a letter could always be regarded as a single event. But the postal service is not quite like that. Even the fastest achievable performance leaves plenty of time for other events to intervene between the posting and delivery of a letter. Letters sometimes get lost. And overtaking is possible, too. A letter I post to you today may reach you after a letter I post to you tomorrow. So if our communication by letter is a part of an application domain to be described, the role of the postal service will be quite explicit. For us the postal service is a *connection domain*.

That means that the postal service must appear as a domain in the PROBLEM CONTEXT. Showing the shared phenomena explicitly, the context diagram looks like this:

The box marked YP represents the phenomena shared between You and the Postal Service; MP represents the phenomena shared between Me and the Postal Service. The little dots mean that YP is entirely contained in the You domain, and also in the Postal Service domain, and MP is contained in the Me domain and the Postal Service domain.

Now, when you write me a letter, we're not thinking of the posting and delivery of the letter as an event shared between you and me. Instead, the posting is an event in YP shared by you and the postal service, and the delivery is an event in MP shared by me and the postal service. The relationship between your posting event and my delivery event for the same letter may be an elaborate chain of events, all but two of which are private to the postal service domain.

When a connection domain forces itself on your awareness in this kind of way, it raises a difficulty. That difficulty is a kind of PROBLEM COMPLEXITY. The original problem can't be solved without recognizing that another problem frame is needed to accommodate the connection: naturally enough, a CONNECTION FRAME. For example, in a problem using the SIMPLE IS FRAME, the *Information Outputs* of the system are required to contain information about the *Real World* domain. But the presence of a connection domain between the *Real World* and the *System* means that the *System* has no direct access to the *Real World*. So either the *System* must compensate for the distortion introduced by the connection domain – and this may be impossible – or less stringent requirements must be accepted. These considerations are a problem in their own right.

It comes to this. When a connection domain forces itself on your attention you have three choices:

(1) Ignore the connection domain, and treat the phenomena on either side of it as shared, in spite of the fact that they don't really correspond closely enough. The disadvantage is that it may be hard to make sense of what seems to be going on in the *Real World*: the customer seems to cancel the order before placing it; the arrow seems to reach its target before being fired; the bank statement shows the withdrawal made on Tuesday but not the withdrawal made on Monday.

(2) Treat the connection domain as if it were itself the domain of interest – in the Simple IS Frame, as if it were itself the *Real World*. Instead of thinking of your mail-order company as dealing with its customers, just think of it as dealing with the telephone company and Federal Express. That way, you're ignoring the true *Real World*. It could make sense in some situations. Perhaps.

(3) Recognize that the connection domain and the domain on the other side of it are both important. Their relationship is a significant sub-problem. Use the Connection frame to deal with it properly. It's more work; but it's probably worth it in the end. Doing things properly usually is.

Connection Frames

In many problems you'll find that you can't connect the machine to the relevant parts of the real world in quite the way you would like. You would prefer a direct connection by SHARED PHENOMENA. But instead you have to put up with an indirect connection through a CONNECTION DOMAIN that introduces various kinds of delay and distortion into the connection. Here are a few simple examples:

- In the Patient Monitoring problem, the machine can monitor the Patients' temperature, blood pressure, and other vital factors only through the Analog Devices, which are known to be unreliable.

- In data processing applications involving keyboard data entry, the 'data entry subsystem' is another part of the machine to be built. In effect it is also to be regarded as a domain connecting the main machine to the real world of interest, where the data originate.

- In mail-order systems the postal service is a domain connecting the mail-order company to those of its customers who use the mail.

- In a communications problem, a noisy channel is a domain connecting the sender to the receiver.

There are many flavours of connection problem. Here's a FRAME DIAGRAM that captures one basic flavour:

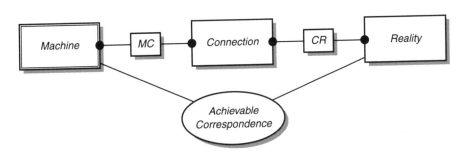

The principal parts are the *Machine* (the double outline shows that you have to construct it); the *Reality*, to which the *Machine* is connected (but only indirectly); the *Connection* domain, which here is regarded as given; and the *Achievable Correspondence*, which is a relationship between the *Machine* and the *Reality*. *MC* and *CR* represent the phenomena shared respectively between the *Machine* and the *Connection* and the *Connection* and the *Reality*. The *Achievable Correspondence* is the best you can provide as a substitute for what you would have preferred: phenomena shared directly between the *Machine* and the *Reality*.

The whole point of treating the connection as a problem to be addressed, rather than just as an unpleasant but unavoidable fact of life, is that you can do better than simply accepting the shared phenomena in *MC* as an inadequate substitute for a direct connection.

The techniques for doing better will vary from problem to problem. For example, in the Patient Monitoring problem the Patients are the *Reality*, and the Analog Devices are the *Connection*. The information provided to the Machine by the Analog Devices can be evaluated against what is known about human temperature, blood pressure, and other vital factors. If an Analog Device indicates that a particular patient's temperature has fallen from 98.2° Fahrenheit to 0.0° Fahrenheit in one minute, the indication must certainly be false. You should design the Machine to take advantage of that knowledge.

If you're building a data-entry subsystem, the appropriate problem frame has the same topology, but a different meaning:

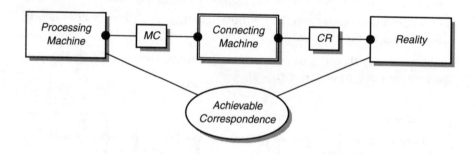

The principal parts are differently named. The *Connecting Machine* (which you must build) is the connection. It connects the *Reality* to the *Processing Machine*, which you are not concerned to build – at least, not in this problem frame. Now, instead of bringing about the *Achievable Correspondence* by a suitable design of the *Processing Machine*, you have to bring it about by suitable design of the *Connecting Machine*.

There's a whole world of connection problems, of many different kinds. Some of them have been pretty thoroughly worked over, especially problems of the kind that arise in telecommunications. But even if you have to start from square 1 to understand your connection problem and to develop a solution, it's a good first step to recognize that it is a separate subproblem, with its own problem frame.

Context Diagrams

Context diagrams have been around for a long time – by software development standards. In *Structured Analysis and System Specification*, published in 1978, Tom DeMarco showed context diagrams like this one:

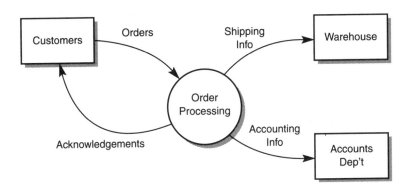

This is the top level of a hierarchical collection of DATAFLOW DIAGRAMS. The circle in the centre represents the system to be developed, thought of as a process. The arrows represent the data flows into and out of the process. The rectangular boxes represent the *sources* or *sinks*: that is, originators or receivers of system data. DeMarco says:

'The Context Diagram documents the domain of study by showing the set of data flows that cross into and out of the domain'.

The 'domain of study' is the system – here, the Order Processing system. This is the focus of interest, and the Customers, Warehouse, and Accounts Department are relatively unimportant. DeMarco says:

'Boxes (representing sources and sinks) are used rather sparingly in Data Flow Diagrams, and usually not in a very rigorous fashion. Since *they represent something outside the area of our major concern*, they exist only to provide commentary about the system's connection to the outside world'.

The italics in the quotation are mine, not DeMarco's. The point I'm stressing is that in Structured Analysis this kind of diagram is called a context diagram because it shows the *context of the system*. The circle in the centre represents DeMarco's area of major concern – what I would call the

MACHINE. The rectangles roughly represent the APPLICATION DOMAIN, structured into separate individual DOMAINS.

It's good to draw context diagrams, but I think it's better to draw them with a different emphasis. I would rather think of a context diagram as showing the context of the *problem*, not of the *system*. That means above all that it should focus your interest on the application domain. In the analysis stages of development – that is, in requirements and specifications – you are concerned with identifying and analysing the *problem*: you have not yet reached the point of developing your *solution*. And the problem is to be found in the application domain, not in the machine.

The context diagram, then, should be the first representation of the PROBLEM CONTEXT. Drawing it gives you an opportunity to structure the problem context as a number of separable domains, together with the machine you intend to build; and to show how the domains interact with each other and with the machine. This structuring of the problem context is an essential first step towards problem analysis, and towards the choice of appropriate PROBLEM FRAMES.

That means that we're going to need a slightly different kind of diagram. In some ways it will show more than the traditional context diagram of structured analysis; in some ways it will show less:

- We will show *all* the domains that may be relevant to the problem requirement, not just those that provide input directly to the machine domain or accept output from it.

- The connections between domains will not represent data flows. Data flows are just one kind of possible communication. At this early stage in our understanding of the problem we don't want to assume that all communication is of the dataflow kind. We will think in more general terms: a line connecting two domains means only that they communicate by SHARED PHENOMENA.

- We won't single out the machine by a special symbol. If your problem turns out to be a MULTI-FRAME PROBLEM, you will often find that some aspects of the machine must be treated as if the machine were a part of the application domain.

Let's look at a context diagram, in this different style, for the familiar Patient Monitoring problem. The patients are in an intensive-care unit in a hospital. Analog devices monitor their pulse rate, temperature, and other vital factors. The system – the machine – is required to check each patient's factors, at specified frequencies, against specified safe ranges. The factors are to be stored in a database, and out-of-range factors reported to the nurse's station. The machine must also check that the analog devices are working correctly, and report failures to the nurse's station.

Here's the diagram:

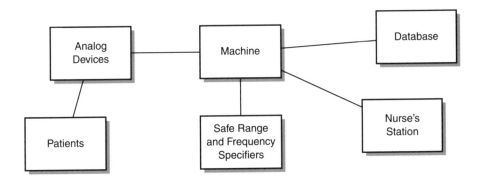

As you can see:

- The Patients domain is included in spite of the fact that they are not directly connected to the machine. Their direct interaction by shared phenomena is only with the analog devices, which in turn interact directly with the machine. But the Patients are of central interest in this problem, and must not be left out.

- The Analog Devices domain is also included, for two compelling reasons. First, the machine must check that the analog devices are working correctly, and report any failure: so they are a part of the problem and hence of the application domain. Second, if you leave out the Analog Devices domain you won't be able to include the Patients, because the Analog Devices are an unavoidable CONNECTION DOMAIN for the Patients.

This context diagram is much more abstract than DeMarco's. It shows less because it doesn't say anything about the domain connections except that they exist: the Machine is directly connected to the Database, and the Patients are directly connected to the Analog Devices, but the Patients are not directly connected to the Machine. It shows more because it shows both the Patients domain and the Analog Devices domain. Its virtue is that it says no more than we really know at this stage, and that it begins to lay the groundwork for choosing a problem frame to fit our problem.

In some problems, one domain may be entirely contained inside another. Think, for example, of a word-processing system. The texts processed by the system are certainly an important part of the application domain. Some of the most important requirements will be about the properties of the texts – paragraph styles, fonts, pagination, spacing, layout. And also about their behaviour – how the pagination and the division into lines should change when a word is inserted, and how the cursor should move horizontally when it is shifted from a longer to a shorter line. Yet the texts will exist only inside the machine.

Containment of one domain by another is represented by a connecting line with a heavy dot at the containing end. Like this:

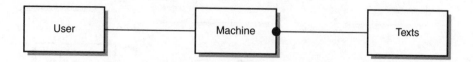

The Texts domain is contained entirely in the Machine domain, in the sense that all the phenomena of the texts domain are also phenomena of the machine domain. The texts have no properties and no behaviour that are not also properties and behaviour of the machine.

You may be wondering why the Texts domain should be recognized as a part of the application domain if it is actually contained in the machine. Surely this containment means that the texts domain is not really separate, and should therefore be omitted from the context diagram? If it's inside the machine, how can you think of it separately from the machine?

Well, that's an interesting and reasonable objection. But I'm still sure it's right to show the texts domain explicitly in the problem context because it's certainly an integral part of the problem. If you omit the texts domain many of the requirements won't be expressible in terms of the application domain. How will you be able to talk about the text layout requirements if you can't talk about the texts? The way the texts are encoded inside the machine will be a part of the solution, but a more abstract view of it is definitely a part of the problem.

When you need to, you can use the same convention of a heavy dot to show other shared phenomena explicitly in a context diagram. Here's a version of the context diagram that shows all the shared phenomena of this problem context explicitly:

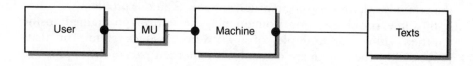

The small rectangle labelled MU represents the phenomena shared between the User and the Machine. You can think of it as a tiny domain, entirely contained in the User domain, and also entirely contained in the Machine domain. This explicit notation for shared phenomena is useful when you need to discuss the shared phenomena in detail, and also when – rather unusually – some phenomena are shared among three domains or more.

Finally, it may seem that we are making a premature implementation decision when we show the same machine connected to all the domains that are capable of being connected to a machine. Not so. Just as the application domain can be structured and subdivided, so can the machine domain. We just haven't done it yet.

Critical Reading

Over 20 years ago, in *The Psychology of Computer Programming*, Jerry Weinberg wrote this about programming:

> 'Programming is, among other things, a kind of writing. One way to learn writing is to write, but in all other forms of writing, one also reads. We read examples – both good and bad – to facilitate learning'.

Reading is no less important in the earlier stages of development, in requirements, analysis, specification, and design, where the descriptions are – or should be – more varied both in form and in content than they are in programming. One virtue of the SADT view of software development, described by Marca and McGowan, is its insistence on reading as well as writing the descriptions produced: in SADT the business of reviewing what has been written is organized in the 'Author/Reader Cycle'. Inspections, and the inelegantly named 'Structured Walkthroughs' are simply another form of purposeful and systematic reading of descriptions.

The Author/Reader Cycle, Inspections, and Structured Walkthroughs encourage reading within the work of one development project. They aim to improve the quality of that work by careful scrutiny. But Weinberg's point is more general. To learn to write well, you must read. Nothing will improve your ability to write good descriptions more than the habit of careful and critical reading. And, above all, active reading. It is all too easy to let your eyes move gently over a text or diagram, enjoying an undemanding intellectual comfort that is readily mistaken for accurate understanding. In software development, reading must be active critical enquiry, not passive acceptance.

As you read a piece of software description, you should be constantly questioning what you read. What kind of description is it? What is it about? What is it for? Does it assert that something is *true*? Then how might it be proved wrong? Or does it state that something is *required*? By whom? How could I check that it really is required? What does the description assume? What does it leave out? Is there something else I must know to understand it? Could it have more than one meaning? How can I check my understanding? Does it define new terms to be used elsewhere? How does it fit with the other descriptions in the same development?

Don't be surprised if you can't answer some – even most – of these questions for many of the documents you come across. Vagueness is one of the commonest defects in software development: that's part of the reason for our frequent failures. Many developers are accustomed to a high degree of uncertainty and vagueness in their descriptions. Surely, they seem to say, it is the very purpose of the earlier stages of development – requirements, analysis, specification, and design – to be more vague. Surely you can become more precise only as you learn more, adding detail and progressing towards the exactness of program texts. Isn't a specification really just a somewhat vague program? Isn't a requirement really just a rather vague specification? Surely it is in the nature of earlier descriptions that they must lack detail. So they must lack precision.

This view is sadly wrong-headed. Its attractions stem from laziness and an uncritical acceptance of TOP-DOWN development and programming. It is hard work to be precise, and vagueness is less demanding for the writer and the reader alike. Reading or listening to a description in the vague, top-down style is not very hard work. If you didn't understand something at a higher level, you don't have to worry. No doubt it will become clearer when a lower level or two has been added. Searching questions would be premature. Don't raise objections at this level of the description. They'll probably be answered later at a lower level, so you can hold them back now in good conscience. Just sit back and listen, or read. And for the writer or speaker too, the duty of precision can be deferred like St Augustine's duty of virtue. 'O Lord, make me virtuous,' he prayed when he was a dissipated young man. 'But not yet.'

Even when you're reading something very precise – perhaps a description in a formal notation – you still can't relax. In fact, the more precise and mathematical the description the more sure you must be to ask yourself the most important question of all: What is being described? And, especially: Is this a description of the machine, or of some part of the application domain?

Z is a very precise mathematical notation, clearly explained in John Wordsworth's book *Software Development with Z*. Z users try to clarify their meaning by insisting, very rightly, on a combination of formal and informal descriptions. But their heart's not in it. In one well-known book on Z – not Wordsworth's – you can read this comment:

> '... the informal text can be viewed as commentary for the formal text. It can be consulted to find out what aspects of the real world are being described ... The formal text on the other hand provides the precise definition of the system ...'

You are left wondering whether the formal text describes the 'real world' or the 'system'. Or are they suppose to be the same thing? You can see something of the same confusion, between describing the real world and describing the system, in many descriptions of object models.

There's a related but different confusion about some dataflow diagrams. When you read a dataflow diagram in which the data flows may represent either pure data or physical things – such as coins in a vending machine, or people in a hospital, or goods in a warehouse – you are often left wondering exactly what each part of the description is about. Do some data flows and stores contain both physical things and pure data? Are some of the processes both physical and computational? Or are there really two diagrams superimposed?

When you know what a description is about, and it seems clear enough, you must guard against making assumptions that the writer never intended you to make. These assumptions often stem from the pictures that a word conjures up in your mind. Look at this finite-state machine:

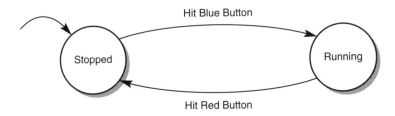

Which of these inferences would you draw from it?

(1) In the *Stopped* state it's impossible to hit the Red Button, and in the *Running* state it's impossible to hit the Blue Button.

(2) You can hit the Red Button in the *Stopped* state, and the Blue Button in the *Running* state, but it has no effect: it doesn't change the state.

(3) You can hit the Red Button in the *Stopped* state, and the Blue Button in the *Running* state, but the effect is unspecified.

Now look at this one:

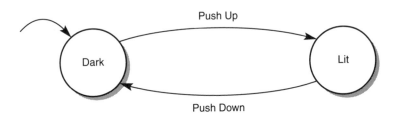

Which of these inferences would you draw from it?

(1) In the *Dark* state it's impossible to Push Down, and in the *Lit* state it's impossible to Push Up.

(2) You can Push Down in the *Dark* state and Push Up in the *Lit* state, but it has no effect: it doesn't change the state.

(3) You can Push Down in the *Dark* state and Push Up in the *Lit* state, but the effect is unspecified.

Meaningful names raise expectations. You'd expect that after a Push Up event the next event would have to be a Push Down, wouldn't you? Perhaps you had a picture of a two-position lever in mind. I did. And you'd expect that after a Hit Red Button you could easily do another Hit Red Button if you wanted to. Perhaps you were thinking of independent buttons like keys on a keyboard. That's very reasonable. But it may be quite wrong. The Push Up/Push Down lever may be spring-loaded so that it returns to a central position after each push, always ready to be pushed either up or down. And the buttons may be located on the two ends of a rocker bar so that you can only hit them alternately. In critical reading you must always be alert to separate your reasonable expectations from what the descriptions are actually saying.

It's often a hard separation to make. A theatre audience waiting for the curtain to rise were horrified to see two men rush in, one threatening the other with a knife. The men were overpowered by theatre staff, and police came to take statements from the audience. Most people said they had seen the big man trying to knife the little man. That was certainly reasonable.

But in fact the men, the theatre staff and the police were all actors taking part in a psychological experiment. What the people had actually seen was the little man trying to knife the big man. They couldn't separate their assumptions from what they actually saw. Software developers must do better.

Dataflow Diagrams – 1

They were all ready to start the walkthrough. Fred had been working on part of the sales accounting system: the problem of matching customers' payments to their outstanding invoices. He had produced a dataflow diagram, and was going to walk through it with Ann and Bill. Jane was there too, because she was new to the team and didn't know about dataflow diagrams. This was a good opportunity for her to learn about them. Fred had invited her, and the project manager said it was a good idea.

'The diagram I'm going to show you,' said Fred, 'expands a process bubble in the diagram at the next level up. Here's the bubble to be expanded.' He showed this viewgraph on the overhead projector:

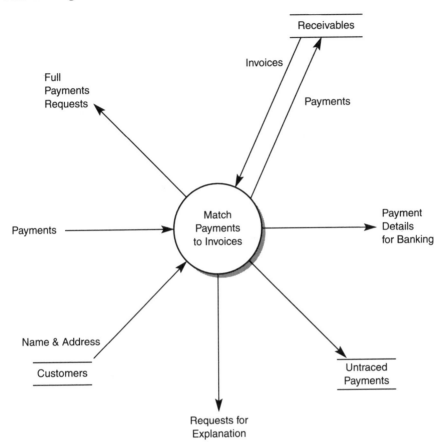

'The payments come in from customers – that's the arrow on the left. Basically, we have to send the payment details to the cashiers for banking – that's the arrow on the right – and put a payment record into the Receivables file on the top right. To do that, we must match the payments with invoices that we get from the Receivables file. If we can't match a payment we put it into the Untraced Payments file, and someone else deals with it. If the payment is not enough to cover the amount in the invoice we send the customer a request to pay in full – that's up at the top left. Oh, and we also send them requests to explain untraced payments. OK so far?'

'I suppose you need the Customer file so you can put names and addresses on the payment and explanation requests,' said Ann.

'Right,' said Fred. 'Now here's the diagram I've done that expands the process bubble.' He put another viewgraph on the projector. It was this:

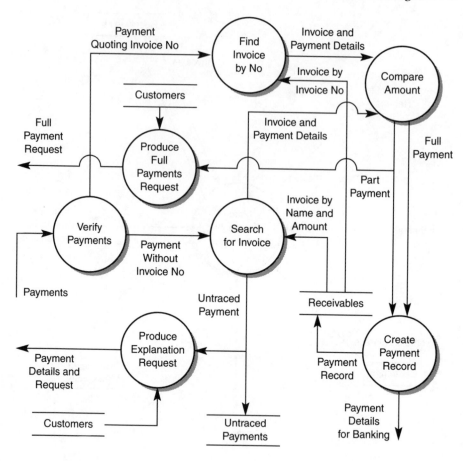

'Looks good,' said Bill. 'Let me see if I can walk through it. The *Verify Payments* process checks to see whether a payment has an invoice number. If it has, you find the invoice – that's the *Find Invoice by No* process at the top of the diagram – and send it with the payment to the *Compare Amount* process. If it hasn't, you have to search for the invoice by using the customer's name and the amount of the payment. If that doesn't work you have an untraced payment. Otherwise you send the invoice and payment details to the *Compare Amount* process as before. Am I on the right lines?'

'Absolutely,' said Fred. 'Right on.'

'The *Compare Amount* process checks the amount paid against the invoice, and whether it's a full or a part payment you send the details to the cashier for banking and put a payment record in the Receivables file. If it's a part payment you also produce a full payment request. Am I right, or am I right?'

'Terrific,' said Fred. 'You just forgot to say that untraced payments go to the *Produce Explanation Request* process so we can send a request to the customer.'

'Sounds good to me,' said Ann. 'We could have an early lunch.'

'Well, wait a minute,' said Jane. 'I haven't really understood what's going on. You said that *Verify Payments* sends each payment either to *Find Invoice by No*, or to *Search for Invoice*, depending on whether it has an invoice number or not. Where does it say that in the diagram?'

'*Verify Payments* has one input data flow and two outputs,' said Ann. 'That's where it says it. It's just like the *Search for Invoice* process. That's got one input data flow of payments without invoice numbers, and two output flows, one for untraced payments, and one for payments with invoices.'

'But the *Create Payment Record* process also has two output flows,' said Jane, 'one for payment records for the Receivables file, and one for payment details for the bank. But it sends each full or part payment to both of those, not just to one.'

'Ann's a bit confused,' said Bill. 'A dataflow diagram doesn't show whether a process writes to one or more of its output flows for each input message. That's at a lower level, probably in the process specification. It's a top-down technique.'

'I'm not at all confused,' said Ann. 'It just depends on your conventions. And I know about top-down as well as you do.'

'All right,' said Jane. 'So we're using Bill's convention. So how *do* you know that *Verify Payments* never writes on both its output data flows?'

'That's a funny question,' said Fred. 'It's obvious, because one flow is named *Payment Quoting Invoice No* and the other one is *Payment Without Invoice No*. You have to read the names. Names are very important in systems analysis.'

'I am reading the names,' said Jane, 'and I don't understand them at all. For example, does "Full Payment" mean the exactly right amount has been paid, or does it include overpayments? And does "Invoice and Payment Details" mean exactly one invoice and one payment? Don't customers sometimes send one payment to cover more than one invoice? And they could send two cheques to cover one invoice, I suppose, as well, couldn't they? And then, what's this *Search for Invoice* process doing? Suppose there are two invoices for the customer, both with the same amount as the payment? Or two invoices adding up to the amount of the payment? Does "Search for Invoice" mean it's only searching for one invoice? Or suppose it finds just one invoice, but it's less than the payment? I don't see how you can work out from the diagram whether these are real possibilities, and, if so, what's supposed to happen when they turn up.'

'Look, Bill's already said it's top-down,' said Fred, 'so you can't expect to answer all these detailed questions now. You'll have to come along to the next walkthrough when I'll have the next level of dataflow diagrams for the more complicated processes here – probably for *Search for Invoice* and *Compare Amount* – and process specifications for the rest.'

'But I don't think these *are* detailed questions,' said Jane. 'The problem is matching payments to invoices, and you're telling me that the diagram doesn't show whether the matching is one-to-one, one-to-many, many-to-one, or many-to-many. I'd have thought that was a fundamental question about a matching problem, not a detailed question. If the diagram doesn't show that, what *does* it show?'

'Well,' said Bill, 'it shows that the function of matching payments to invoices needs seven processes connected by the data flows you can see. That's what it shows.'

'I don't understand,' said Jane. 'It seems to me that it just shows that *Fred thinks* that seven processes connected like that would be useful. But to find out what the function is, or what the processes are, we have to wait till the next level. So the diagram shows that Fred thinks seven processes would be good for the function, but we don't know *what* function and we don't know *what* processes. That *can't* be right, surely?'

'Hold on,' said Fred. 'We're going way off track here. The questions Jane is asking about the matching problem are all good questions, and the whole point of the dataflow diagram is that it makes you think about the good questions – just like Jane is doing. She's got the idea pretty fast,' he said, ingratiatingly. 'That's what a walkthrough's all about.'

'Nice of you to say so,' said Jane, 'but I'm still lost. Suppose we *do* discuss and think about these questions, would we be able to show the answers in the diagram? From what everyone's been saying, we wouldn't be able to. We'd have to wait till the next level. But I don't see how you'd do it at the next level either. Until you get down to the process specifications you keep talking about. I suppose you could tell from *them* what it's all about, but if there are lots of levels you might have to wait a long time. The dataflow diagrams in the levels above don't seem to be much use. They're just vague pictures suggesting what someone thinks might be the shape of a system to solve a problem, and no one's saying what the problem is.'

'Jane, that's offensive,' said Bill. 'Everyone uses dataflow diagrams here, and everyone knows that top-down is the right way to do things. There just isn't any other way. You have to start with the big picture and work your way down to the details.'

'Perhaps,' said Jane, 'but the big picture isn't much use if it doesn't say anything you can understand. You're all just *guessing* what Fred's diagram means. It wouldn't mean *anything at all* to you if you didn't already have a pretty good idea of what the problem is and how to solve it.'

They went to lunch after that. It was a rather uncomfortable lunch. After lunch Bill and Fred were walking together back to the office they shared. 'I don't understand Jane,' said Fred. 'No,' said Bill. 'I don't think we should invite her to the next walkthrough, do you?'

Dataflow Diagrams – 2

Jane had been pretty rude. That was no way to make friends and influence people. But some of her criticisms and objections are hard to answer. They really centre around the following question. When you see a named process symbol in a dataflow diagram, like this:

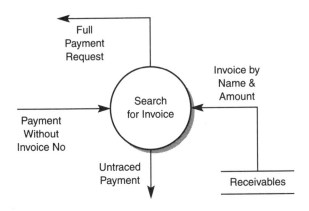

how much *reliably unambiguous* meaning can you get from the symbol and its name, in the context? What does the circle mean? And what does 'Search for Invoice' mean? The key point, of course, is in the phrase *reliably unambiguous*. You can read as much meaning as you like into the diagram from your own assumptions and expectations. But other people will bring different assumptions and expectations to their readings. What matters is the meaning that you can be sure of.

Let's start with the circle. The circle denotes a dataflow process. A dataflow process takes in data packets from its input data streams, and produces data packets on its output streams. It may be either active or passive in dealing with each stream. For example, this process is probably active in getting the *Invoice by Name & Amount* packets from the Receivables data store, and passive in accepting the packets of the *Payment without Invoice* No input stream. And, as Jane pointed out, there's nothing in the symbol to indicate any relationship among the input and output packets. For example, you mustn't assume that the process repeatedly takes in one packet from each input stream and produces one packet on each output stream, or anything like that.

So the process symbol represents something very general. Some users of dataflow diagrams even use them to represent continuous processes. For them, the input and output flows are continuous, like water flowing in a pipe, rather than in discrete packets, like records in a serial file on a magnetic medium.

Some notations used in other disciplines give more precise meaning to their symbols. Logic network diagrams use these symbols:

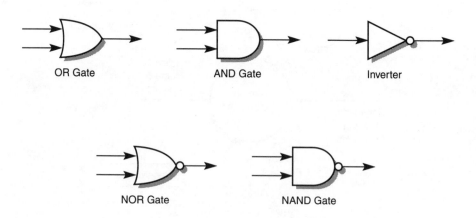

Each input and output is either 1 or 0. The output of the OR Gate is 1 iff (if and only if) at least one of its inputs is 1. The output of the AND Gate is 1 iff both of its inputs are 1. The output of the Inverter is 1 iff its input is 0. The output of the NOR Gate is 1 iff both its inputs are 0. And the output of the NAND Gate is 1 iff at least one of its inputs is 0. Because these symbols represent particular kinds of logic gate, rather than just any general logic gate, a diagram using them has a precisely defined meaning. This diagram represents the device called a half-adder.

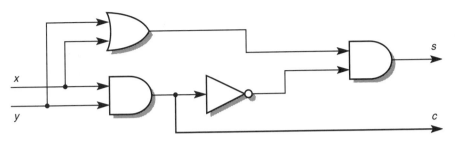

Given two inputs, x and y, each 1 or 0, it produces their sum s and the carry c. The function of the device depicted can be precisely and reliably understood from the diagram. You can calculate it from the symbols and their connections.

Because the meaning of the process symbol in a dataflow diagram is so general, much of the weight must be carried by the names written in the symbols and on the data flows. A lot depends on the meaning of 'Search for Invoice' and 'Compare Amount' and 'Full Payment' and 'Invoice and Payment Details'. How much weight can such names carry?

There's a fundamental distinction that's important here. It's the distinction between describing something that has previously been fully defined and describing something that is still just a vague idea. If you're describing something that's just a vague idea, the names you write in your diagram are not really names at all. They are really very brief descriptions, intended to convey various parts of the idea. Fred's processes are still in the vague idea stage. That's why he has to keep telling Jane to wait for the next level. He hasn't decided himself what the *Search for Invoice* process does: it just does something that can be roughly indicated by the name 'Search for Invoice'.

When you're describing something that is fully defined, and perhaps even already exists, then the situation is quite different. The names you write in your diagram can be truly names: they denote things that can be explored, inspected, and exhibited. That makes all the difference. You can build perfectly reliable descriptions in dataflow diagrams, provided you're describing something that is already known and understood.

In the early days of Structured Analysis, dataflow diagrams were used for several purposes at different stages of a development. Tom DeMarco explains the steps in his 1978 book *Structured Analysis and Specification*. The first step was the Current Physical Data Flow Diagram, showing the existing system as implemented in clerical and automated operations. Here's a fragment of the kind of thing it might have been:

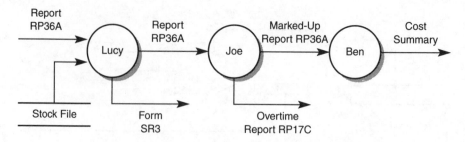

This diagram would have been derived from a study of the existing system. It's a picture of a particular department. They work in room 42, and to draw this diagram you would go to room 42 and talk to them. There are three people in room 42, called Lucy, Joe, and Ben. When you ask them what they do, they describe their jobs. They talk about passing the reports and forms to each other; about marking them up; about looking in the Stock File; and about sending the Cost Summary and the SR3 Forms and the RP17C Report on to other departments.

So the diagram was a REFUTABLE DESCRIPTION. You could look at the world it described. Nobody is quite sure what 'Search for Invoice' refers to. But everybody knows what 'Lucy' refers to. Go and visit her. Look at a Form SR3 and riffle through the cards of the Stock File and see what's written on them. Show the description to Lucy, Joe and Ben. Perhaps they will tell you it's not true. They might say that Joe doesn't mark up the report, but Ben does – Joe just does the overtime report and passes the unmarked RP36A report on to Ben. There's no invention or imagination here: just straight-forward description of the world.

After the Current Physical Flow Diagram came:

- the Current Logical Flow Diagram, showing a more abstract view of the existing system;

- the New Logical Flow Diagram, showing an abstract view of a new system, derived by modifying the existing system; and, finally

- the New Physical Flow Diagram, showing an implementation of the new system.

Each diagram was quite closely related to its predecessor; and the first diagram was related to the reality of the existing system.

But the whole procedure of going through the four stages came to seem too cumbersome; and often there was no existing system to provide the starting point. So Ed Yourdon, in *Modern Structured Analysis*, says:

'... the systems analyst should *avoid* modeling the user's current system if at all possible. The modeling tools should be used to begin, *as quickly as possible*, to develop a model of the *new* system that the user wants'.

Nobody seems to have noticed that this modern change undermined the whole basis for using dataflow diagrams in Structured Analysis. The Current Physical and Current Logical diagrams may have been old-fashioned and a bore and a nuisance, but they laid a foundation for the logical and physical diagrams of the new system. Their removal left a building without foundations. But then, that's Top-Down, isn't it?

Definitions

Each term you use in a description must be defined somewhere. Otherwise your readers won't know what you're talking about – and you may not be so sure yourself, either.

One way to define a term is to give a Designation. That means giving a recognition rule for recognizing some class of phenomenon that you could observe in a domain. In the domain of human biological relationships you might write these designations:

x is a human being (homo sapiens)	$\approx$ Human(x)
x is male	$\approx$ Male(x)
x is female	$\approx$ Female(x)
x is the biological (genetic) mother of y	$\approx$ Mother(x,y)
x is the biological (genetic) father of y	$\approx$ Father(x,y)

'Human(x)' is the term you're going to use for the phenomenon 'x is a human being (homo sapiens)', and so on. The terms Human, Male, Female, Mother, and Father are now well enough defined by the recognition rules you have given – if they're not, you should get a biologist to help you to improve the descriptions. You can use the designated terms in Refutable Descriptions that make assertions about the domain. Here's an assertion in Predicate Logic:

$$\forall\, x,y \bullet (\, (\, \text{Human}(x) \wedge \text{Mother}(x,y)\,) \rightarrow (\, \text{Female}(x) \wedge \text{Human}(y)\,)\,)$$

Whatever x and y you choose, if x is human and x is the mother of y, then x is female and y is human. All human mothers are female and their children are all human.

Now suppose that you want to make some assertions about grandparents, and aunts and uncles, and cousins and brothers and sisters. You don't have any designations for these terms, but it will be very inconvenient and difficult to do without them. There are two ways of making them available for use in your descriptions. One way is to write some more designations. For example:

---

x is the genetic full brother of y	$\approx$ Brother(x,y)
x is the genetic full sister of y	$\approx$ Sister(x,y)

Sometimes this is the right thing to do. But probably it's not the right thing here. The right thing here is to do it the other way: to give a formal definition of each of the new terms, using the terms you have already designated. Here are definitions for brother and sister:

$$\text{Brother}(x,y) \triangleq \text{Male}(x) \wedge \exists f \bullet (\text{Father}(f,x) \wedge \text{Father}(f,y))$$
$$\wedge \exists m \bullet (\text{Mother}(m,x) \wedge \text{Mother}(m,y))$$
$$\text{Sister}(x,y) \triangleq \text{Female}(x) \wedge \exists f \bullet (\text{Father}(f,x) \wedge \text{Father}(f,y))$$
$$\wedge \exists m \bullet (\text{Mother}(m,x) \wedge \text{Mother}(m,y))$$

I'm using the symbol $\triangleq$ as the definition symbol. The definition of brother says that Brother(x,y) is true if and only if x is male and x and y have the same father (f) and the same mother (m). The definition of sister is similar.

The terms brother and sister add convenience to your descriptive language. They don't add any new phenomena, or any new observations, to your domain. Ultimately, statements that use the defined terms can be 'unpacked' into exactly equivalent statements that use only the designated terms. Of course, you can build further levels of definition if you want to. Here's a definition of uncle, built on the definition of brother:

$$\text{Uncle}(x,y) \triangleq \exists p \bullet ((\text{Father}(p,y) \vee \text{Mother}(p,y)) \wedge \text{Brother}(x,p))$$

Uncle(x,y) is true if and only if there is some p that is the father or mother of y and has x as a brother. Statements that use the term 'uncle' can be unpacked into statements that don't use 'uncle' and don't use 'brother' either.

Why is it better to give a formal definition of brother and sister – and uncle, too – than to write more designations? Because they are not really separately observable phenomena. 'Brother' really *means* 'a male who has the same mother and father'; and 'uncle' really *means* 'a brother of a parent' – no more and no less. By giving a definition, you achieve an important benefit. You bring the meaning within the formal part of your description instead of leaving it in the informal left-hand side of a designation.

There's another benefit, too. Careful use of definition helps you to keep the number of designations as small as possible. Then your designations will form only a NARROW BRIDGE between the informal domain in the real world and the formal descriptions in your software development. That will make it much easier to understand your descriptions, and to check whether they are true.

Definitions are different from designations. But they're even more different from refutable descriptions. Let's look at another little example. Developing a system to control the filling of a chemical vat, you decide to designate these two phenomena:

By time t, the total volume of chemical that has flowed
   into the vat through the inlet pipe is x litres $\approx$ Inflow(x,t)
By time t, the total volume of chemical that has flowed
   out of the vat through the outlet valve is x litres $\approx$ Outflow(x,t)

Now you add a definition:

$$\text{Netflow}(c,t) \triangleq \exists\, i,o \bullet (\text{ Inflow}(i,t) \wedge \text{Outflow}(o,t) \wedge (c = i - o)\,)$$

The term Netflow(c,t) is defined to mean that at time t, there is some total volume i that has flowed into the vat through the inlet pipe, and some total volume o that has flowed out of the vat through the outlet valve, and c is the amount by which i exceeds o. Like all formal definitions, this definition just makes a convenient term available for use in descriptions. It asserts nothing whatsoever about the chemical plant. There would be no sense in asking whether the definition is true or false: a definition can only be well-formed or badly formed, and useful or not useful.

Now suppose instead that you had decided to make another designation:

At time t, the total volume of chemical
   in the vat is x litres $\approx$ Contains(x,t)

Contains(x,t) is a new observable phenomenon in the chemical plant domain. You could observe it, perhaps, by using a dipstick, or a sight tube connected to the vat.

You add a refutable description:

$$\forall\, c,t \bullet \text{Contains}(c,t) \leftrightarrow \exists\, i,o \bullet (\text{ Inflow}(i,t) \wedge \text{Outflow}(o,t) \wedge (c = i - o)\,)$$

This description *asserts* that for any c and t whatsoever, Contains(c,t) is true if (and only if) c is the excess of inflow over outflow up to time t. This is an important assertion in your description of the chemical plant. It's not true if there is leakage or evaporation of the chemical. Someone who wanted to falsify it would make careful observations of the vat and produce their observations as evidence. 'Look,' they would say, 'I observed at time 12:59 that Contains(843,12:59) and Inflow(965,12:59) and Outflow (106,12:59). But $965 - 106 = 859$, not 843. So your assertion is untrue.' If you can't show that their observations are faulty, you would have to agree with them.

Although the definition (of Netflow) and the assertion (about Contains) look very similar, they are really quite different. It's very important not to confuse them. Just remember: formal definitions are just about language. They don't say anything about the domain.

A last word. A definition must be complete. That's what I meant by the 'if and only if' in the explanation of the definitions:

$$\text{Brother}(x,y) \triangleq \text{Male}(x) \wedge \exists f \bullet (\ \text{Father}(f,x) \wedge \text{Father}(f,y)\ )$$
$$\wedge \exists m \bullet (\ \text{Mother}(m,x) \wedge \text{Mother}(m,y)\ )$$

and:

$$\text{Uncle}(x,y) \triangleq \exists p \bullet (\ (\ \text{Father}(p,y) \vee \text{Mother}(p,y)\ ) \wedge \text{Brother}(x,p)\ )$$

Definition completeness means that you can never give a definition that says 'such-and-such is defined to be true in these circumstances – oh, and there may be other circumstances, yet to be specified, in which it's defined to be true also'. That kind of partial definition wouldn't be very useful, because almost anything you said using the partially defined term might become false when the definition is later completed.

Dekker

In his 1968 paper *Cooperating Sequential Processes* Dijkstra acknowledged the Dutch mathematician Thomas Dekker as the author of the first solution of the *mutual exclusion* problem. The problem is illuminating and humbling. It is very simple, and the solution is easy to understand. But it is not easy to devise a solution, and there are many ways of failing. Nancy Leveson and Clark Turner showed in their paper *An Investigation of the Therac-25 Accidents* that a programmer's failure to solve this problem was responsible for several deaths: the Therac-25 was a software-controlled radiation therapy machine that killed several patients in the 1980s because its software was faulty.

In its simplest form the problem concerns two concurrent processes, P1 and P2:

P1: begin	P2: begin
...	...
...	...
end *P1*	end *P2*

The two processes run on the same hardware processor. They are executed concurrently by a scheduler which switches the hardware processor between them so that each seems to be running on its own, slower, processor. The processes communicate by sharing access to variables in the processor's RAM.

The text of each process contains a *critical region*. The critical region may be inside a loop; so it may be executed many times. The problem is to ensure that the critical regions are mutually exclusive: that is, that the two processes are never both in their critical regions at the same time. This mutual exclusion is necessary if the critical regions perform complex updates to a shared data structure in disk or RAM, and the updates would get in each other's way if they were both going on at the same time.

A scheme is needed, using shared variables in the store, that will guarantee the necessary mutual exclusion. Here is a scheme that uses two shared boolean variables, *flag1* and *flag2*. The idea is that each *flagi* has the value true when the corresponding process *Pi* is trying to enter its critical region.

Version1:
var *flag1, flag2*: *boolean* := *false*;

P1: **begin**	P2: **begin**
...	...
flag1 := *true*;	*flag2* := *true*;
while *flag2* **do**;	**while** *flag1* **do**;
<critical region 1>	<critical region 2>
flag1 := *false*;	*flag2* := *false*;
...	...
end *P1*	end *P2*

Clearly *flagi* is set to true throughout the period in which the process *Pi* is in its critical region. And, equally clearly, each process waits, at its null **while** loop, until the other process has left its critical region. So the problem is solved. Isn't it?

Not quite. The scheduler may interleave the process executions like this:

```
P1:                          P2:
    set flag1 to true
                                 set flag2 to true
    check flag2 (true)
                                 check flag1 (true)
    ...
```

And so on indefinitely. Now they're stuck: each process waits forever at its **while** loop. That's called *deadlock*. But we can fix it:

```
Version2:
var flag1, flag2: boolean := false;
   P1: begin                        P2: begin
       ...                              ...
       flag1 := true;                   flag2 := true;
       while flag2 do                   while flag1 do
          begin                            begin
             flag1 := false;                 flag2 := false;
             flag1 := true;                  flag2 := true;
          end;                             end;
          <critical region 1>              <critical region 2>
          flag1 := false;                  flag2 := false;
       ...                              ...
   end P1                           end P2
```

The processes can't both be stuck, because each gives the other an opportunity to go ahead by turning its own flag off and then on again. Well, this still isn't right. The process executions may be interleaved like this:

```
P1:                          P2:
    set flag1 to true
                                 set flag2 to true
    check flag2 (true)
                                 check flag1 (true)
    set flag1 to false
                                 set flag2 to false
    set flag1 to true
                                 set flag2 to true
    check flag2 (true)
                                 check flag1 (true)
    ...
                                 ...
```

And so on indefinitely. Although there are times when each process's flag is set to false, the other process may never be lucky enough to check it at such a time. It's just possible that each process may wait for ever at its **while** loop. That's *livelock*. Not acceptable for a safety-critical system.

Both versions have another defect, too. One of the processes may possibly execute its critical region and set its flag to false, but then return so quickly to the point in its text at which it sets its flag to true again that the other, waiting, process never checks the flag and finds it false. (Remember that the critical regions are probably inside loops.) This might happen repeatedly, the first process always shutting out the second. That's called *starvation*, for obvious reasons.

Here's Dekker's solution:

```
Version3:
    var flag1, flag2: boolean := false;
        turn: 1..2 := 1;
        P1: begin                          P2: begin
              ...                                ...
            flag1 := true;                     flag2 := true;
            if turn = 2 then                   if turn = 1 then
                while flag2 do;                    while flag1 do;
            else                               else
                begin                              begin
                    flag1 := false;                    flag2 := false;
                    while turn = 2 do;                 while turn = 1 do;
                    flag1 := true;                     flag2 := true;
                    while flag2 do;                    while flag1 do;
                end;                               end;
            <critical region 1>                <critical region 2>
            turn := 2;                         turn := 1;
            flag1 := false;                    flag2 := false;
              ...                                ...
        end P1                             end P2
```

The *turn* variable establishes a priority that is used to resolve contention between the processes and to avoid the possibility that one process may repeatedly exclude the other. Can you find anything wrong with it? No, of course not – I began by saying that Dekker's was acknowledged to be the first solution. Do you think you would have found Dekker's solution yourself? Can you prove – and I mean *prove* – that Dekker's solution is correct? And what do you think of this fourth version?

```
Version4:
    var flag1, flag2: boolean := false;
        turn: 1..2 := 1;
        P1: begin                          P2: begin
              ...                                ...
            flag1 := true;                     flag2 := true;
            turn := 2;                         turn := 1;
            while flag2                        while flag1
```

```
            and turn = 2 do;                    and turn = 1 do;
            <critical region 1>                 <critical region 2>
            flag1 := false;                     flag2 := false;
            ...                                  ...
            end P1                               end P2
```

It seems simpler than Dekker's solution. Do you believe that this fourth version is correct? Or is it not? Would you be willing to stake your life on your answer? A little humility is in order, I think. Whenever you are tempted to think that small problems can't be very difficult, or that MATHEMATICS is irrelevant to your work, just look again at the mutual exclusion problem and think of Thomas Dekker.

Descriptions

The central activity of software development is description. Software developers need to master the techniques of description, and to understand what makes a particular description suitable or unsuitable for a particular purpose.

Descriptions are the externally visible medium of thought. For software developers, the old joke 'How can I know what I think until I hear what I say?' must be rephrased: 'How can I know what I think until I see what descriptions I write?' If you understand how descriptions work, and how one description differs from another, you can use this understanding to improve your techniques for thinking about problems. Thinking about descriptions is thinking about thinking.

The first step in understanding descriptions is to recognize that there are – at least – four important kinds of description: designations; definitions; refutable descriptions; and rough sketches.

- A DESIGNATION singles out some particular kind of PHENOMENON that is of interest; tells you informally – in natural language – how to recognize it; and gives a name by which it will be denoted. Here is a designation:

    'The human genetic mother of x is $m \approx$ Mother(x,m)'

    The *designated phenomenon* is the relationship of genetic motherhood between two people; it will be denoted in descriptions by using the predicate Mother (x,m). So Mother(Joe,Lucy) will mean that the genetic mother of Joe is Lucy.

- A DEFINITION gives a formal definition of a term that may be used by other descriptions. Here is a definition:

    'Child$(x,y) \triangleq$ Mother$(y,x) \vee$ Father(y,x)'

    It defines the term 'Child(x,y)' to mean exactly the same as 'Mother(y,x) or Father(y,x)'. A definition cannot be true or false: it can only be well-formed or not well-formed, and useful or not useful. A designation, of course, is rather like an informal definition. But it's convenient to reserve the word *definition* to mean a *formal* definition expressed in terms *previously defined*. A designation is always informal, because the world where the phenomena are to be recognized is informal.

- A REFUTABLE DESCRIPTION describes some DOMAIN, saying something about it that could – in principle – be refuted or disproved. Whether it could in practice be disproved is another matter: the important thing is that it could make sense to disprove it, as it can't make sense to disprove a definition. Refutability depends on the fact that the description ultimately refers to designated phenomena of the domain being described. Here's a tiny refutable description, expressed in PREDICATE LOGIC:

$$\forall\ m,x \bullet \text{Mother}(x,m) \rightarrow \neg\ \text{Mother}(m,x)\text{'}$$

It says that whatever m and x you choose, if m is the human genetic mother of x, then x is not the human genetic mother of m. To refute it you would have to find a pair of mutual genetic mothers. Inconceivable. But not nonsensical.

- A ROUGH SKETCH is a tentative description of something that is in process of being explored or invented. It uses undefined terms to record vague half-formed ideas. It's useful at a development stage when you want to say 'well, perhaps something like this might be right' without devoting much time or effort to saying exactly what you have in mind. Here's a tiny rough sketch:

'Everyone really belongs to just one family.'

We don't know, and we haven't been told, what 'really belongs to' means, or what 'family' means. It's hard to make any exact sense of this description, but it might possibly be a useful intermediate stage towards saying something refutable.

Any software development needs many descriptions. One reason is that it makes good sense to keep the different kinds of description separate: for instance, not to mix designations with rough sketches. Another, more important, reason is that you can't say everything in one description. The complexity of most software problems does not allow you to think about the whole problem at once. So at any one time you identify an aspect or part of the problem that can be considered separately, and leave the rest aside until another time. This *separation of concerns* is reflected in a separation of your thoughts into a number of separate PARTIAL DESCRIPTIONS.

There are many ways of separating concerns into partial descriptions: how you do it will have a decisive effect on your development project. It determines the structure of everything you do in the development.

Modularizing your requirements or specifications is at least as important as modularizing your programs.

For a description to be useful, you must know its SCOPE: that is, what it's about. First, you must know what domain – what part of the universe of interest – is being described. If you are looking at a map, you need to know whether it is a map of the earth or a map of the moon. And then you must know what phenomena of the domain are being described. Is it a rainfall map, or a population map? You say what phenomena are being described by associating a set of designations with the description. For a rainfall map you would designate phenomena like 'The average annual rainfall in area a is r'; for a population map you would choose phenomena like 'The population per square kilometre of area a is p'.

A description also has a SPAN: that is, the particular subset of the designated phenomena it includes. Knowing the span of the population map means recognizing the part of the world's surface that is depicted, and knowing whether it is the population in 1990 or in 1800 that is shown. Similarly, the span of the rainfall map might be the Jurassic period or the present century.

These ideas – of partial description and description scope and span – can help when things get difficult. Stop and ask yourself: Am I making the right kind of separation? Am I using the wrong scope, or the wrong span? Sometimes a problem that seems hard is just an easy problem surrounded by irrelevant and confusing material.

Here is a well-known puzzle:

> 'In a Knock-Out Tennis Tournament, if the number of competitors is a power of 2 – say, 2 to the nth power – then there will be n rounds. In each round, half of the players in the round are eliminated, and the other half go forward to the next round, in which there will be only half as many matches. Eventually, there will be a round with only one match, and the winner of that match is the winner of the tournament. If the number of competitors is not a power of 2, then some of them miss the first round, and proceed directly to the second round; from the second round onwards, everything continues as normal. The question is: If there are 111 competitors, how many matches are there in the whole tournament?'

The difficulty of the puzzle – if there is a difficulty – arises solely from the background information given in the preamble to the question. The victim is inundated with explanations of the ordering of the rounds, of the decreasing number of matches from one round to the next, and of the arrangements necessary when the number of competitors is not a power of 2. There is a large scope of description here, and you are easily drawn into assuming that it is necessary:

'Let me see. The smallest power of 2 that is not less than 111 is 128, which is 2 to the power 7; so this is a tournament with 7 rounds, and 17 – that is, 128 minus 111 – players miss the first round. Now, how many matches must there be in a tournament with 7 rounds? . . .'

And so on. But the question is really much easier. Each match played eliminates one competitor; 110 competitors must be eliminated to find the eventual winner; so there must be 110 matches.

If you always keep the ideas of description scope and span in mind, you'll find it easier to avoid confusing yourself with too much information. You're trying to answer the question: How many matches are there in a tournament with 111 competitors? Somewhere, you've got to make use of a relationship – direct or indirect – between a competitor and a match. What's the smallest possible scope relating competitors and matches? A competitor *plays in* a match. A competitor *loses* a match or *wins* a match. What's the smallest span? One match.

Think a little about that before rushing to enlarge the scope and span of your description. It may come to you: in each match exactly one competitor loses, and is eliminated from the tournament. The playing of the matches in a certain order, their arrangement in rounds, and the association of the rounds with powers of 2 can all be excluded from the scope of your descriptions. They're all irrelevant to the question you're trying to answer. They give you an unnecessarily – and damagingly – large *scope* and *span*.

Confusion and difficulty in software development will not often yield so easily. But thinking about descriptions, and about their separation, and their scope and span, is an important and versatile way of attacking them.

Designations

Lewis Carroll was a logician. His fantastic and whimsical writings about Alice, in *Alice's Adventures in Wonderland* and *Through the Looking-Glass and What Alice Found There*, deal with many profound topics of philosophy and logic. One of the most important topics concerns the meaning of words. In a famous exchange, Alice questions Humpty Dumpty's cavalier approach. 'The question is,' said Alice, 'whether you *can* make words mean so many different things.' 'The question is,' said Humpty Dumpty, 'which is to be master – that's all.'

Later, Alice finds a poem, *Jabberwocky*, in a book in the Looking-Glass room. Here are the last four verses:

> And, as in uffish thought he stood,
> The Jabberwock, with eyes of flame,

Came whiffling through the tulgey wood,
And burbled as it came!

One, two! One, two! And through and through
The vorpal blade went snicker-snack!
He left it dead, and with its head
He went galumphing back.

'And hast thou slain the Jabberwock?
Come to my arms, my beamish boy!
O frabjous day! Callooh! Callay!'
He chortled in his joy.

'Twas brillig, and the slithy toves
Did gyre and gimble in the wabe:
All mimsy were the borogoves,
And the mome raths outgrabe.

Carroll continues:

'It seems very pretty' she said when she had finished it, 'but it's rather
hard to understand!' (You see she didn't like to confess, even to herself, that she couldn't make it out at all.) 'Somehow it seems to fill my
head with ideas – only I don't exactly know what they are! However,
somebody killed *something*: that's clear, at any rate –'.

Her confusion may remind you of the feeling you get from many software
documents: they fill your head with ideas, only you don't know exactly
what they are. Later Alice encounters Humpty Dumpty again, and asks him
to explain the poem. Explaining the last verse, Humpty Dumpty says that:

- *'brillig'* means four o'clock in the afternoon – the time when you begin
  broiling things for dinner;
- *'slithy'* means 'lithe and slimy';
- *'toves'* are something like badgers – they're something like lizards – and
  they're something like corkscrews;
- *'wabe'* is the grass-plot round a sun-dial; it's called *'wabe'* because it
  goes a long way before it, and a long way behind it, and a long way
  beyond it on each side.

Humpty Dumpty has exactly the right idea of how to explain the poem. He
knows that Alice understands English: she just doesn't know the meanings
of the difficult words. So he does not paraphrase the whole poem, or individual verses or lines. Instead, he provides a set of definitions, one for each
difficult word.

This is exactly what you need in software development when you are
describing a domain. A description states some relationship – existing or

required – among certain PHENOMENA: to understand what the description means in the domain you must be able to identify the phenomena. It's not enough to learn that the borogoves were all mimsy: you must be able to recognize a borogove when you see one, and to say reliably whether it is mimsy or not. The tool you need is a *designation*. Here's one of Humpty's designations, slightly reorganized:

Recognition Rule	$\approx$ *Designated Term*
x is something like a badger, something like a lizard, and something like a corkscrew	$\approx$ Tove(x)

On the left is the *recognition rule*. It's an informal natural language rule for recognizing the phenomenon being designated: in this case, that something – x – is a tove. On the right, following the designation symbol $\approx$, is the *designated term* – Tove(x) – that will be used to refer to the phenomenon in descriptions. In practice the headings *Recognition Rule* and *Designated Term* are omitted.

A designation serves two purposes. It works in both directions. When you're starting out to describe something, a designation singles out a kind of phenomenon as being of interest, and gives it a name. Later, when you've written some descriptions, the designations tell you what the terms in the descriptions mean.

Suppose you're developing a database system about literary history. Here is a designation set with which you can describe certain literary relationships:

x is a nineteenth-century English novel	$\approx$ Novel(x)
x is a named human character in the novel y	$\approx$ CharacterIn(x,y)
x is the author of the novel y	$\approx$ AuthorOf(x,y)

This designation set contains three designations. It says that the phenomena they designate are of interest in your system: you're going to be talking about authors and characters of nineteenth-century English novels. It also says that in any description using this designation set 'Novel' does not refer to just any work of fiction, but only to nineteenth-century English novels. *Oliver Twist* and *Pride and Prejudice* are in; *The Catcher in the Rye*, *La Peste* and *The Grapes of Wrath* are out. And 'Character' does not refer to animals or anonymous human characters: *Nancy* and *Oliver* are in; Bill Sykes's dog *Bull's-eye* is out.

The essence of a good designation is phenomena that are clearly and unambiguously recognizable in the domain, and recognition rules that tell you well enough how to recognize them. Because most interesting domains are informal you mustn't demand perfect precision in a recognition rule. There are always difficulties. What about a novel written in 1799 and published in 1801? What about joint authorship? Is 'The Artful Dodger' a *named* character? The point is to do it *well enough* for the purposes of the system you're building. If you can't write a good recognition rule you have probably chosen an unsuitable phenomenon. Take a lot of care in choosing and writing designations: they are the foundation of your descriptions.

A designation set is not at all the same thing as a data dictionary, or its grander cousin, the data encyclopaedia or repository. First, it conveys no information about the domain except, perhaps, that the designated phenomena are recognizable in the domain. From the designation set above, you may not infer that Novels are not themselves Authors of other Novels; nor that Characters can't be Authors; nor that every Novel has at least one Author; nor even that if X is the Author of Y then Y must be a Novel. These truths, if truths they are, must be explicitly stated in REFUTABLE DESCRIPTIONS. Designations, in short, are not assertions.

Second, you certainly don't want designations for all the terms used in your development descriptions. On the contrary, your aim should be to build a NARROW BRIDGE between the domain and your descriptions, writing designations for as few phenomena as possible and defining other terms on the basis of those few. For example, you may find it useful to define such terms as: WroteAboutCharacter(x,y) – *Charles Dickens* wrote about *The Artful Dodger*; or ShareCharacter(x,y,z) – *Framley Parsonage* and *Dr Thorne* share the character *Miss Dunstable*; or BothInSameNovel(x,y) – *Bill Sykes* and *Nancy* both appear in *Oliver Twist*. All of them can be defined on the basis of the already designated phenomena. It would be a mistake to write designations for them.

Third, a designation set is *local* in the sense that it is associated with one particular domain; but is not tied to particular descriptions. Different descriptions can be applied with the same designation set to describe different relationships among the same phenomena. And by applying the same description with different designation sets you can assert that the same relationships hold among different collections of phenomena in the same or in different domains. That's a large part of what MODELS are about.

Confusion about the meaning of terms is an endemic risk in software development. Every systems analyst knows that ten different users will have at least ten different ideas about the meaning of 'product', and that 'sale' will mean different things according to whether you ask the people in accounts or the people in sales or the people in the warehouse. It's essential to bring this confusion under control, since otherwise when you make descriptions you are building without foundations. Of course, you aim – or you should aim – to write precise descriptions, and to avoid the ambiguities of natural language by using more formal notations and languages. But that's not enough: you need explicit designations too.

As John von Neumann observed in *The Theory of Games*, 'There is no point in using exact methods where there is no clarity in the concepts and issues to which they are to be applied'. In a crisper conversational version he said more simply, 'There is no sense in being precise when you don't know what you are talking about'.

Deskilling

When structured programming was fashionable in the 1970s, some people said that it took all the skill and all the fun out of programming. They said it was like Scientific Management, developed by Frederick Taylor and others in the early years of the twentieth century to deskill the jobs of engineering production-line workers. Taylor completed the process begun by the industrial revolution 150 years earlier. Mill owners of the early nineteenth century found the carefree and independent attitudes of cottage craft workers inconvenient for the rigorous discipline of their mills and inconvenient for their profits. They aimed to turn the self-employed hand-loom weavers into tightly regimented and controlled mill hands.

Philip Kraft saw the same process at work in software development. In 1977, in *Programmers and Managers*, he wrote:

> 'Managers have therefore adapted the principles of structured programming – orderliness, simplicity, economical and standard language – to facilitate control over a social process rather than to enhance an intellectual activity'.

He recognized that there was another aspect:

> 'Indeed, Dijkstra and Gries have stressed in their writings that they see in structured programming the possibility of enlarging, rather than diminishing, the skills, knowledge, and understanding of the average programmer. I have no doubt whatsoever that they believe and hope this to be the case'.

But his broad analysis was unequivocal. If you're a programmer, structured programming is bad news, and you should not let your boss impose it on you:

> 'Briefly, programmers using structured programming would be limited to a handful of logical procedures which they could use – no others were permitted. They could call for only certain kinds of information; they could ask only specified questions about that information; ... No deviation from this logical sequence is allowed ...'

Obviously, this process of deskilling has been going on since long before the industrial revolution. In Roman times, and in Western Europe until 800 years ago, multiplication of two numbers – often necessary in a mercantile counting house – was a difficult problem, and division demanded intellectual brilliance of a high order. Multiplying DCCXLIII by MCMXXIV is a serious task, even with the help of the primitive abacus that some counting houses had. The work was done by skilled people. No doubt they adopted an independent attitude and were not easily controlled by the counting house manager.

Then the West learned about the number zero, and about positional notation, from the Hindus and the Arabs. And with it they learned standard methods for multiplication and division, which would now need only a handful of logical procedures. The problems of division and multiplication were suddenly taken out of the category that demands brilliance and put into the category that every well-educated person can solve easily. Multiplying 743 by 1924 wasn't at all hard when you knew how to do it.

Perhaps the Philip Krafts of the time complained bitterly. But they would have been missing the point. There's no shortage of problems in arithmetic: finding large prime factors is a hotter topic now than multiplication or division has ever been. Nor is there any shortage of problems in software development. The point of learning a good development method is not to reduce software developers' skills and devalue their talent. Quite the opposite. It is to free the developers to apply their skill to problems that can give it a proper reward, instead of wasting it on self-inflicted confusions and on techniques and notations that no one could use effectively.

Whether your boss is treating you properly is one thing. Whether you should resist learning more systematic methods is another thing altogether. You shouldn't. It's sad to see an intelligent person struggling with the software equivalent of a long multiplication problem.

Domain Characteristics

A word-processing program deals with *texts* and the *users* who create and edit them. A switching program deals with *telephone calls*. A process-control program deals with a *chemical plant*. These are some of the DOMAINS in the PROBLEM CONTEXTS of their respective programs. The most important thing about them is that they are all different. *Texts*, and *users*, and *telephone calls*, and *chemical plants* have very different domain characteristics.

The characteristics of a domain determine how it can interact with other domains and with the machine. They play a crucial role in fixing the shape and character of the software development problem, the kinds of solution it can have, and the kinds of method you can use to solve it. A method that is good for developing a word-processing program probably won't be good for telephone switching or for process control, because their domains are so different. So you must always pay a lot of attention to the characteristics of the domains you deal with.

There is no standard comprehensive taxonomy of domain characteristics. What's important will vary from domain to domain, from problem to problem, and – most important – from method to method. But some distinctions stand out because they are almost always important.

First, the distinction between *static* and *dynamic* domains. In a dynamic domain there is a time dimension. Things happen, and things change. It's important to know whether one event happened before or after another event. There is a notion of *state*: a state is everything that is true at a particular time. As time passes and events occur, the domain progresses through different states. We usually think of the progress of time as a progress through a sequence of alternating events – happenings that cause change – and intervals – the gaps between events in which everything remains the same.

But a static domain has no time dimension. There are no events, nothing happens, and nothing changes. If you're thinking in terms of events and intervals, a static domain has no events. And it has either no intervals or only one interval, depending on how you want to look at it.

For a particular problem it may be right to take a static view of a dynamic domain. When you plan a journey by road you think of the road network as fixed. Although the roads do change over time, you expect them to change only very slowly, over a period much longer than your journey time. But a civil engineer working on the design and construction of a new traffic intersection thinks of the surrounding part of the road network quite differently. As the construction of the intersection progresses through its various stages, the intersecting roads must be diverted or closed, then restored to their new routes and reopened. For the engineer, the road network is definitely a dynamic domain.

The government of the United Kingdom provided a nice example in the 1981 census of how to treat a dynamic domain statically. Households were asked to complete a census form with the rubric:

> 'You must answer the questions in this form so that your answers are true at midnight on 4th/5th April 1981'.

The census gave a snapshot of the United Kingdom at that one moment. Because there was only one moment, analysis of the information returned could not possibly be concerned with anything happening, or with anything changing. Nothing could change, because there was only one moment: no before, and no after.

A domain – whether it's static or dynamic – may have a *one-dimensional* structure, or it may be *multi-dimensional*. A single-string necklace of beads is a one-dimensional domain, but a road network is multi-dimensional. A file of records on magnetic tape, or organized as a sequential file on disk, is one-dimensional, but a relational database is not. A single railway line without branches or loops or crossings is one-dimensional, but the worldwide telephone system is multi-dimensional. The text of the Bible is one-dimensional, and so is the program text of a C function; but a graphic image is not. A communication channel, in which messages are transmitted in time order, is a one-dimensional domain. One-dimensionality is an important property because one-dimensional structures are much simpler than multi-dimensional structures.

A lot of what we do in software development is imposing one-dimensional structures on multi-dimensional domains. Domain characteristics depend, of course, on the selection of relevant phenomena within each domain. The program text of a C function is one-dimensional if you look at it from a narrowly syntactic point of view, ignoring the identifier values. But it's multi-dimensional if you use the identifier values to look at data dependences.

Another important distinction is between *tangible* and *intangible* domains. The texts in a word-processing system are intangible: they have no physical manifestation except that provided by the MACHINE by which they will be created and manipulated at the user's command. In fact, the texts may be thought of as existing inside the machine: all the phenomena of the texts are phenomena of the machine. This is often true of an intangible domain, such as a matrix of numbers or the position in a chess game. If it is to play a role in the completed system, it must be given an existence inside the machine, either as data or as program.

The chemical plant in the process-control system, on the other hand, is very tangible indeed. It is a physical thing in the world, with all that that entails. Inevitably, it is informal. That means that you must be specially careful in choosing the phenomena to be captured in DESIGNATIONS. You have to choose the phenomena that you can describe exactly enough to be reliably recognized in the domain. It also means that domain properties hold only approximately. Whatever relationships you describe among phenomena of an informal domain, there can always be exceptions. Informal domains are *unbounded*, in the sense that you can never be sure that you have covered all the cases, or considered all the factors. There can always be some other case, or some previously ignored factor that turns out to be relevant.

Dynamic tangible domains are also subject to physical constraints. Things can't happen at just any speed. You have to wait for the chemical in the vessel to reach its boiling point, or to cool down, or to flow out through the evacuation pipe. Any dynamic physical domain in the problem context introduces real-time considerations into the development.

Some very important distinctions concern causality and control. These domain properties are often ignored in software development – that is, they are treated implicitly and never explicitly described. Formal methods often abstract from these distinctions, because they are hard to capture in the mathematical languages that formalists love. Informal developers have an opportunity to do better here. But for both, the distinctions are usually simplified to a single distinction between the machine's inputs and its outputs. It's really a lot more complex and subtle than that.

One distinction is among *inert*, *reactive*, and *active* dynamic domains. A dynamic domain is inert if it never does anything of its own accord. It does have a time dimension, and things can change. But they change only when they are changed by an outside agent. Think about the texts in the word-processing system. They just lie there in the machine, doing absolutely nothing. But the machine can insert, delete, move, and change the text as the user commands. This inert character of the texts is very important in the WORKPIECES FRAME that is suitable to this kind of problem. A reasonable method for building a word-processing system assumes that the text will not change except when the machine is changing it.

One step up the evolutionary ladder from the inert dynamic domain is the reactive dynamic domain. A domain is reactive if it does perform some actions of its own, but only in response to external stimulus. A vending machine that dispenses chocolate bars or fizzy drinks is a reactive domain. When a customer inserts coins and presses a selection button, the vending machine responds by delivering the chocolate or can of drink and possibly some change. Then it relapses into its normal lethargic state, waiting for the next customer to arrive.

At the top of the ladder is the active dynamic domain, which performs actions without external stimulus. An active domain is always busy on its own initiative. The user of the word-processing program is an active domain. From the point of view of the software developer, the user is continually executing actions for which no external stimulus has occurred. The cause of the actions, so far as the software development problem is concerned, is entirely internal to the user domain. The actions appear to occur spontaneously. For a meteorological program the atmosphere is an active domain: air pressure, humidity, temperature, and wind speed all change spontaneously.

Domain characteristics depend a lot on how you structure the problem context by dividing it into domains. The vending machine domain is reactive; but if you include the vending machine's customers in the same domain, it becomes an active domain, because the customers supply the active character.

An important distinction in active dynamic domains is the distinction among *autonomous*, *biddable*, and *programmable* domains. An autonomous active domain is a law unto itself. There is no means by which its actions can be in any way controlled, although their effects in other domains can often be restricted or even frustrated. The patients in the Patient Monitoring problem are like this. They raise and lower their blood pressure and temperature, their pulse rate and their skin resistance, without so much as a by-your-leave. It may be that the analog devices attached to the patients can't register all the changes as they occur: some changes may happen too quickly or fall outside the range that the device can sense. But the changes will occur nonetheless, and you have to consider them in developing the system.

The users of the word-processing system are, by contrast, a biddable active domain. In some respects this may not mean very much, because they may fail to do what they are bidden to do. But the developers of the system do have the freedom to insist that the users must cooperate if they want the promised results. The system must be capable of accommodating extreme forms of user behaviour, but it need not deliver the texts that the user wants if the user refuses to play the assigned role.

The most obvious example of a programmable active domain is, of course, a general-purpose computer. The whole enterprise of software development depends on the programmability of the computer. By programming it you convert it into the special-purpose machine that you need to solve your problem. Whenever your problem contains a programmable domain that you are allowed to program, it becomes in effect a part of the machine you are building.

The distinction between a reactive domain and a biddable active domain is important in applications like railway control. An electric railway in which the controlling computer can switch the power on and off for each track segment provides a reactive domain. Subject only to equipment breakdowns, the computer can guarantee to maintain safety by ensuring that two trains are never in the same segment. It's a control problem. But a steam or diesel railway can't be controlled like that. The drivers of the trains are at best biddable. The computer can't guarantee that they will obey the signals. It's a different problem.

Understanding the characteristics of your domains is always a large part of understanding what kind of problem you're dealing with.

Domain Interactions

We structure the APPLICATION DOMAIN into a number of distinct but possibly interacting domains. That means that we will consider them – to some degree, at least – separately. But what determines whether this separate consideration is a practical possibility? How can we judge whether our structuring is good? And what does it mean to say that one domain interacts with another or with the machine?

Let's start with the familiar Patient Monitoring problem. Here is a CONTEXT DIAGRAM depicting the DOMAINS and their interactions:

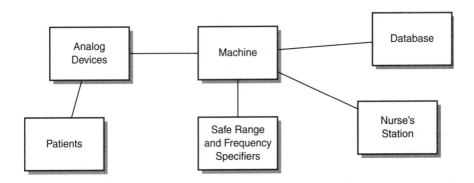

The purpose of the Machine is to monitor the Patients' vital factors – blood pressure, temperature, and so on – reading them at Specified Frequencies from the Analog Devices and storing the readings in the Database. When any reading falls outside the Safe Range Specified for the Patient, or an Analog Device fails, an alarm message is sent to the Nurse's Station.

All five domains are needed to cover the subject matter of the customer's requirements. We chose to divide the whole application domain into these five for largely intuitive reasons. But there is something more precise underlying our intuition. The domains are separate because their PHENOMENA are largely or entirely separate. Where domains interact, the interaction takes the form of SHARED PHENOMENA. Where a domain is isolated from others, it is a central purpose of the Machine to interact with it and with the other domains. By sharing phenomena with them all, the machine establishes relationships among the separate domains.

Think, for example, about an event in the Patients domain in which the temperature of the patient John Doe rises from 101° to 102° Fahrenheit. Because John Doe is directly connected to analog device i, this event in the Patients domain is a phenomenon shared with the Analog Devices domain: in the same shared event, the resistance of the electrical sensor in device i rises by 0.5 ohm. The analog device is designed so that this increase in the sensor resistance causes the numerical value in a register in the device to change from 100.9 to 102.1 (the accuracy of the device being, inevitably, imperfect).

John Doe's temperature increase would have no further results within the system in the absence of the machine. But the machine is present, and it interacts with the analog device. The reading obtained by executing an instruction ReadDevice(*i, temp*) is the numeric value 102.1 in the register in device *i*: both the operation executed and the resulting value are phenomena shared between the analog device and the machine. In due course, the machine compares this value with appropriate values selected from the Safe Range and Frequency Specifiers domain, writes it to the Database, and, perhaps, displays it on the Nurse's Station.

There are two kinds of link in this chain. The shared phenomena provide one kind of link. They carry the interactions between the machine and a domain and between one domain and another. The other kind of link is provided by the internal properties and behaviour of the machine and of each domain. The analog device links the changes in its sensor temperature to changes in its register value; and the machine links the register value to a field written in a database record or an alarm message. You can see from this that a full understanding of the requirements and how they could be satisfied depends on understanding both kinds of link: both the domain interactions and the internal properties of each domain.

Let's go back to one of the questions we started with. What determines whether our structuring of the application domain is a good one: that is, whether in practice each domain can be considered separately? What are the criteria for domain separation? The answer is that the internal properties and behaviour of each domain must be largely independent. They will be constrained to some extent by shared phenomena: interacting domains constrain each other. But the constraint imposed by shared phenomena must be small in relation to the significant internal properties and behaviour.

For example, the separation of the Patients domain from the Analog Devices is a good separation. There's a lot to say about human vital factors in the Patients domain – about their interrelationships, about their maximum and minimum values and about their possible rates of change. And there's a lot to say about the internal electrical properties of the Analog Devices. But relatively little of this is constrained by the shared phenomena at their interface.

If you're an enthusiast for Structured Design, you can think of this as a kind of *coupling and cohesion* criterion. Interacting domains must be weakly coupled, and each domain must be strongly cohesive. But remember that the criteria are not being applied to the processing functions of the system, but to the domains and their phenomena.

Domains

Like so many other terms used in computing, the word *domain* has several meanings. The domain of a mathematical function is the set of argument values for which the function defines result values. For a practitioner of domain analysis, a domain is a general class of system for an application area such as resource management, or airline reservations, or banking, or production control. Sally Shlaer and Stephen Mellor, in their book *Object Lifecycles*, use the word in another sense. They say:

> 'In building a typical large software system, the analyst generally has to deal with a number of distinctly different subject matters, or *domains*. Each domain can be thought of as a separate world inhabited by its own conceptual entities, or objects'.

My use of the word is closest to Shlaer and Mellor's. I use it to mean a particular part of the world that can be distinguished because it is conveniently considered as a whole, and can be considered – to some extent – separately from the other parts of the world.

In every software development problem the PROBLEM CONTEXT has at least two clearly distinct domains: the APPLICATION DOMAIN – the environment or real world or subject matter – and the MACHINE. The application domain is where the customer's requirement exists; the machine provides a solution to the problem by interacting in some way with the application domain. You can think of the application domain as *what is given*, and of the machine domain as *what is to be constructed*.

The first step in problem analysis is to structure and analyse the application domain – to separate it into a number of domains in Shlaer and Mellor's sense: a number of distinctly different subject matters.

To some extent this structuring can be done intuitively, dividing the application domain along obvious lines suggested by the problem and the context. And intuition, as so often happens, can be supported, refined, and corrected by a little theory. Let's start with the intuition. Here's a statement of a well-known problem, adapted from a 1974 account by Stevens, Myers and Constantine of *Structured Design*:

> 'Patients in an intensive-care ward in a hospital are monitored by electronic analog devices attached to their bodies by sensors of various kinds. Through the sensors the devices measure the patients' vital factors: one device measures pulse rate, another temperature, another blood pressure, and so on. A program is needed to read the factors, at a frequency specified for each patient, and store them in a database. The factors read are to be compared with safe ranges specified for each

patient, and readings that exceed the safe ranges are to be reported by alarm messages displayed on the screen of the nurse's station. An alarm message is also to be displayed if any analog device fails.'

The application domain to be structured is, roughly, the intensive-care ward. From the problem statement, and some vague knowledge of hospital wards, you can see that these three domains are important:

(1) the Patients

(2) the Nurse's Station, and

(3) the Analog Devices.

Why can you be sure of these domains? Because the customer's REQUIREMENTS are expressed in terms of them. The Patients must be monitored according to the specified frequencies and safe ranges. The Nurse's Station must be notified by alarm messages if anything is wrong. And the Analog Devices must be monitored and any failure reported at the Nurse's Station. You are applying the fundamental principle for identifying and structuring the application domain:

● *The Principle of Domain Relevance*
  Everything that's relevant to the requirements must appear in
  some part of the application domain.

There's an important consequence of this principle. The application domain is not limited to the parts of the world that are directly connected to the machine. The Analog Devices are a part of the application domain that is directly connected to the machine. But the Patients themselves are also a part of the application domain, although they are not in direct contact with the machine.

Monitoring and reporting on the Patients is a central requirement. If you leave them out of the application domain you will not be able to describe and deal with that requirement properly. The physiological principles governing the states, and state changes, of the Patients' vital factors – temperature, blood pressure, skin resistance, and others – must be elucidated and described as a part of your study of the application domain. Studying what the machine can sense at the other end of the Analog Devices isn't the same thing at all. The point is reinforced in this particular problem, because the failure of an analog device is a possibility that must be explicitly considered and dealt with.

Is it all right, then, to leave out the Nurses and include only the Nurse's Station? Yes, because the requirement is not at all concerned with the nurses themselves; not even with their actions in response to the alarm messages displayed on the Nurse's Station.

Is the structuring of the application domain now complete? Not really. There are two more domains: the Safe Range and Frequency Specifiers; and the Database. You can regard the Safe Range and Frequency Specifiers as a tangible domain: then they are the medical staff who decide on the safe ranges for each patient's vital factors, and on the frequency with which they should be monitored. Or you can regard them as an intangible domain: then they are the ranges and frequencies themselves. But whether tangible or intangible, they are clearly necessary by the Principle of Domain Relevance. If you leave them out there will be no part of the application domain to which requirements about the ranges and the frequencies could refer. From an implementation point of view, there will be no source from which the ranges and frequency specifications could reach the machine. Certainly they will not reach the machine through the analog devices or through any other domain.

You may be thinking that the Database domain is a little dubious. After all, is it not really a part of the machine? It may be. The right answer to the question depends on how you interpret the sentence

'A program is needed to read the factors ... *and store them in a database*'.

You can interpret it in two different ways:

(1) The mention of the database is just a mistake. The writer presumed that the program implementation would need a database, and made the mistake of describing an implementation of the solution instead of describing the problem. It wouldn't be the first time.

(2) The mention of the database is purposeful and correct. The program is required to store the factors in a database, to be used by other programs whose requirements are given separately elsewhere. If the program does not store the factors in the database it will be failing to satisfy an explicit requirement just as much as if it did not send alarm messages to the Nurse's Station.

Of course, you can't really choose between these two interpretations by analysing the text: you must discuss the issue with your customer. (In fact, it is somewhat absurd to discuss the problem at all on the basis of the brief description we are using here. The absurdity is – possibly – justifiable here, because I am using a small example to explain development ideas. But it's certainly not justifiable in a real development.)

So our intuition – aided by the Principle of Domain Relevance – has led us to structure the application domain in five domains: Patients; Analog Devices; Nurse's Station; Safe Range and Frequency Specifiers; and Database. We can draw a simple CONTEXT DIAGRAM to show the identified domains and how they are connected to each other and to the machine:

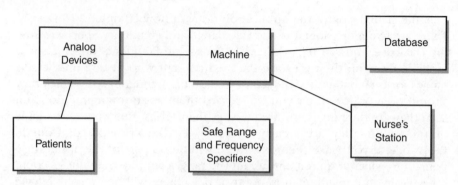

Now the next step is to examine each domain and understand its
DOMAIN CHARACTERISTICS. You must also examine the DOMAIN INTERACTIONS,
with each other and with the machine. This exploration of the parts of the
problem context will lay the essential basis for the appropriate choice of
PROBLEMFRAME.

Entity–Relation Span

Here is a small description in the form of an entity–relation diagram:

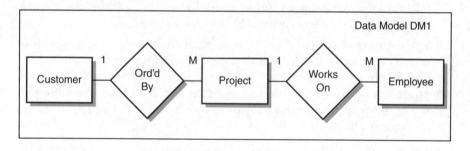

Employees work on projects, which are ordered by customers. Each
employee works on only one project, but a project may have many employees working on it. Each project is ordered by one customer, but a customer
may order many projects. This seems clear enough, and indeed it is. What is a
little less clear, perhaps, is the SPAN OF DESCRIPTION: how much, exactly, of the
world does the description describe? In particular, what is its span in time?

One way of interpreting the description is as an *invariant*: something
that is *always* true. Think of the description as a description of a conceptual database; then it describes what must be true before and after every

transaction. Or think of it as a description of the real world of the application domain, and think of the flow of time as an alternation of EVENTS AND INTERVALS: then the description makes an assertion about *each interval considered in isolation* – that is, between any two consecutive events that change the state of the world:

$$\forall \, v : \text{Interval}(v) \bullet (\text{Data Model } DM1(...,v,...))$$

Whatever interval v you choose, the Data Model DM1 is true of that interval. You can think of the whole description in two parts. One is the enclosing wrapper – the quantifier $\forall v : \text{Interval}(v)$ – asserting that DM1 is true of every interval. This quantifier spans all intervals. The other part is DM1 itself. DM1 has a span of just one interval.

The interval parameter v is not explicit in the diagram. The diagram talks about Employees and Projects and Customers, but it says nothing explicit about intervals. If you translate the assertions of the diagram into predicate logic, you can put the v parameter back. For example, you could translate the M-to-1 multiplicity of the Employee-WorksOn-Project relationship like this:

$$\forall \, e,p,q,v \bullet ((\text{WorksOn}(e,p,v) \land \text{WorksOn}(e,q,v)) \rightarrow p=q))$$

Whatever Employee e, Projects p and q, and interval v you choose, if e works on p in interval v, and also e works on q in interval v, then p and q are identical. That is, no employee can work on two different projects in the same interval. Of course, employees can be transferred between projects, so one employee can work on two different projects in *different* intervals. The description doesn't say that can't happen.

If you restore the interval argument like this, you can avoid thinking that the description says more than it actually does. Translating the M-to-1 multiplicity of the Project-OrderedBy-Customer relationship you get this:

$$\forall \, c,d,p,v \bullet ((\text{OrderedBy}(c,p,v) \land \text{OrderedBy}(d,p,v)) \rightarrow c=d))$$

Whatever Customers c and d, Project p, and interval v you choose, if p was ordered by c in interval v and also p was ordered by d in interval v, then c and d are identical. No project can be ordered by two customers in the same interval. The description doesn't say that one project can't be ordered by two different customers in *different* intervals. But probably you wish it did. It doesn't make sense to think of two different customers ordering the same project, even at different times. You would like to omit the interval argument and assert:

$$\forall \, c,d,p \bullet ((\text{OrderedBy}(c,p) \land \text{OrderedBy}(d,p)) \rightarrow c=d))$$

But the description doesn't say that. You might think of indicating the difference between the two relations by an annotation on the diagram. But that isn't really a good idea at all. The span of the description DM1 is quite clear: it's just one interval. So it can't possibly say that anything – the association between a customer and a project – is constant over more than one interval. The great virtue of good diagrams is simplicity. Entity–relation diagrams are no exception. If a description says less than you want to say, that's not so bad: you can always make another description, in another language. But if you destroy the simplicity of a notation you can't recover it by adding something. Less is more.

Events and Intervals

Time is mysterious. Marvin Minsky, in *Computation: Finite and Infinite Machines*, quotes Poinsot's statement:

> 'If anyone asked me to define time, I should reply: Do you know what it is that you speak of? If he said Yes, I should say, Very well, let us talk about it. If he said No, I should say, Very well, let us talk about something else.'

But in software development we must talk about time. Most of the domains we deal with have a time dimension; and the temporal properties of the machines we build are of central importance.

An important complication in talking about time is that the talking itself takes place at some point in time. In English, as in many other languages, this complication is happily embraced and woven into the language. We use different tenses of verbs – I *will eat* an apple, I *am eating* an apple, and I *ate* an apple – for a statement about the future, the present, and the past, where future, present, and past are all relative to the time at which the statement is made. We use time words like 'now', 'yesterday', and 'soon' in the same kind of way.

When you talk about time like this, the interpretation, and so the truth, of what you say depends on when you say it. But in software development it's very inconvenient if the truth of your descriptions changes between the writing and the reading, or between one reading and another. You must pin down the butterfly of time. One way of doing this is to treat each point in time explicitly as an individual. Then you can capture the PHENOMENA of time itself in two simple DESIGNATIONS:

---

p is a point in time	$\approx$ TimePoint(p)
The point p precedes the point q in time	$\approx$ Precedes(p,q)

Designations of facts involving points in time must have a variable corresponding to a point in time. Here are designations for a description of a very simple traffic light:

The North–South light is red at time point p	$\approx$ NSRed(p)
The North–South light is green at time point p	$\approx$ NSGreen(p)
The East–West light is red at time point p	$\approx$ EWRed(p)
The East–West light is green at time point p	$\approx$ EWGreen(p)

The lights are never green together, and no car is forced to wait for ever. In PREDICATE LOGIC:

$$\forall\, p \bullet (\, \text{TimePoint}(p) \rightarrow (\, (\, \text{NSRed}(p) \vee \text{EWRed}(p)\,)$$
$$\wedge\, (\, \text{NSRed}(p) \rightarrow \exists\, q \bullet (\, \text{Precedes}(p,q) \wedge \text{NSGreen}(q)\,)\,)$$
$$\wedge\, (\, \text{EWRed}(p) \rightarrow \exists\, q \bullet (\, \text{Precedes}(p,q) \wedge \text{EWGreen}(q)\,)\,)\,)\,)$$

It's true of every point p in time that: either the North–South light is red at p, or the East–West light is red at p, or both; if North–South is red at p there is another point q, which p precedes, at which North–South is green; and similarly for East–West.

This way of treating time is sometimes convenient, but it doesn't let you talk about events. You can talk about states – about what is true in the world at each particular point in time – but you can't easily talk about the events in which the world changes. One way of bringing events into your view of the world is to recognize *events* as individuals, and to talk about *intervals* instead of points in time. The general idea is that events are atomic and instantaneous, and that between successive events there are intervals of time in which nothing happens – that is, there are no events.

Here are appropriate designations for events:

e is an atomic instantaneous event	$\approx$ Event(e)
The event e occurs before the event f	$\approx$ Earlier(e,f)

An event is 'atomic' and 'instantaneous' only when you can regard it as having no parts and no duration in time. One event 'occurs before' another means that one event is finished, is entirely in the past, before the other is started. We shall insist that 'occurs before' applies to all pairs of distinct events. That is, we will never regard two distinct events as occurring simultaneously: one of them must occur before the other.

The idea of an event is severely restricted. Any action, or performance, or occurrence, that has an internal time structure must be regarded as two or more events. The key restriction is that an event represents a transition of the world from one state to another *without passing through any intermediate state*.

Of course, in any real world this view is an abstraction: you choose to ignore some details and aspects of reality as irrelevant. Different abstractions are useful for different purposes. Think about a move in a chess game. A physiotherapist, or a robot designer wanting to emulate the player's arm movements, sees an elaborate performance of moving the arm towards the piece, grasping the piece, lifting it, transporting it to its new position, and placing it there on the board. But the players engaged in the game see each move as an atomic event, ignoring any substructure of the physical act of moving the piece. For them the move is an indivisible transition between successive board positions: that is, between successive significant states of the world. To a chess player, it makes no sense to ask: What happened *during* White's fifteenth move?

Chess moves are instructive examples of events in another respect. In most moves, all that happens is that one piece moves from one board position to another. But in a capture, an enemy piece is also removed from the board. The captured piece may be the enemy piece that had been occupying the destination square (but in certain moves this is not so – for example, in an *en passant* Pawn capture). And in some moves, the moved piece is promoted and becomes a different piece as a result of the move – a Pawn becomes a Queen (or any other piece except a Pawn or King) on reaching the eighth rank. In a castling move, two pieces are moved instead of one: the King and Rook move past each other.

Although each special move is in some sense more elaborate than the most common moves, it is still regarded by the players as an atomic event. When a piece is captured there is no intermediate state in which the capturing piece has moved but the captured piece has not yet been taken off the board. When a player castles, there is no intermediate state in which the King has moved but not the Castle. When a Pawn reaches the eighth rank there is no intermediate state in which it is on the eighth rank but is still a Pawn.

In the same way, a bank may choose to treat a transfer from one account to another as a single transaction. There is no intermediate state in which the money has left the source account but has not yet reached the destination account – or *vice versa*. The debiting of the source account and the crediting of the destination account are one and the same event.

Events are INDIVIDUALS; so they are described, like all individuals, by facts in which they play a part. For example, the bank domain may have phenomena designated like this:

In event e account a is debited cash amount m	$\approx$ Debit(e,a,m)
In event e account a is credited cash amount m	$\approx$ Credit(e,a,m)

If a particular event E is a transfer of a cash amount M from account A to account B, then both of the following facts are true:

   Debit(E,A,M) and   Credit(E,B,M)

You could define the predicate Transfer(e,a,b,m):

   Transfer$(e,a,b,m) \triangleq$ Debit$(e,a,m) \wedge$ Credit(e,b,m)

(Tom DeMarco asked what happens if you do Transfer(E,A,A,M). Does the balance on account A dip by M, however briefly? Definitely not, *if the bank chooses to treat a transfer as a single event*. If they try to pay you less interest because your balance was momentarily reduced, tell them to buy a copy of this book. No – make that 100 copies, just to be sure.)

The Event–Interval View also has intervals. They, too, are individuals. An interval is the period between successive events when nothing happens and therefore nothing changes. Here are the designations, including the two designations for events, repeated from above:

e is an atomic instantaneous event	$\approx$ Event(e)
The event e occurs before the event f	$\approx$ Earlier(e,f)
v is an interval of time in which no event occurs	$\approx$ Intvl(v)
The event e begins the interval v	$\approx$ Begins(e,v)
The event e ends the interval v	$\approx$ Ends(e,v)

Each event ends one interval and begins another. Events and intervals alternate in the way you would expect. An event begins the interval that follows it, and ends the interval that precedes it. You can define initial and final intervals:

   InitIntvl$(v) \triangleq$ Intvl$(v) \wedge \neg \exists e \bullet$ Begins(e,v)
   FinalIntvl$(v) \triangleq$ Intvl$(v) \wedge \neg \exists e \bullet$ Ends(e,v)

InitIntvl(v) is defined to mean that v is an interval and there does not exist ($\neg\,\exists$) an event e that begins it; FinalIntvl(v) is similarly defined to mean that there is no event e that ends it. Each definition makes the predicate (InitIntvl or FinalIntvl) available for use, without implying that there is any individual interval of which it is true.

It is fundamental to the event–interval view of time that nothing changes except when an event occurs. So in each interval the set of facts remains constant. To express changeability over time you must use a predicate in which at least one variable is to be replaced by a reference to an interval. A predicate with no interval argument, like this:

Lecturer t teaches course c	$\approx$ Teaches(t,c)

generalizes facts that never change. If Teaches(Dr Jones, Physics) is a fact today, then it must always have been a fact in the past, and will always be a fact in the future. This is surely not what we really mean. Almost certainly, our readers would be grateful for a little more precision – and Dr Jones for a little relief:

Lecturer t teaches course c in interval v	$\approx$ Teaches(t,c,v)

Reformulating descriptions to make the interval arguments explicit in this way will often help to make them clearer.

Here is a very simple example of a description in terms of events and intervals. A light is either on or off. (That is to say, it is either on or off in any particular interval.) There is only one kind of event that changes its state: pressing the button. The designations are:

In interval v the light is on	$\approx$ On(v)
In interval v the light is off	$\approx$ Off(v)
In event e the button is pressed	$\approx$ Press(e)

The light can be described by a finite-state machine:

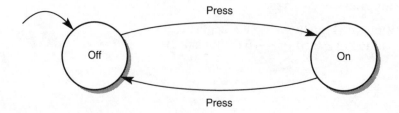

You can translate this description into predicate logic as follows. First:

$$\forall\, v \bullet (\, (\, \text{On}(v) \to \neg\, \text{Off}(v)\,)$$
$$\land\, (\, \text{Intvl}(v) \to (\, \text{On}(v) \lor \text{Off}(v))\,)$$
$$\land\, (\, \text{InitIntvl}(v) \to \text{Off}(v)\,)\,)$$

On and Off are mutually exclusive. In each interval the light is either On or Off. In the initial interval it is Off. And:

$$\forall\, v,w,e \bullet (\, (\, \text{Ends}(e,v) \land \text{Begins}(e,w)\,) \to$$
$$(\, (\, (\, \text{On}(v) \land \text{Off}(w)\,)) \lor (\, \text{Off}(v) \land \text{On}(w)\,)\,)\,)\,) \leftrightarrow \text{Press}(e)\,)$$

Consider any three individuals v and w and e. If v and w are consecutive intervals separated by event e, then the state of the light changes between the intervals v and w if and only if e is a Press event.

Notice that other events, not mentioned in this description, may occur at any time; but they will not cause the state of the light to change. There may be many intervals between the initial interval and the first Press event, and between successive Press events. In general, each visit to a state in a finite-state machine occupies many intervals.

Existence

The statement *x exists* has two quite different kinds of meaning. One is the meaning of the existential quantifier built into PREDICATE LOGIC:

$$\exists\, x \bullet (\text{Divides}(x,10) \land \text{Divides}(x,15))$$

means that there exists an x such that x divides *10* and x divides *15*. In the whole population of INDIVIDUALS you can find at least one individual – in fact, the number 5 – satisfying the descriptive clause. Here's a similar statement about the family of Adam and Eve:

$$\exists\, x \bullet (\text{ChildOf}(x,\text{Adam}) \land \text{ChildOf}(x,\text{Eve}))$$

Possible choices of x are Cain, Abel, Seth, or any of their sisters. They are all children of Adam and Eve. The statement is clearly true.

The other kind of meaning of *x exists* is multifarious. It is many meanings, depending on what x you have in mind, and on what you're saying about it. If x is a building, you may mean that x has been built and not yet demolished; or that x was actually constructed and not just imagined. If x is a human being, then by *x exists* you may mean that x is real and not mythical. Or that x is alive today. In that sense, no child of Adam and Eve *exists*.

These multifarious meanings are not built into any language. To capture them, you need a separate DESIGNATION for each one. And if your meaning involves time, you must make the time explicit:

| The person x is alive on date d | $\approx$ AliveOn(x,d) |

Then this statement is clearly false:

$\exists\, x \bullet$ (ChildOf$(x,$Adam$) \wedge$ ChildOf$(x,$Eve$) \wedge$ AliveOn$(x,$1Jan1900$))$

The only built-in notion of existence that is built-in and not to be designated is the first notion, captured by the existential quantifier $\exists$. $\exists\, x$ just
means that you can find an individual x somewhere in the domain you're
talking about. Talk about arithmetic, and x can be a number. Talk about fiction or myth, and your x can be an imaginary creation. Talk about the
whole of human history and it can be an x who died long ago or hasn't yet
been born. The existential quantifier is timeless.

Frame Diagrams

Frame diagrams are an extension of CONTEXT DIAGRAMS. A context diagram
shows the structuring of the APPLICATION DOMAIN into a number of constituent domains, and shows how those domains interact with each other
and with the MACHINE domain. The domains are represented by rectangles,
and interaction between two domains is represented by a line connecting
their two rectangles. Here's a simplified context diagram for a compiler
construction problem:

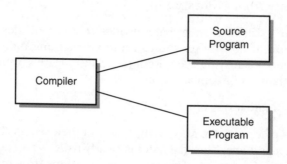

There's a little more to context diagrams than that, but not much more.
As its name implies, a context diagram shows the context of a problem. But
it doesn't show what the problem is.

A frame diagram adds two things to the context diagram that contribute
to identifying the problem. First, it picks out the machine domain – the
part of the world that you have to construct. In a frame diagram the

machine domain is shown by a double outline. Second, it includes and names domain relationships. A domain relationship is a condition among domains that is required to hold in a system. It is shown as an ellipse, connected by lines to each related domain. Here's a frame diagram for the compiler problem:

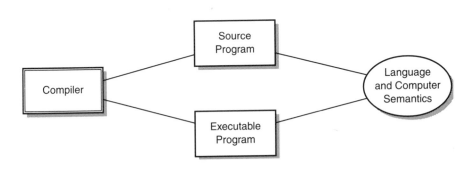

In a problem to develop a compiler, the requirement is that the Source Program and Executable Program must be related by the semantics of the Source Program Language and of the target language of the computer on which the Executable Program will run. This requirement appears in the frame diagram, but not in the context diagram. The frame diagram also shows that the problem is to construct the compiler itself. The problem is not, as it might have been, the problem of constructing a source program from which a given compiler would produce a given executable program. That would be a *decompilation* problem.

This diagram is called a frame diagram because it shows the principal parts of a PROBLEM FRAME: domains and domain relationships. A problem frame is a structure to be imposed on a problem. When you want to discuss or explain a problem frame in its general form, you show it in a frame diagram divorced from any particular problem. For example:

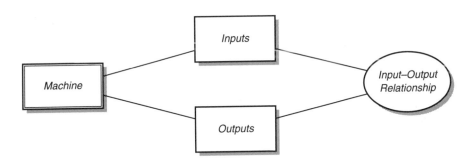

The names used in this frame diagram are generic: *Machine*, *Inputs*, *Outputs*, and *Input–Output Relationship*. This frame fits the compiler problem; but it might also fit the problem of producing an analysis of a stream of email messages. That's why the names are generic, rather like the names of the formal parameters of a procedure.

It's often useful to draw a frame diagram to show how a generic problem frame fits a particular problem context, especially where you are dealing with a MULTI-FRAME PROBLEM. To do that, you have to draw the frame diagram on top of all or part of the context diagram. Here's how I do it:

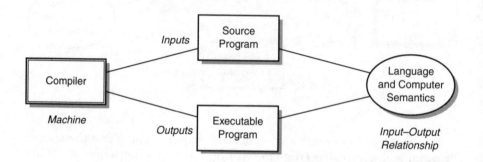

The specific names from the context diagram and requirement are written inside the symbols for the domains and the relationships. The names from the generic problem frame are written alongside or underneath the symbols they are associated with. Here's the frame diagram for the problem of analysing the stream of email messages:

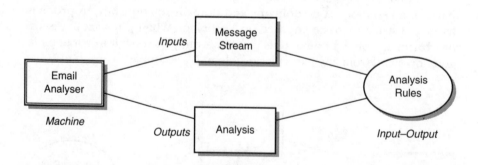

It's exactly like matching the actual parameters to the formal parameters in a procedure call.

You could introduce many variations and elaborations into these diagrams. One elaboration that seems especially attractive is to indicate the DOMAIN CHARACTERISTICS of the various domains, because they are an essential factor in determining whether a frame fits a problem context. But it's not clear how to do this in any reasonable way: there is no well-established taxonomy of domain characteristics.

And, anyway, it's better not to try to put too much into one diagram. Frame diagrams, like all diagrams, should always be kept as clean and simple as you can: they are at their best when they show information that you can grasp quickly and easily.

The Fudge Factor

Have you ever seen one of those pictures of the human body in which the pictured size of each part is proportional to its importance in your self-consciousness? Hands and mouth are huge. Toes are so small that they are almost invisible.

You could try to draw that kind of picture of your development project. The tiny bits are the bits you fudge. There's always something that has been fudged – treated very approximately, left to chance, postponed because it seemed too difficult, ignored because it seemed unimportant or trivial or, frankly, just not very interesting.

Different developers fudge different things. Object-oriented developers pay a lot of attention to class hierarchies and competing paradigms of object interaction, but they don't bother much with correctness. The fragmentation of their systems into class definitions encourages local browsing, but makes it hard to analyse larger patterns of behaviour. Formal method practitioners are very careful about correctness and precision in a mathematical sense. But they don't bother much about the relationship between the mathematically precise software and the real world in which it will operate. It's not a topic of serious mathematical interest, so they treat it as unimportant.

One form of fudging is making do with a slightly ill-fitting problem frame. Suppose that you are developing an administrative system for a library, and you have decided to use the SIMPLE IS FRAME. So you are treating the system as an information system. The *Real World* is the world of the library, with its books and members. You are busy describing the *Real World*. You have just described the alternation of Borrow and Return events for each book: a book that has been Borrowed must be Returned before it can be Borrowed again. This is a truth about the world, guaranteed by its physical properties, and not depending in any way on the operation of the system you are building.

Then you come to consider the borrowing limit. No member may have more than six books out on loan at any one time. Is this a truth about the world? No. It's a REQUIREMENT: a property of the application domain that the system must enforce. Unfortunately, the simple IS frame has no place – no principal part – that can accommodate this little piece of description. You really should be using some variant of the SIMPLE CONTROL FRAME, which provides a *Desired Behaviour* principal part specifically for this kind of description.

But this is making a mountain out of a molehill, isn't it? Surely all you need to do is to ensure that the system will never issue a Borrowing acknowledgement for the forbidden seventh loan. Without a Borrowing acknowledgement the book is not allowed to be taken out of the library. Then the borrowing limit will be implicit in the description of the *Information Outputs* and the *Information Function*. Not quite so clear as putting it into a description of the *Real World*, but hardly a serious defect.

True enough. It's a tiny and unimportant fudge. The library administration is not exactly an information system problem, but it's close enough for practical purposes.

Daniel Jackson told me about a similar difficulty that arose on a software development course. The problem was to specify an Air Traffic Control system using a formal method. One vital function of an Air Traffic Control system is to maintain certain minimum horizontal and vertical separations between planes. Some students specified the desired separations as an *invariant* of the system: something that was always true. But that made it logically impossible for the system specification to say what must happen when a plane deviates from the desired minimum separation. The deviation would contradict the invariant, and the whole specification would become meaningless. So their specification had to fudge the description of how deviations would be corrected.

They were fudging the central function of the system. That's definitely a mountain, not a molehill. I don't think that one should be fudged. The students needed to find a way of describing both the target the system was aiming at – no deviation – and the reality – deviation and subsequent correction.

There will always be something fudged in any development. Don't think you can avoid it. What you can do is to make sure that the fudging is confined to places where it doesn't threaten the project's success, or – much more serious – human wellbeing. Remember this principle:

- *The Principle of Commensurate Care*
  The care taken in each aspect of a development should be
  proportional to $P{\times}D$, where P is the probability that it will
  go wrong, and D is the size of the disaster if it does.

If D is very small, you don't need much care because P can't be bigger than 1. In your personal database system for local eating places, the worst disaster that can happen is that you end up at the wrong restaurant, or miss your dinner altogether. D is very small indeed, and you don't really need to take much care about getting the system right. But in the central functioning of a life-critical system, where D is enormous, you must take a lot of care even if P is very small.

It's a matter of assessing and managing risks. Barry Boehm makes risk management a central theme in his *Spiral Model of Software Development*. He deals with the whole range of management problems: personnel shortfalls, unrealistic schedules, and failures by subcontractors, as well as some method-oriented problems such as constantly changing requirements and failure to develop the right user interface. Within the sharply focused concerns of development method there is the same need to ask yourself: What can go wrong? How likely is it to go wrong? How severe is the penalty if it does go wrong? And to place the fudge accordingly, where it will do no serious harm.

Graphic Notations

To plan a journey from Hampstead to Wimbledon you look at a London Underground map. Wimbledon is on the District Line, which is shown in green; Hampstead is on the Northern Line, which is shown in black. Run your eye down the black line and see where it meets the green line. Easy. It's easy because the map is a graphic description. The same information presented as a set of lists, each list showing the stations of one Underground line in order, would be impossibly difficult to use.

In the same way, a graphical representation of a finite-state machine by a state-transition diagram is much more immediately understandable than a list of its states and transitions. But good graphic descriptions are hard to make. For any description, graphic or textual, you have to decide what to show and what to ignore. The designer of the original London Underground map decided to ignore distances: the map is topological, not topographical. For a graphic description you also have an extra task: deciding how to place the symbols. This can be an unwelcome complication, especially if you feel sure that there shouldn't be any crossings.

But much the greatest difficulty is to stop yourself from drowning in a sea of vagueness. Here's a diagram describing something to do with controlling a lift:

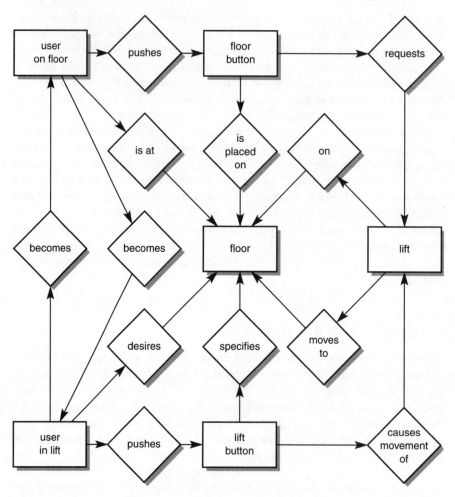

It's a kind of entity–relationship diagram. The notation is a little unusual. It uses arrows instead of plain lines to connect the rectangles (representing entity classes) to the diamonds (representing relations). This departure from the usual convention is helpful: it tells you to how to read the relations. For example, you should read the *specifies* relation as 'a lift button specifies a floor' rather than as 'a floor specifies a lift button'. The notation is clear; the difficulties lie elsewhere.

You can read the diagram to yourself, following the arrows: 'a user in a lift *becomes* a user on a floor; a user on a floor *is at* a floor', and so on. But in itself this is just an extremely informal natural language description. The purpose of a formal description is to say something more exact than you can easily say briefly in natural language. The Underground map is a formal description, with an exact, consistent and perfectly clear meaning. When you try to extract an exact and perfectly clear meaning from this entity–relationship diagram, unfortunately, you find it doesn't make a lot of sense.

For example, an entity–relationship diagram usually implies that the entity classes are disjoint: no individual can be both a floor button and a lift button, or both a floor and a lift. But this supposition is false here: a user on a floor is not a different individual from a user in a lift. But, you may say, the point is that the same individual cannot be both a user on a floor and a user in a lift *at the same time*. Very well. But then you can only conclude, in the same way, that one individual cannot be both a lift and a floor at the same time: a lift, may, perhaps, turn into a floor.

What about the relations? Two entity instances associated by a relation must both exist – in some sense – at least while the relationship between them exists. So the relationship *is at* can apply only to an existing user on a floor and an existing floor. But what about 'user on floor becomes user in lift'? Does it imply that one and the same individual can, after all, exist both as a user on a floor and as a user in a lift at the same time?

And what do the relations *pushes* and *moves to* mean? The relationships in a relation must persist for some time: perhaps *moves to* should really be renamed *is moving to*. But what about *pushes*? 'A user on a floor pushes a floor button' sounds much more like an instantaneous event than a relationship. Should *pushes*, perhaps, be renamed *has pushed*?

The difficulty is that the graphic notation itself is perfectly clear, but the meaning of the boxes and diamonds and lines is very obscure and uncertain. Perhaps you might find the diagram useful as a guide map to an informal description written in natural language. Then the rectangles just represent nouns in the description, and the diamonds represent verbs. Well, that's possible. But I'm sure it's not what was intended by the diagram's creator. And it's certainly not the kind of interpretation you would give to the Underground map. I think the diagram may look all right at first sight, but it is too vague to be really useful.

Graphic notations are, in fact, formal languages. Yet they seem to carry a higher risk of vagueness than textual languages. Perhaps lines and boxes suggest less need of rigour than identifiers and functions and expressions and assignment statements because they don't usually come with a compiler. This vagueness leads some people to despise graphic notations – although they still like to indent their program texts. But the cure for vagueness is not to avoid the use of graphic notations altogether. They're much too useful for that. The cure is to be very careful when you write a description in any language, and to be twice as careful again if it's a graphic language. You don't want to land up at Trafalgar Square when you meant to get to Wimbledon. You'll miss the tennis.

Hierarchical Structure

After the participants had introduced themselves, the software design course began with an explanation of hierarchical structuring.

'Hierarchical structure is a very important idea,' said the instructor. 'It separates concerns very well, because the parts of the structure have no relationships except through the lines of the hierarchy. For example, a hierarchical management organization makes life easier for the managers:

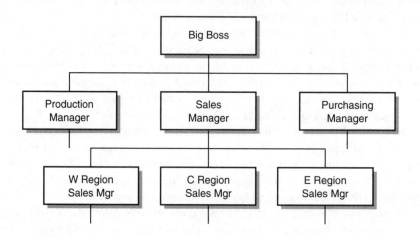

'The Big Boss talks only to the three Senior Managers. The Sales Manager talks only to the three Regional Sales Managers. Everyone interacts only with the manager immediately above and the managers immediately below. The Big Boss doesn't have to be concerned with the regional structure of the sales organization: that's the responsibility of the Sales Manager. And the Sales Manager doesn't have to know about the organization within each sales region: that's the responsibility of the Regional Sales Manager for that region.

'We'll see that you can get the same elegance and simplicity in software development. You all know about structuring programs as hierarchies of modules, interacting only by the procedure calls through which each manager module invokes its immediate subordinates. The purpose and behaviour and properties of each module can be understood in isolation, because the procedure header tells you everything you need to know about its interaction with its parent, and the calls that appear in the module text tell you everything you need to know about its interaction with its children. That means that you can write and test each module independently.

'The hierarchical idea works for systems as well as programs. Every system can be decomposed into subsystems; and it is itself a subsystem of a larger system. In fact, you can think of the whole universe as a hierarchy of systems. Look at this diagram:

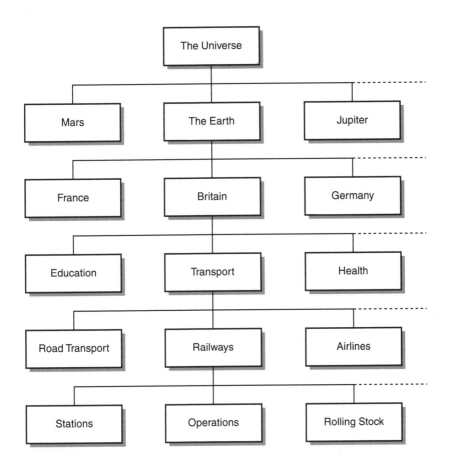

'Hierarchical structure is also the key to understanding classification. Everything in the world belongs to some class, and every class is a subclass of a bigger class. This is called the 'IsA' hierarchy: a dog *Is A* mammal; a mammal *Is A* vertebrate; a vertebrate *Is An* animal; and so on. It works for software as well: just look at the class hierarchy in Smalltalk or any other properly object-oriented language.

'In fact,' he went on, 'hierarchical structure is the key to problem solving in general. We solve problems by breaking them down into a hierarchy of sub-problems, level by level, until the sub-problems at the bottom level are simple enough to solve directly. This is how to master complexity, and mastering complexity is the central activity – it's what software design is really about. Any questions so far?'

'Yes,' said Joe. 'I have a question.' There's always someone like Joe in every class. Can't – or won't – accept the simplest and most obvious ideas without a big fuss and a lot of discussion. Everyone knows how important hierarchical structuring is. Why can't we just get on with the course?

'What do the connecting lines in the diagram mean?' said Joe.

'They mean that the lower box is a part of the upper box,' said the instructor. 'Jupiter is a part of the Universe; Britain is a part of the Earth; the Education system is a part of Britain; and so on. That's all.'

'I don't understand how the Education system is a *part* of Britain,' said Joe. 'It seems to me that it's sort of spread all around. And what about international air travel? And what about the Channel Tunnel trains? Are they part of the British Transport system or the French Transport system? And what about the cars and lorries that are carried on the trains? Are they part of French Road Transport, or of British Railways, or what? You said that the parts of the structure have no relationships except through the lines, but that's obviously not true.'

'Yes, I was wondering the same thing about the organization chart,' said Pamela. 'Everyone knows that organizations are never really hierarchical, because people in different parts of the organization at the same level must communicate with each other if things are to work at all. The hierarchical organization chart is a fiction. So perhaps there are other kinds of structure,' she said. 'Just like organizations don't have to be hierarchical, perhaps problems can have matrix structures, or network structures, or something like that.'

'Surely there are really several structures in any organization,' said Joe. 'There are always lines of communication that cut across the reporting structure, and there's always an informal structure of people talking to each other just as they need to. Doesn't hierarchy originally mean the organization of a priesthood? There's no sense in pretending that there's one structure that's divinely appointed. There are always many structures. And,' he added, 'hardly any of of them are hierarchies.'

'That's right,' said Pamela. 'The structures you find in practice are more likely to be networks of different kinds, because a network is a more general pattern of relationships.'

'But you're forgetting,' said the instructor, 'there is always the question of how the many network structures fit together. The hierarchical structure is important there, and what you're talking about is the lower-level detail within the hierarchically arranged parts.'

'No,' said Pamela. 'The network structures fit together in an arrangement of layers. It's like overlays in a complicated transparency. You might have one overlay showing roads and cars and lorries, and another overlay showing railway lines and trains. You put one on top of the other and they have to fit properly at the places where a road crosses a railway, or a car or lorry is carried on a train, or anything like that.'

'Wait a minute,' said the instructor. 'These are good points, and I'm glad you raised them.' Actually, he didn't look at all glad. He was beginning to look rather annoyed. 'The key point is just that you have to deal with complexity, and the main idea is breaking problems down into sub-problems, and that sort of thing. I think we should stop this discussion now, and get on with the course. I think we're wasting too much time on this.' He looked at his watch. The coffee break wasn't for another hour and a quarter. Not a very good start to a course, really.

'Sub-problems and that sort of thing,' whispered Joe to Pamela. 'I hope it's not all going to be like this.'

Identity

To say that X is *identical to* Y is to say that they are one and the same INDIVIDUAL: anything that is true of X must inevitably be true of Y, because X is Y and Y is X. This notion of identity is built into any view of the world that pays attention to individuals. In the language of PREDICATE LOGIC, where it is called *equality*, there is a special symbol for it: to say that X *is identical (or equal) to* Y, you write $X=Y$. Three obvious properties of identity are that $X=X$ is always true (identity is reflexive); that if $X=Y$ is true then $Y=X$ is also true (identity is symmetric); and that if $X=Y$ and $Y=Z$ are both true then so is $X=Z$ (identity is transitive).

Identity is quite different from similarity or equivalence. To say that X *is similar (or equivalent) to* Y is to say that they are distinct individuals that share some property, or characteristic, or attribute, or quality. They might be of the same size, or the same colour, or have the same birthday, or be alike in any other way you could imagine. The definition of X *is equivalent to* Y is not usually built into our view of the world. You have to define whatever different kinds of equivalence or similarity you need. Predicate logic has no special symbol for equivalence or similarity: you invent predicate names as you need them, designating or defining predicates such as AreSameSize(X,Y), and OfEqualWeight(X,Y), and whatever else you need. Notice that if you and I are *similar* because we have the *same* birthday, then your birthday and my birthday are *identical*.

Programming languages that have a notion of individuals always have a built-in notion of identity or equality. In Smalltalk it is called equality, and denoted by the symbol ==. Smalltalk also has a notion of equivalence or similarity; it is defined separately for each object class, and is denoted by the symbol =.

Some programming languages have no effective notion of identity. In Fortran, the condition 'X .EQ. Y' means similarity. The variables X and Y are distinct individuals, but contain the same value. In the same way, COBOL uses the relational condition *X equal to Y* to mean a kind of similarity. In COBOL, the meaning of *X equal to Y* is greatly complicated by the implicit conversion between numeric and non-numeric types. For example, if the variable X contains the five-digit integer *00123* and the variable Y contains the three-digit integer *123*, then *X equal to Y* is true, and so is *Y equal to X*. But if a third variable Z contains the character string '123', then *X equal to Y* is true, and *Y equal to Z* is true, but *X equal to Z* is not true. In COBOL, equality is reflexive and symmetric, but not transitive.

There is some scope for confusion between identity and similarity. The concepts themselves are easily distinguished, but often you must take great care to be quite sure which one you mean. It depends on which individuals you are talking about. Would you say that the fifth and seventh, and first and sixth, characters in the word 'Identity' are identical or similar? That will depend on what individual you mean by a 'character in a word'. Let's say that the word 'Identity' has eight distinct individual *elements:* in the days of metal type it would have been made up from eight separate pieces of metal. And that the English alphabet has 26 distinct individual *letters*. And that the upper-case I and lower-case i are distinct individual *symbols*.

Then by 'fifth character' you might mean: *the fifth element;* or *the letter associated with the fifth element;* or *the symbol associated with the fifth element*. If you mean *element*, then the fifth and seventh characters are certainly not identical. But they are similar – if you define similarity of elements as having the same *letter*. If by 'character' you mean *letter*, then the fifth and seventh characters are identical, and so are the first and sixth. If you mean *symbol*, then the fifth and seventh characters are identical, but the first and sixth are not identical. But the first and sixth symbols are similar – if you define similarity of *symbols* to mean that they represent the same alphabetic *letter*.

Sometimes the individuals in question may be events. In an electronic mail system you might find yourself looking at a screen display showing a list of messages received. 'Look,' you say, 'the fourth one is the same as the sixth one.' What does it mean to say that two messages are 'the same'? Does it mean that their texts consist of the same character string? Or, perhaps, that they were originated by one individual *send event* whose output has somehow been duplicated in transmission?

Another kind of problem concerning identity arises from the use of natural language phrases that sound like – but are not quite – direct references to individuals. Here is a passage from William Kent's brilliant 1978 book *Data and Reality*:

> 'Sometimes two distinct entities are eventually determined to be the same one, perhaps after we have accumulated substantial amounts of information about each.
>
> '. . . At the beginning of a mystery, we need to think of the murderer and the butler as two distinct entities, collecting information about each of them separately. After we discover that "the butler did it", have we established that they are "the same entity"? Shall we require the modelling system to collapse their two representatives into one? I don't know of any modelling system which can cope with that adequately'.

The phrases 'the butler' and 'the murderer' seem to be of the same kind: both seem to be direct references to individuals. But they are not. 'The butler' does refer directly to an individual: the individual known to the family and their guests as Jones. But 'the murderer' refers, at best, to a person or persons unknown: to whoever it was that committed the murder. If you find a red hair by the victim's body, and are able to conclude with certainty that the murderer has red hair, you might record your conclusion in predicate logic:

$$\forall x \bullet (\ \text{IsMurderer}(x) \rightarrow \text{HasRedHair}(x)\ )$$

Whatever x you choose, if x is the murderer, then x has red hair. There is no simpler formulation. (The philosopher and logician Bertrand Russell proposed a more complex formulation in his *theory of definite descriptions*.) But if the butler has red hair, that fact can be recorded rather more simply:

HasRedHair(Jones)

Kent was focusing on data modelling and database technology. The 'modelling system' he speaks of is a database system, of the kind that was in use in the 1970s. In such a system the butler's red hair can be easily recorded as an attribute of an entity record; but it's a mistake to try to fit the murderer's red hair into an entity record. The problem hasn't gone away since Kent wrote in 1978 – it's still being written about in the object-oriented world. There's an argument here in favour of logic programming. In Prolog the butler's red hair is a *fact*; but the murderer's red hair is a *rule*. Unfortunately, database systems of the 1970s had no place for rules.

A question before you move on. What do you think Heraclitus might have meant when he said, 'You can't step into the same river twice'?

Implementation Bias

The distinction between WHAT AND HOW is often said to be the distinction between SPECIFICATION – which comes earlier in software development – and implementation – which comes later.

One reason for concentrating initially on *what* a system should do, before turning our attention to *how* it should do it, is that we want our system specifications to be free of *implementation bias*. That means that the description of what the system will do should not be biased or distorted, or confused or contaminated, by considerations of how it might do it. An unbiased specification should be easier to understand. It allows developers and their customer to focus discussion on the customer's requirements, without introducing irrelevant and distracting material about the workings of the computer system. And when the implementation stage of development is reached it allows the developers more freedom because their implementation choices have not been pre-empted in the specification.

Steve McMenamin and John Palmer wrote a book called *Essential Systems Analysis*. The essential system is the system purged of implementation bias. It is the system described in a way that eliminates all implementation details such as redundant data, unnecessary files, and arbitrary sequencing choices for the system's actions. These details, say McMenamin and Palmer, arise from the imperfect technology that is available in practice; you eliminate them by imagining that you have perfect technology – infinitely capacious, infinitely fast, infinitely cheap – and describing the system as it would then be.

But it's not quite so easy to eliminate implementation bias. The idea of perfect technology isn't easy to work with. Suppose, for example, that you are specifying a library system. The external operations are *StartNewLibrary, AcquireBook(b), LendBook(b), and ReturnBook(b)*. The system will have to remember which books are out on loan and which are available in the library. Would it be perfect technology to store the book records in arbitrarily chosen positions in an array, for which you have an infinitely fast sequential search? Or in a hash table, for which you have an infinitely fast access to home and overflow entries? Or in a hash table that never has collisions? Or none of these? It's not an easy question to answer.

Cliff Jones provides a different perspective in his book *Systematic Software Development Using VDM*. A VDM specification of a system is a description of its *external behaviour* – that is, its responses to a succession of *external operations*. What the system remembers in order to produce the correct responses is its *internal state*. For each operation you must describe its arguments, how it changes the internal state, and the result returned to the user.

VDM provides an objective test for implementation bias in the internal state. A VDM description of internal state is biased if there are distinct values of the state that can't be distinguished by looking at the results of subsequent external operations. By this criterion, both the sequential array and the hash table with collisions are implementation biased. If you swapped the positions of two array entries, there would be no detectable effect on the results of subsequent operations. The same would be true if you swapped an overflow entry with the home entry having the same hash value.

Applying this criterion is a significant part of the VDM method. Jones says:

> 'The precision of this test makes it possible to use it as a proof obligation. A model is *sufficiently abstract* (to be used as a specification) providing it can be shown to be free of bias'.

But there are limitations. Implementation bias in the VDM state is relative to a particular set of external operations. Suppose that you had chosen to store the book records in a sequential array, in acquisition order. By the criterion this choice was biased: none of the operations *AcquireBook(b), LendBook(b), and ReturnBook(b)* would return a different result if the array were differently ordered. Now suppose that you decide to add a new operation *AcquiredBefore?(b1,b2)*. The result of this operation is a message telling the user which of the two books *b1* and *b2* was acquired first. Adding the new operation eliminates the implementation bias in your previous choice of internal state, because different arrangements of the array are now distinguishable by *AcquiredBefore?(b1,b2)* operations. This makes the test difficult to apply in a practical project, where the population of external operations may be continually changing.

I think the central point is just this. Essential Systems Analysis and VDM are both, in their very different ways, trying to describe the internals of the MACHINE. McMenamin and Palmer want to avoid bias by describing a *perfect machine*, to which any actual design must be only an approximation. Cliff Jones wants to avoid bias by describing an *abstract machine*, of which any actual design will be a concrete realization. Both approaches suffer from the same disadvantage: they are both describing the machine.

VDM describes the machine's internal state in terms of abstract data structures. Essential Systems Analysis describes the machine's internal behaviour in terms of processes and data flows and data stores. But the internals of the machine – however described – are inherently an implementation concern. You can't describe *what the system must remember* in an unbiased way, because the whole idea of the system remembering anything is inherently an implementation idea.

If any state must be described in a specification, it should be only the state of the APPLICATION DOMAIN, not of the machine. Describing the library books as being in a certain order is absolutely fine, provided it's an order that's observable in the domain or definable purely in terms of phenomena that are observable in the domain. Suppose that *PublishedOn(b,d)* is a domain phenomenon, recognizable when book *b* was published on date *d*, and *EarlierDate(d,e)* is the domain phenomenon that date *d* is earlier in time than date *e*. Then there is no implementation bias at all in talking about *EarlierInBookSequence(b,c)*, meaning that book *b* is earlier in the sequence than book *c*, if you define it in terms of observable domain phenomena:

EarlierInBookSequence(*b,c*) ≙
  ∃ *d, e* • PublishedOn(*b,d*) ∧ PublishedOn(*c,e*) ∧ EarlierDate(*d,e*)

One book is earlier in the book sequence than another if it was published on an earlier date.

It doesn't matter whether the book sequence, or the publication dates, or even the time ordering of the calendar is necessary to your system, or even relevant. Anything you say about it is a description of the domain.

A description of the domain could be false; or it could be irrelevant; or it could describe states that your customer wants to avoid rather than achieve. But it can't be implementation-biased.

Individuals

Domain PHENOMENA are facts about individuals. The essential characteristic of individuality is that each individual is identical to itself, but distinct from every other individual. You must be able to say confidently of two individuals: 'I'm talking about *this* one, not *that* one'.

The archetypal example of an individual, of course, is an individual human being. We use the word 'individual' in everyday language to mean just that. Whatever doubts we may have on other matters, we have a strong sense of our own individuality: each one of us is an individual person, distinct from all others. Macabre science fiction imaginings and jokes – If you were to be involved in a brain transplant would you rather be the donor or the recipient? – serve only to emphasize the unthinkability of our not being distinct and separate individuals.

Decisions to treat certain things as individuals are not objective. You choose to recognize just those individuals that are useful to your purpose and easily enough distinguishable in practice. A person, a bank account, and a book may all be individuals. So may a number, a colour, a date, a speech, an invoice, a birth, a marriage, an explosion, a company, a purchase, a school, a season, a musical note, an idea, a name, a word, a keystroke, or a character. In short, individuals may be any things you choose, so long as you can distinguish one from another. But it is often hard to make workable decisions about what to regard as individuals.

One common problem is self-inflicted. Nine teachers and 23 alumni are coming to the school meeting. How many coffee cups do you need? There's no reason to assume that 32 is the right answer. Three of the teachers are alumni. A bank customer's accounts participated in 19 withdrawals and 7 deposits in a period. How many transactions were there? 25. One transaction was a transfer, which is both a withdrawal from one account and a deposit in another. There were 42 employees, 16 shareholders, and 3 directors at the company's annual general meeting. How many chairs were needed?

The point is obvious but easily forgotten. Very few classification schemes partition the world's individuals into disjoint sets. So you can't enumerate individuals by enumerating members of the classes. You wouldn't assume that HasRedHair(x) and LikesCheese(x) are disjoint – that is, that they can't both be true of the same x. It's no more reasonable to assume that IsEmployee(x) and IsShareholder(x) are disjoint. Declaring them as entity types, or as base sets in a formal notation like Z, doesn't make them disjoint. It just assumes that they are disjoint. Wrongly, no doubt.

More serious difficulties arise because the real world about us is fuzzy and informal. While the identity and distinctness of individual human beings is clear enough, many other kinds of individual are hard to pin down. For example, it seems obvious that motor cars can be treated as individuals. But William Kent, in *Data and Reality*, points out that two friends, both expert mechanics, might start to exchange parts of their cars, which are of the same manufacturer and model. First they exchange wheels, then engines, then transmissions, then doors, then body shells. At what point have they exchanged cars? At what point did the individual that began life in one garage move to the other garage?

You don't have to be as inventive and fanciful as William Kent to find many other similar examples:

- An airline flight may be regarded as an individual. But two flights may be merged into one journey made by one aeroplane. Or one flight may have intermediate stops between its starting and ending airports, with different planes used for different sections of the same flight.

- A road may be regarded as an individual. But years of small layout changes may give rise to such curiosities as discontinuities, gaps and right-angle bends. Different stretches of one road may have different names or road numbers. One physical stretch may be regarded as a part of two different roads. I once saw a delicious sign on an American highway: it said simply '161 is 524'.

• A phone call may be regarded as an individual. But suppose A calls B, B uses the 'conference call' feature to introduce C into the conversation with A, and B then drops out, leaving A talking to C. How many calls is that? How many calls are there on a 'chat line', where an ever-changing population of teenagers dial into an unending conversation?

What is in question in these examples is IDENTITY. In Kent's motor car example, it is clear at each stage that there are two motor cars: but it is not clear which is which. When you are sitting in an airline seat next to another passenger, it is clear that you are both on a flight: but is it possible that one of you is on flight AB123 and the other on flight AB456? If you are forced to take a view of the world in which you cannot reliably distinguish one motor car from another, or one airline flight from another, then motor cars and airline flights cannot be individuals.

These difficulties are evidence that the real world is an irreducibly INFORMAL DOMAIN: whatever rules and definitions you make, there will always be room for exceptions and new hard cases you had not previously thought of. But there are several ways of dealing with the informality, and you must choose the most appropriate for each case.

Sometimes you can substitute a surrogate individual. Kent points out that for vehicle licensing purposes some authorities substitute the engine block for the car: the engine block is virtually indivisible and it carries an identifying number that is virtually indelible. From the authority's point of view, the two friends exchanged cars when they exchanged engine blocks. Of course, some people do contrive – usually for purposes of thievery – to change the number on an engine block; perhaps some virtuoso might even cut two blocks in half and weld together halves from different blocks to make two new blocks; and surely someone has built a car with two engines? But for enough of the cases the problem is solved: engine blocks are sufficiently distinct to serve as the individuals needed.

Often the best solution is reductionist. Forget about the recalcitrant things that refuse to behave as individuals should, and focus your attention instead on simpler and more clearly recognizable phenomena. It may be hard to recognize individual telephone calls, but it's easy to recognize the events of lifting the receiver, hanging up, dialling a digit, and being connected to another subscriber. It may be hard to recognize an individual airline flight, but it's easy to recognize the events of a plane taking off and landing, and passengers embarking and disembarking. It may be hard to recognize an individual road, but it's easy to recognize an unbroken stretch of carriageway between intersections.

But can you really discard such concepts as airline flights and roads? What about their identifiers? There are road numbers and flight numbers: surely they must refer to individuals of some kind? Not necessarily. The identifiers are themselves individuals. They participate in facts – in their associations with unbroken stretches of carriageway, or with episodes in an aeroplane's life that begin with a take-off and end with a landing. But the relationship between road numbers and carriageway stretches is many-to-many; and the relationship between flight numbers and episodes is many-to-many. There are no recognizable individuals in the domain with which the identifiers are in one-to-one correspondence. In short, they may be called identifiers, but they do not identify.

Informal Domains

Computer programs are formal. They describe machines that have limited and precisely describable behaviours and properties, constructed from a small and well-defined repertoire of machine operations and state components. Although the physical machines themselves are not formal, they usually work well enough and reliably enough for their informality to be ignored while we are developing software. And if their informality forces itself on your attention, as it does for developers of fault-tolerant software, you simply formalize a little more: the repertoire of machine operations is extended by one or more failure operations, such as halting unexpectedly or producing an arbitrary result from an otherwise reliable operation.

Because you want your formal programs to compute about the real world, you must also give formal descriptions of the parts of the world that are important to you. But this is harder than formalizing the behaviour of computing machinery, because the world is much less limited than a computer. Effectively, the world is infinite: however much you describe, there is always more. 'Every rule has an exception', we say. However careful you are in framing a rule, however careful to take every consideration into account, there is always something you have left out that can make nonsense of your rule.

So rules and formalizations about the informal real world are always very imperfect. Some, of course, are more imperfect than others. A Punch cartoon, printed in March 1869, shows a railway passenger, intending to travel with her menagerie of pets. She has asked how the railway's formal rules about fares will be applied to her animals, and a porter, holding a tortoise, is telling her the station master's answer. The caption reads:

> 'Station Master says, Mum, as Cats is "Dogs", and Rabbits is "Dogs", and so's Parrots; but this 'ere Tortis is a Insect, so there ain't no charge for it!'

The railway's formal rules seem to classify all living things as human passengers, dogs, and insects – although the last are, perhaps, an extension invented by the porter. Reality does not fit very well into this classification.

You encounter the same kind of situation, in a lesser degree, when you try to determine exactly what your customer for a data processing system means by a 'supplier' and find that there are at least ten different meanings in use, none of them convincing. The company that supplies domestic gas to my house operates a budget scheme. They estimate monthly usage and charge monthly on that basis. At the end of each half-year, if the discrepancy between the amount charged and the amount spent exceeds £200, a cash payment is made. Once, surprisingly, they had to pay me. They sent me their cheque, and with it came a purchase order carrying my name as the supplier: my Supplier Identifier was 000000. Because I was being paid I clearly had to be either an employee or a supplier. The railway company would have understood.

Confronted by these apparent stupidities, developers may be tempted to wash their hands. This nonsense is none of our business. Let the customers work out for themselves what they mean by 'dog' and what they mean by 'supplier', and call us in when they're ready to discuss their problems sensibly.

Nothing could be a greater mistake. The difficulty of formalizing the informal is real. Doing it right is a large part – sometimes the largest and most important part – of what is needed to build a good system.

Is

One of the most versatile words in English, and one of the most misleading, is the little word *is*. You should always be wary of it: its user may be trying to slip something past you while you're not on guard.

'Software development is description,' I may have said in the preface to this book, implying that it is only description, and that anyone who claims that software development is engineering, or software development is mathematics, must be simply wrong. Challenged, I could retreat and justify the statement by denying the implication: 'Of course, what I meant you to understand is that software development is description and it's also many other things.' But the denial is suspect.

Particularly beautiful examples of the misuse of *is* can be found in software texts written by mathematicians. Explaining the formal specification of a small telephone system, its authors write: ' ... a subscriber is a sequence of digits. Let *Subs* be the set of all subscribers

Subs: $\mathbb{P}$ (*seq*[*Digit*])

... certain digit sequences correspond to unobtainable numbers, and some are neither subscribers, nor are they unobtainable'. A subscriber *is a sequence of digits*, indeed! The shortening of 'we assume that each subscriber has exactly one directory number, and we will represent subscribers in our development by their directory numbers, which are sequences of digits' to 'a subscriber is a sequence of digits' is breathtaking: only a mathematician could treat the real world with such audacious disdain.

In this respect mathematicians are inclined to behave like administrators. As John Gall explains in *Systemantics*, the Second Corollary of the Fundamental Law of Administrative Workings is:

> 'To those Within a System, The Outside Reality Tends to Pale and Disappear'.

Fortunately, soon after I first encountered the telephone system example, British Telecom helpfully provided an antidote: they ran an advertising campaign based on the slogan 'To us you're not just a number'. Indeed not.

JSP Frame

JSP is a program design method. Program design is not a central concern of this book; but I think JSP is worth saying something about. Partly because it's my own baby – I wrote about it in *Principles of Program Design* – and partly because it exemplifies some very desirable characteristics of method. All good parents think their own babies are beautiful.

The PROBLEM FRAME for JSP is very simple:

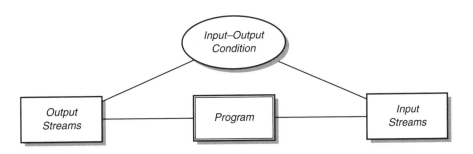

The machine to be built is called the *Program*. The *Input Streams* and *Output Streams* principal parts are domains directly connected to the *Program*. The *Input-Output Condition* is a relationship among the phenomena of the *Input Streams* and *Output Streams* domains. It may specify relationships within the *Output Streams* domain as well as between the two domains. The solution task, of course, is to construct the *Program* to produce the *Output Streams* from the *Input Streams* so that the *Input–Output Condition* is satisfied.

As always, the FRAME DIAGRAM shows only an outline of the frame. The substance depends on the characteristics of the principal parts. The strength of the JSP method comes from the very tightly defined characteristics that it demands of the principal parts of the frame. The *Input Streams* and *Output Streams* must have these properties:

- They must be respectively given and created domains, as you would expect.
- Each one must also be one or more sequential structures of elements – for example, sequential files of records on disk, or streams of messages in a channel, or sequences of characters or words input at a keyboard, or sequences of signals such as mouse clicks and movements, or printed lines on a document.
- Their sequential structures must be describable in regular expressions over the element types. That is, they must be describable using sequence, selection, and iteration.

The *Input–Output Condition* must also have some tightly defined properties:

- It must relate subexpressions of the regular expressions that describe the stream structures.
- It must be simple enough to be expressed as correspondences, each among a small number of subexpressions. It must not specify very elaborate correspondences involving many subexpressions of one stream and many subexpressions of another.

Here is a very small JSP problem. There are two file directories, A and B, both sorted by filename. The program to be written, P, must produce a list, also sorted by filename, of the files that appear in both directories.

The two directories A and B are given, and the list is created. They are all sequential structures, describable in regular expressions. The rule for collating the two directories and selecting the parts to be listed has the properties demanded of the Input–Output Condition. So this is indeed a JSP problem. Here is a frame diagram for the problem, made in the usual way by superimposing the generic JSP problem frame on the problem's CONTEXT DIAGRAM:

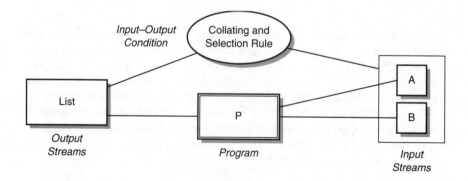

JSP exploits its very tightly fitting problem frame to give a very prescriptive design procedure:

(a) Describe each of the streams in a Tree Diagram. JSP tree diagrams are, essentially, regular expressions.

(b) Draw the correspondences among the tree diagrams specified by the *Input–Output Condition*.

(c) Put the stream tree diagrams together, in a Composition, to give the structure of the *Program*.

(d) Write down the operations needed to produce the outputs from the inputs, and put them in their proper places in the program structure.

(e) Work out the condition needed for each loop (iteration) and if-else or case (selection) component of the program structure.

(f) Convert the program structure, with the conditions and operations, into a program text.

Because the problem frame is so tightly constrained, there are very clear rules for checking whether each step has been done correctly. For example, you check your program structure composition at step (c) by pruning it back to each of the stream structures in turn from which you made it. And if you can't complete a step correctly, you can identify the reason:

- The streams and correspondences can't be described as stipulated in steps (a) and (b). You have a problem frame Misfit.

- You can't form the program structure at step (c). There is a *structure clash* among the stream structures – they might, for example, be like the structures of the Calendar.

- You can't find suitable iteration and selection conditions at step (e). Probably there is a *recognition difficulty* – the input cannot be parsed by just looking at the next element.

JSP has techniques – 'advanced JSP'– for classifying and solving structure clashes and recognition difficulties. But for a problem frame misfit the only solution is to try another problem frame, and another method. That's how it should be.

Logical Positivism

A vital tool for avoiding vagueness and worse is the Designation set, in which you say which Phenomena of the domain you are talking about and how you are referring to each one. Given a domain description in unambiguous language, and a designation set defining each term used in the description, you can then look at the domain and see exactly what the description is saying, and ask yourself whether it is true or false. In short, the test of truth and falsehood is a phenomenological test, to be applied in the described domain.

The point is closely related to the central argument of the Vienna Circle of Logical Positivist philosophers. Rebelling against what he regarded as the meaningless statements of metaphysicians and of some other philosophers, A J Ayer wrote in *Language, Truth and Logic* in 1936:

> 'We say that a sentence is factually significant to any given person, if, and only if, he knows how to verify the proposition which it purports to express – that is, if he knows what observations would lead him, under certain conditions, to accept the proposition as being true, or reject it as being false.
>
> '. . . On the other hand, such a metaphysical pseudo-proposition as "the Absolute enters into, but is itself incapable of, evolution and progress" is not even in principle verifiable. For one cannot conceive of an observation which would enable one to determine whether the Absolute did, or did not, enter into evolution and progress'.

Ayer later came to think that the view he expressed here was too uncompromising. In his introduction to the 1946 edition of his book he wrote:

> 'In the ten years that have passed since *Language, Truth and Logic* was first published, I have come to see that the questions with which it deals are not in all respects so simple as it makes them appear; but I still believe that the point of view which it expresses is substantially correct'.

Ayer's view is too uncompromising and too simple because along with the despised 'metaphysical pseudo-propositions' of philosophers such as F H Bradley – the despised sentence about the Absolute was taken from Bradley's book *Appearance and Reality* – it sweeps away most of human discourse on aesthetics, morals, art, and literature. Karl Popper, also a member of the Vienna Circle of philosophers, took a more discriminating view. He asked himself the question: What is science? He did not dismiss all non-scientific subjects as worthless, but he wanted to distinguish scientific subjects such as chemistry and physics from subjects which he considered to be non-scientific, such as religion, or pseudo-scientific, such as astrology.

Popper's criterion of a scientific subject is that its practitioners form falsifiable theories about the world. Typical scientific theories cannot be conclusively verified, but they can be falsified by observation. In some unusual cases conclusive verification is possible. A theory that an individual with certain properties must exist can be conclusively verified by finding the individual. The planets Neptune, Uranus and Pluto were found in this way. But a typical scientific theory deals with a general law, not with the existence of an individual, even one on the scale of a planet.

Popper pointed out that scientific experiments put theories at risk: the scientist who puts forward a theory invites other scientists to falsify it by experiment. The theories of a pseudo-science, by contrast, cannot be falsified by any observation or experiment. The newspaper astrologer tells you that 'financial concerns will be of positive interest this week', but carefully refrains from telling you which horse will win the big race.

Vague descriptions created in software development are certainly not 'metaphysical pseudo-propositions'; nor is the making of those vague descriptions a 'pseudo-science'. They do have a legitimate place in software development, as ROUGH SKETCHES. But a vague description must not be offered when what is needed is a precise description that we would call a REFUTABLE DESCRIPTION. Vague descriptions are usually not meaningful by Ayer's criterion of meaningfulness, nor, probably, scientific by Popper's criterion of science. A precise description makes a clear and falsifiable statement about the domain it describes. In Ayer's words, you know what observations would lead you to accept it as being true or reject it as being false. That's still a good test to apply.

Machines

Software development is engineering. When you build software you're building a machine. You don't build the physical fabric of the machine: the hardware engineers do that when they build the computer. But you build the behaviour and the properties of the machine that will make it useful for some particular purpose.

In the 1940s and early 1950s, the electronic computer was an elaborate device waiting to be told what to do by a human operator – to *obey* prepared programs of *commands*, or *orders*, or *instructions*. Gradually the importance of programming as an intellectual discipline became more widely acknowledged. As Dijkstra wrote in 1976:

> '. . . slowly the programming profession was becoming of age. It used to be the program's purpose to instruct our computers; it became the computer's purpose to execute our programs'.

But there was a further step to take. We should add:

> 'It used to be the computer's purpose to execute our programs. It became the computer's purpose to embody the machine that each program describes'.

As software developers we write a very exact description of the character and behaviour of the machine we want. A general-purpose computer takes this description – the program text – and magically embodies, or turns itself into, the special-purpose machine we described. The general-purpose computer can do this because it has three properties: it is *programmable*; it can *calculate*; and it is equipped with *standard interfaces*.

There were programmable machines long before computers. Large church clocks were sometimes decorated with carved figures of saints, the striking of the clock being accompanied by a mechanical procession of these figures. The procession was controlled by a rotating cylinder fitted with pegs, much like the barrel of a music box. Clocks like this were constructed in Europe as long ago as the fourteenth century, and at least one animated clock was built in China in the eleventh century. Their programmability was conceptual rather than practical: changing the program would have involved dismantling the machine far enough for the rotating cylinder to be replaced. But the crucial idea – that the mechanism for moving the figures could be separated from the mechanism for programming the moves – was clearly present.

Towards the end of the seventeenth century people began to think about programmable weaving looms. In the simplest form of weaving, the warp threads, which lie along the length of the material, are held taut, while successive cross threads, called the weft, are inserted, passing above some warp threads and below others. To insert the weft in each pass, the warp threads that will be above it in the pass are raised, while those that will be below it are lowered. In the space between, called the shed, the weft can be easily carried across the width of the cloth by the shuttle. Patterns are produced by selecting the warp threads to be raised and lowered for each pass of the weft. The problem was to devise a mechanism that would let the sequence of warp thread selections be prepared in advance, and performed accurately and quickly, however complicated the pattern.

A man named Broesel made the first serious attempt, at the end of the seventeenth century. His device used a program in the form of a linen strip bearing small wooden bars. Later inventors used paper rolls, or punched cards linked to form a chain. Joseph Marie Jacquard perfected a design using punched cards and patented it in 1801. A famous woven portrait of Jacquard himself needed about 24 000 cards; repetitive patterns needed many fewer cards, arranged in an endless loop. Looms with Jacquard programming mechanisms are still at work today.

Calculation was not originally associated with programmability. The earliest successful mechanical calculators, devised in the seventeenth century by the mathematicians Pascal and Leibniz, and by others, were not programmable. The initial entry of the operand numbers for each calculation, achieved by setting the positions of wheels or rods, was a primitive form of data entry, but not of programming. There was no idea that the behaviour of the machine, once those numbers had been initially entered, might be under any form of programmed control.

Charles Babbage, who was born in 1791, conceived the idea of a programmable calculating machine with internal storage. His difference and analytical engines, designed in the years from 1820 to 1860, were too ambitious for their purely mechanical implementation, and only parts of the machines were ever built. But they show that he understood more about programming than most of the pioneers of electronic computing a hundred years later. Babbage used Jacquard's scheme of endless loops of punched cards to hold both the program (the 'Operation' and 'Combinatorial' cards) and the input data (the 'Number' cards). He saw the value of being able to output intermediate results that could be used as input data for later computations, and provided a card punching apparatus for this purpose.

Babbage even had the notion of a compiler. He saw that creating the Jacquard cards for a program would be an error-prone task, and that the encoding system for the cards – Babbage's machine language – was cumbersome. So he thought of creating another program – in effect, a compiler – to make the machine calculate and punch the encoded cards from inputs of a more convenient form, Babbage's higher-level programming language. This notion, that a programmable calculator can calculate about its own programs, is the essential idea for a general-purpose computer. A Universal Turing Machine calculates by interpreting its programs rather than compiling them, but the essential idea is the same.

Still something more is needed. Because we want to build machines that we can install in the world to interact with it, our computers need a repertoire of interaction operations that can be executed just as we wish within our programs. Sometimes we want our machine to raise or lower a warp thread in a loom; sometimes we want it to make St Peter move past St Paul; sometimes we want it to display a picture on a video screen, or accept a keystroke from a keyboard, or move a control surface of an aeroplane's wing, or dispense cash.

Babbage understood this need very well, at least so far as it concerns output operations. He intended originally to equip his machine with three output devices: a single-copy printer; a device to produce copper plates from which many copies of computed results – such as astronomical tables – could be printed offline; and a graph plotter that would print graphs on paper or engrave them on copper plates. But it soon occurred to him that a more general interface to such devices would be preferable, and that the card punch, originally intended for producing intermediate results to be used as input in a later execution, could provide such an interface. He wrote:

'Since however the invention of the number cards these modes of
printing or engraving have ceased to become integral parts of a
Calculating Engine. The absolute certainty of every printed result can
now be obtained although the printing mechanism be totally detached
from the calculating portion of the Engine, an improvement which it
was impossible to make untill that point of the enquiry was attained.
'The cards on which the results are punched may themselves be
placed in a distinct machine and from the holes formed in them the
new machine may either engrave or print them as it may have been
prepared to operate.'

The 'integral parts of a Calculating Engine' need not, therefore, include
devices for raising weft threads, moving statues of saints, or even for dis-
playing pictures on a screen: such devices can be attached by a general
interface. Today we use serial and parallel ports, and other interactive interfaces rather than Babbage's batch interface of punched cards, but the
principle is the same.

Mathematics

Some mathematicians who write about software development say that programs are mathematical objects and that software development is therefore
mathematics. The key software development activities, in their eyes, are
abstraction and formal mathematical reasoning, best done by manipulating
symbols according to the rules of a calculus. Their justification for this view
is that software is complex, and the only intellectual tool we have for han-
dling complexity of that kind is to think and reason with as much precision
and rigour as we can.

That kind of thinking and reasoning, they say, is mathematics. Without
the precision and rigour of mathematics it is impossible to solve some
kinds of problem, impossible to write correct programs for some tasks. The
terrible accidents in which the Therac-25 radiation therapy machine killed
several patients were largely due to programming errors. Some of these
errors were in faulty concurrent access to shared variables, the *mutual
exclusion* problem that had been definitively solved by the Dutch mathematician DEKKER many years before the Therac software was written. But
the Therac-25 programmer was not, apparently, aware either of the difficulty of the shared variables problem or of the existence of a solution.

Yet traditionally most practising software developers have regarded a
mathematical approach to their work as either irrelevant or too difficult.
Some have even regarded mathematics and mathematicians with a degree
of contempt. A leading US company in structured development methods
once advertised one of their seminars like this:

'Building workable software systems is not a "science". So-called computer scientists try to convince us that our systems are really directed graphs or n-tuples of normalized forms or finite state automata . . . their pronouncements are more relevant to Zen than to the no-nonsense business of building useful, maintainable programs and systems. They have no answers to real-life problems like users who change their minds or requirements that are in a constant state of flux.

'In place of academic approaches, we require a set of hard-nosed practical methods that deal squarely with the fallible nature of project personnel, users, machines, maintainers and the development process. Such a set of methods is called *Software Engineering*. Use of proven Software Engineering techniques is the subject of this seminar.'

This is invective, not argument. But it must have struck a sympathetic chord in the breasts of many practising, or would-be, software engineers, for the advertisement pulled in over 5000 bookings for the seminar. Behind the dismissive sarcasm about 'so-called computer scientists' and 'academic approaches' you can hear faint echoes of a serious criticism of some of the advocates of a mathematical approach. Viewing a program as a finite-state automaton, or a database as a directed graph, is an *abstraction*. Abstraction, above all, is what mathematics is about: stripping away inessential detail and going to the heart of the matter in hand. But it is a particular kind of abstraction. Abelson and Sussman, in *Structure and Interpretation of Computer Programs*, quote Herman Weyl:

'We now come to the decisive step of mathematical abstraction: we forget about what the symbols stand for. . . . [The mathematician] need not be idle; there are many operations he may carry out with these symbols, without ever having to look at the things they stand for'.

Operating on symbols, without ever looking at the things they stand for, is the essence of formal mathematical reasoning. Thinking about a database structure as a directed graph, or about a program as a finite-state automaton, allows formal reasoning that is simply impossible if you insist on thinking all the time about the disk sectors and the record pointers, or about arithmetic overflow and the details of the programming language. But it is vital to remember that the abstraction is just that: it is one abstract way of looking at the reality in hand, and it ignores all the other ways of looking at it, which have their own importance and validity.

The seminar company should have said: Yes, a program can be described as a finite-state automaton. But it is not *only* a finite-state automaton – it has other properties too, and they must not be ignored. Yes, a database can be regarded as a directed graph. But it is not *only* a directed graph – it is also a collection of records on disk, linked by record address pointers. And sometimes these other aspects of programs and databases will be more important than the aspects captured by the first or most obvious mathematical abstractions. The mathematicians know this too. It's just that they often forget it, or forget to say it, because they are so carried away by the sheer excitement of mathematical reasoning.

Mathematics, and mathematical abstraction, is an important tool in software development. Where formal correctness is the crucial issue, as it is in some parts of some developments, we must be mathematicians, dealing in proofs and theorems and calculi. If we cannot do the mathematics ourselves, we must seek the help and advice of those who can: that is what the Therac programmer should have done.

But formal correctness is not always the crucial issue. The word-processing system I use is full of programming errors. It doesn't always deal correctly with paragraphs that flow from one page to the next. It sometimes inserts a spurious hyphen at the end of a line. It doesn't repaint the screen correctly after some kinds of text deletion. And sometimes it even crashes the operating system. I wouldn't want to fly in an aeroplane whose avionics software was as bad as this. But I can live with these errors quite easily in a word processor. I have learned to avoid them most of the time. Given the choice between a reduction in the number of errors and an improvement in the annoyingly slow scrolling speed on a 50-page document, I would choose the faster version without hesitation.

For software developers, mathematics is only a tool: not the whole of their trade, not the greater part of it, not even the most important part. The central emphasis in software development – especially in requirements and specifications – is not on proof and logical deduction, but rather on separation of concerns and the clarity that makes a truth obvious. It is not on mathematical abstraction, but rather on identifying and describing the PHENOMENA of the PROBLEM CONTEXT in which the machine must function. Above all it is not on calculation, but rather on description. Software describes a machine that must fit into the world of concrete reality, not into a world of Platonic abstractions and ideals. If software development is the goal, the mathematician who likes to forget what the symbols stand for must forget only very briefly, and only very occasionally.

Method

Tom DeMarco, in *Controlling Software Projects*, says:

> 'As I get older and crankier, I find myself more and more exasperated with the great inflexible sets of rules that many companies try to pour into concrete and sanctify as methods. The idea that a single method

should govern even two different projects is highly suspect: the differences between projects are much more important than the similarities.'

Being old and cranky myself, I agree. I do think that a whole class of *programs* – of moderate size – can be similar enough for one method to govern the task of designing them all: JSP works well for most programs that consume and produce ordered streams of messages or records. But a software development big enough and complex enough to be called a *project* will need a combination of specially chosen or tailored methods.

For developers, that raises the stakes much higher. Instead of just learning and applying method M, you must consider some larger issues. Is method M good for this problem? How can we make best use of method M? What about method N? What are the good features of method P? Is method V better than method W? Why doesn't method X ever seem to work for me? Can we combine method Y with method Z? Instead of being just a user of one method, you must become a *methodologist*. You must study and analyse and criticize methods. You must understand and assess their virtues and vices. And, above all, you must relate them to the kinds of problem they can solve.

If you have only one development method at your disposal, you won't need to devote much effort to these topics. Everything had better look like a nail, because all you've got is a hammer. That's why – I suppose – so many advocates of software development methods say nothing about how to classify problems and how to recognize when the method they are advocating can be profitably applied. Their unspoken assumption is that their method is equally useful for every problem. In some cases that's true. But not quite in the way they meant it.

You should always remember and observe this principle:

- *The Principle of Dispassionate Methodology*
  Don't get your method advice from a method enthusiast. The best advice comes from people who care more about your problem than about their solution.

Thinking about the relationship between problems and methods is a central theme of this book. A method is associated with a PROBLEM FRAME; if your problem fits the frame you can use the associated method. So an essential question to ask about any method is: What is its problem frame? A method that recommends you to 'define the user operations' is assuming that in your problem you can identify 'users' and 'operations' performed by the users. That will be true of a word-processing package or an interactive query system, but not of a process-control system. It will be true – to a certain extent – of a system to control a lift, but not of a batch payroll system.

For any realistic problem you will need more than one method. You will have to see the problem as a complex of several overlapping problems, one superimposed on the other like colour separations. The key concept here is the concept embodied in the logical connective *and*. Your problem is not likely to be a method X problem *or* a method Y problem. It's much more likely to be a method X problem *and* a method Y problem – *and* a method W *and* a method Z problem as well, no doubt. A realistic problem is almost always a MULTI-FRAME PROBLEM.

When you're examining a software development method, always be critical. The notion 'If it's in a published method it must be soundly based' is about as sensible as the notion 'If it's in the newspapers it must be true'. Don't be too ready to accept that the recommended kinds of description are precise enough, or that their meaning in the real world is well enough defined. Probe for weaknesses. Object-oriented methods are tied to a computational paradigm: that is likely to hinder you in describing your problem. Formal methods tend to drift off into mathematical abstraction: formalists often forget the need to tie their descriptions to the reality they describe. Informal structured methods are likely to score very high on the vagueness and waffle scale: whenever you hear the phrase TOP-DOWN you should be on your guard.

When you're looking critically at a particular method, you can apply some general principles. One important principle has already been mentioned in the INTRODUCTION, but bears repetition:

- *The Principle of Close-Fitting Frames*
  The purpose of a problem frame is to give you a good grip on the problem. So the frame must define and constrain the problem very closely indeed.

A method that relies on a very loose problem frame can only be a very loose method. It can't give you a good grip on your problem, so it can't give you much help in solving it. That's why functional decomposition is so feeble. What system doesn't have a function? And what function can't be decomposed? Functional decomposition has no constraining power.

A related principle is that a method should make good use of the properties of the problem, as constrained by the problem frame:

- *The Principle of Frame Exploitation*
  A method should exploit the stipulated characteristics of the principal parts of its problem frame.

One method might say: Describe the data. A better method might say: Describe the *Input Data Streams* by giving a *Finite Automaton* to recognize each stream. The better method is referring to its problem frame: the *Input Data Streams* are principal parts of the frame. And it is exploiting the stipulated characteristics of the parts: the problem frame stipulates that each *Input Data Stream* must be recognizable by a *Finite Automaton*. Not all sequential streams are recognizable by finite automata. Not all problems have sequential input streams. But if your problem – or one aspect of it – does fit this frame, you can expect more help from this method.

A good method must clearly distinguish description of what is *given* – the PROBLEM CONTEXT and the customer's REQUIREMENT – from description of something new that has to be *invented*. It's easier to check that you have correctly described something given than something invented, because there's always someone you can ask, or some place you can look. And what is given constrains what you must invent, rather than the other way around. So this is another important methodological principle:

- *The Principle of Deferred Invention*
  Invention should be delayed until description of what is already given has been completed.

Good methods place invention as late as possible in development; and follow each bout of invention as soon as possible by a test of what has just been invented. Or, even better, cast the inventive activity as a *derivation* of what is needed from what you have already described.

Finally, always look for the *difficulties* in a method. Ask whether it explicitly acknowledges that things may not go smoothly. Does it state stringent limitations on its applicability? Does it sometimes tell you 'At this step you may encounter a difficulty'? Are there places at which it says 'The operation you need to carry out here may prove impossible'? Does it say 'There are two reasons you may get stuck at this point'?

If it does, rejoice. Explicit limitations and difficulties are the most valuable part of any method:

- *The Principle of Beneficent Difficulty*
  Difficulties, explicitly characterized and diagnosed, are the medium in which a method captures its central insights into a problem.

A method without limitations, whose development steps are never impossible to complete, whose stages diagnose and recognize no difficulty, must be very bad indeed. Just think about it. A method without limitations and difficulties is saying one of two things to you. Either it's saying that all problems are easily solved. You know that's not true. Or else it's saying that some problems are difficult, but the method is not going to help you to recognize or overcome the difficult bits when you meet them. Take your choice. Either way it's bad news.

Misfits

Misfits are uncomfortable. Buy a pair of shoes that are too small, or too shallow, or too narrow, or too big, and you will have no peace until you get rid of them. PROBLEM FRAMES are like that. Choose the wrong frame for a problem – or for a part of a complex problem – and it will hurt as much as the wrong pair of shoes. Progress is not impossible, but it's painful, and as you go farther along your path the pain may become crippling.

There are ways of alleviating the pain. You can stretch or chop the problem to fit the frame. That's the PROCRUSTES approach. Your customer probably won't like it. Instead, you can stretch or chop the frame, or add new bits on, to make it fit the problem better. That's a more humane policy. But remember that you chose the method because it goes with the frame. As the frame becomes more distorted you must expect that the method you chose will become less useful.

You can check whether a frame fits a problem by four informal tests. The tests are not entirely independent of each other. A frame that fails to fit on one test will often fail on another test too. And if you stretch a point to pass one test you'll usually find that you have made things worse for another test. If a shoe is not long enough, you can bunch your toes up a bit to make your foot shorter. But then you'll find that the shoe is too shallow.

You should always carry out these tests when you're deciding on a problem frame and a method: it's like checking the fit of a pair of shoes before you take them out of the shop. Do it while there's still time to change your mind.

The separability test

You must be able to separate out the principal parts of the problem frame. Suppose you were considering using the WORKPIECES FRAME for developing a program that conducts an interactive dialogue with its users. Then presumably you would be thinking of each user input as an *Operation Request*, and the *Machine*'s response would be seen as the result of the program performing the operation as requested, in accordance with the specified *Operation Properties*.

But a real dialogue can't usually be separated into request–response pairs in this way. In a typical realistic dialogue, the interaction is much more complicated. The initiative in the dialogue is sometimes with the user, and sometimes with the machine. When the machine is interrogating the user, the user's responses can hardly be seen as *Operation Requests*. The dialogue has a larger and more complex structure than a simple iteration of user–machine exchanges. Attempts to separate out the *Operation Requests* are doomed to fail.

The completeness test

Every part of the problem – and that means every domain of the PROBLEM CONTEXT and every part of the REQUIREMENTS – must be accommodated in a reasonable and natural way in some principal part of the frame. More than one part of the problem can be fitted into one principal part of the frame, but nothing must be left out. If there's something left out, then you need a different frame – either instead of the frame you're considering, or in addition.

So if you are considering using only the SIMPLE IS FRAME for a control problem, you should think again. The Simple IS frame has a *Real World* principal part, in which no doubt you are thinking of accommodating the domain to be controlled. Now, in a control problem, however simple, you will need to give two distinct descriptions of this domain. One description, in the indicative MOOD, to describe the domain's properties and behaviour that it has regardless of the activities of the machine that you are building and another, in the optative mood, to describe the properties and behaviour that the machine is going to bestow on it.

But the Simple IS frame provides for just one description of its *Real World* domain, because the domain is assumed to be autonomous. The *System* can't affect it. Its events and state changes are all internally caused. The single description describes the resulting *Real World* behaviour from the point of view of an external – and purely passive – observer. So your indicative description fits in just fine. But there's nowhere to put the other, optative, description. The whole idea that the *System* might affect the *Real World* is missing from the frame; so there's no provision for describing how it ought to affect it. You have failed the completeness test. You'll need another problem frame.

The part characteristics test

The parts of the problem and its context must have the characteristics demanded of the principal parts to which they are assigned.

Suppose, for example, that you are wondering about the possibility of using the Workpieces frame for your control problem instead of the Simple IS frame that you have just so wisely rejected. Presumably, the domain to be controlled is going to be accommodated as the *Workpieces* principal part of the frame.

Sorry. It can't be. The *Workpieces* principal part must be an inert dynamic domain. It's dynamic because things happen: there are events, and changes of state. But it's inert because nothing happens except in response to externally controlled events. If you leave a *Workpiece* alone, it will just lie there like a couch potato, waiting for something to happen. A method associated with this frame won't give you anywhere to describe what the *Workpiece* does when no one's looking, because it doesn't do anything. A domain to be controlled isn't like that. The passengers of a lift keep pushing buttons, and a motor car slows down when it comes to a hill or the driver applies the brakes, and the chemicals in a chemical plant keep boiling and cooling and flowing and evaporating. It's no use thinking of the chemical plant or the car or the lift domain as *Workpieces*. If you want to avoid a serious misfit you need a different problem frame.

The proportionality test

When you fit the parts of the problem into the principal parts of a frame, you should fill the principal parts roughly equally. You don't want one part filled to overflowing, while another is almost empty. This is important because the associated methods will distribute their emphasis, and the help they can give you, in a roughly equal way over the parts.

Suppose that you are considering a little program design problem. The program will be given an integer N, and must determine and print out P_N, the Nth prime number. Your favourite program design method is – naturally – JSP. How does your problem fit the JSP FRAME?

The *Input Streams* principal part is easy. It's just the integer N. You can certainly regard it as a sequence of one element, and that's a perfectly good regular expression. In the same way, the Nth prime number fits happily into the *Output Streams* principal part. The program you're trying to write is, of course, the *Program*. All that's left is the *Input–Output Condition*. It's needed to give the relationship between the *Input Streams* and the *Output Streams* domains.

Unfortunately, this *Input–Output Condition* contains the whole of the problem. The relationship between the input integer N and the output integer P_N is very elaborate, because it contains the whole of the definition of primality of numbers. But the structures of the input and output are as trivial as it is possible to be. This is a failure of proportionality. Try a different method. Even JSP isn't always right.

Models

The word 'model' has a fine ring of purpose and quality. Who would not want to make – or to be – a model? Major-General Stanley, in *The Pirates of Penzance*, claimed to be 'the very model of a modern Major-General'. The result of the 1644 reorganization of the parliamentary army was the New Model Army. Car makers offer their sparkling new cars in different models. Economists make models of their national economies. Shipbuilders make models of ships, and architects make models of buildings. Mathematicians and logicians are interested in models of their mathematical and logical theories. Children play with model cars and aeroplanes and trains. And, of course, computer scientists and software developers are the most inveterate modellers of all, making data models, process models, dataflow models, object models, computational models, and system models of all conceivable kinds.

But what, exactly, is a model? How should you use the word? Whatever you do, don't adopt the usage of mathematicians and logicians and – unfortunately, of some computer scientists. They speak of the real world as a model of their theories. For them, the theory is fundamental, and the world is secondary. The frustrated airline customers waiting to check in are merely a model of `queue`. The wobbling pile of plates in the cafeteria is merely a model of the abstract data type `stack`. Their intellectual lives are lived in the ideal world of mathematical abstractions, away from the messy real world. Naturally, this Platonic attitude hampers their ability and desire to think carefully about the real world we live in. That is why you should take their pronouncements about software engineering with a large pinch of salt. How much faith would you place in a cartographer who told you that the world is a model of his map?

For many software developers the word *model* has almost the opposite sense. In *Modern Structured Analysis*, according to Ed Yourdon:

> 'The systems analysis models ... are, for the most part, *paper* models of the system-to-be, that is, abstract representations of what will eventually become a combination of computer hardware and computer software'.

And David Marca and Clement McGowan, in their book *SADT*, say that:

> 'An SADT system description is called a "model".... An SADT model is a complete, concise, and consistent description of a system which is developed for a particular reason.'

They are both using the word *model* to mean a description or representation. Well, that's all right, I suppose. It's in the dictionary, and lots of people in software development do it. But it's not clear why they don't just call them *descriptions*, which is what they are. If dataflow diagrams or SADT diagrams describe your system well, then keep on using them. But perhaps you should just call them *descriptions*. If you're going to call them models, you should be ready to explain clearly how they are more than just descriptions, or different from descriptions.

R L Ackoff gives a careful account of what the word *model* means. In his book on *Scientific Method* he distinguishes three kinds of model: *iconic*, *analogic*, and *analytic*. A model aeroplane, in his view, is iconic: it's an *icon* of a real aeroplane. An electrical network modelling the flow of liquid through a network of pipes is analogic: the wires are *analogous* to the pipes, and the flow of current is *analogous* to the flow of liquid. A set of differential equations claiming to describe how prices change is analytic: it's a description that expresses the economist's *analysis* of the relevant part of the economy.

I like to use the word 'model' for what Ackoff calls *analogic* models. That's the common usage of architects, shipbuilders and children. For them, models are not mere icons or descriptions: they are important physical objects in their own right. A self-respecting child would be contemptuous if a picture of an aeroplane were offered as a birthday present when a model aeroplane had been promised. The famous Admiralty ship models were not drawings or plans: they were pieces of wood, fashioned to the shape of the hull of a proposed ship. An architectural model is not a set of plans: usually it is a construction on a table, made of cardboard and wood. A model railway is certainly not just a description of a railway.

The point about such models is that they are *analogues* of the things they model. They share some interesting properties with them, and some structure. Sometimes, this may just be external appearance: the iconic and analogic classes of model overlap. But a good model aeroplane – in spite of Ackoff's claim that model aeroplanes are *iconic* – can also fly; and a good model railway has working points and crossovers and signals and trains that behave very like the real thing. You might say that the model embodies a *simulation* of the real thing.

This is the kind of model that is often built into a computer system. Developing an object-oriented system to control the lifts in a building, you might create objects corresponding to the buttons, doors, and lift cars. These objects exist in the MACHINE. The objects, their behaviour, their states, and the relationships among them form an *object model* of the APPLICATION DOMAIN of the lifts. In exactly the same way, if you create a database about nineteenth-century English novelists, you are building a *database model* inside the computer of the real world of the novelists. Some of the real-world relationships – those that you choose to model – among the real novelists, their fictional characters, and their novels will also hold among the novelist records, the character records, and the novel records in the database. The machine becomes a model of the reality. Information about the state of the reality becomes much more conveniently accessible to the machine and to its users. Instead of looking at the reality directly, you can look at the model of reality inside the machine.

The essence of this kind of model is twofold. First, there is some description that applies both to the machine and to the reality it models, and captures what they have in common. Second, there is a correspondence between individuals in the machine and individuals in the reality.

Let's look at the description first. When you write a description of any domain, you use terms in the description to denote individuals and facts in the domain. You can make these denotations explicit by writing DESIGNATIONS. Then you can easily use the same description with different sets of designations. It looks like this:

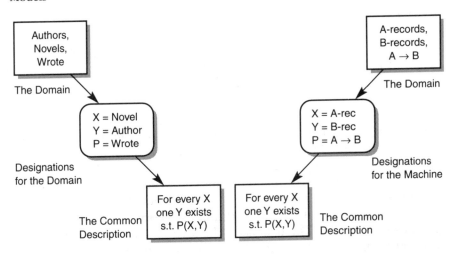

The domain has two kinds of individuals: Authors and Novels. Each fact in the domain is that a particular Author Wrote a particular Novel. In the machine, the individuals are A-records and B-records; and there is one kind of fact – A→B, meaning that a certain A-record contains a pointer to a certain B-record. The description says that for every individual that is an X, there is one individual that is a Y such that P(X,Y) is true. You apply the description to the domain by using the appropriate designations. If you take X to mean a Novel, Y to mean an Author, and P(X,Y) to mean that the Author Wrote the Novel, then the description says that for every Novel there is one Author who Wrote that Novel. You can apply it to the machine by using the other designations. Then it says that for every A-record there is one B-record that the A-record Points to.

To make the model work properly, so that it contains useful information about the domain, you also have to establish correspondences between the individuals in the machine and the individuals in the domain. In practice that will mean that each A-record will have a 'Novel-name' component, whose value will be the name of the corresponding Novel; and each B-record will have an 'Author-name' component containing the name of the corresponding Author. If you want to know who wrote *Middlemarch*, you find the A-record whose Novel-name is *Middlemarch*, and follow its B-record pointer; the Author-name in the B-record is *George Eliot*. The database simulates the domain.

Are you thinking that my explanation of the description and the two designation sets and the simulation is ridiculously over-elaborate? Yes, of course. You wouldn't do it like that at all. You would just make a data model something like this:

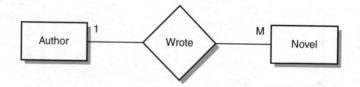

When you're thinking about the domain, the terms in the data model – Author, Novel, and Wrote – mean the real person, the real book, and the real authorship. When you turn your attention to building the database the same terms mean the records and the links between them. You switch from one set of designations to the other, but only in your mind.

Easy, isn't it? Yes, it is. But you must be aware that there's some danger of confusion. The database, like a child's model aeroplane, is a physical thing in its own right. It has its own phenomena and its own relationships among those phenomena. The common description or data model deals with some of these phenomena and relationships. But not all of them. The database has a physical disposition: it is arranged on disk sectors and cylinders and volumes. It is periodically saved, and may be restored from the saved copy. Disk storage is managed by deleting records that seem no longer useful. The records may be held in a certain order to make common access patterns faster. These phenomena and relationships have nothing whatsoever to do with the reality of nineteenth-century English novelists. And, of course, the converse is true as well: there's an unbounded complexity of phenomena and relationships in the real world of the novelists that has no counterpart in the database.

Using a single description, and switching mentally from one set of designations to another, risks confusing three different descriptions:

- the description that is true (with different appropriate designation sets) of both domain and machine;

- another description that is true only of the domain; and

- another description that is true only of the machine.

So you have to be very careful to avoid this confusion. When you're discussing the meaning and effect of record deletion, or the permissibility and significance of null values in record fields, you should always pause and ask yourself which description you're concerned with now. You can remind yourself of the three descriptions from a little picture:

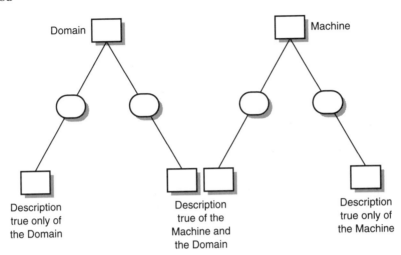

The picture is easy to remember: M is for Modelling.

Mood

The classical grammarians distinguished several *moods* of verbs. 'You sing' is in the *indicative* mood: it asserts a fact. 'Are you singing?' is in the *interrogative* mood: it asks a question. 'Sing!' is in the *imperative* mood: it conveys a command. 'You might sing' is in the *subjunctive* mood: it describes a possible state of affairs. And 'May you sing!' is in the *optative* mood: it expresses a wish. When Alexander Graham Bell spoke his famous first words into the telephone on 10 March 1876 – 'Mr Watson, please come here. I want you' – he was using both imperative and indicative moods in one utterance.

In modern English, the optative form of verbs scarcely exists at all: 'May you sing!' sounds archaic: 'I wish you would sing' is a more likely utterance. But in the chaotic and constantly changing verb forms of English there are still many distinctions of mood, and they are often subtle and obscurely expressed. At school I was taught two sentences that illustrate the confusing uses of 'shall' and 'will':

'I shall drown. No one will save me'

is a desperate cry for help, while:

'I will drown. No one shall save me'

is the proud proclamation of a determined suicide.

It's not a good idea to introduce the uncertain linguistic subtleties of English verbs into system development documents. But some ill-conceived software development standards demand just this. Contractors on some US Government system development contracts may be required to observe these linguistic rules in requirement documents:

> 'Absolute tense "shall": a binding, measurable requirement ... observable when a system is delivered ... in terms of an ... output.

> 'Future tense "will": a reference to the future, ... describing something ... not under control of the system being specified.

> 'Present tense: for all other verbs ... in all other cases'.

This is confusion worse confounded.

But distinctions of mood are necessary in serious software development, and we must find effective ways to express them. In developing a system to control a lift you might want to make clear descriptions of the following roughly stated properties:

(a) The lift never goes from the nth to the $n+2$th floor without passing the $n+1$th floor.

(b) The lift never passes a floor for which the floor selection light inside the lift is illuminated without stopping at that floor.

(c) If the motor polarity is set to *up* and the motor switch setting is changed from *off* to *on*, the lift starts to rise within 250 msecs.

(d) If the *upwards* arrow indicator at a floor is not illuminated when the lift stops at the floor, it will not leave in the *upwards* direction.

(e) The doors are never open at a floor unless the lift is stationary at that floor.

(f) When the lift arrives at a floor, the *lift-present* sensor at the floor is set to *on*.

(g) If an *up* call button at a floor is pressed when the corresponding light is off, the light comes on and remains on until the call is serviced by the lift stopping at that floor and leaving in the *upwards* direction.

You can classify these properties as indicative and optative. Indicative properties are those that the lift domain possesses regardless of the behaviour of the controlling machine. For example, property (a) is true whatever the machine does, because the lift moves in a fixed shaft. Property (c) is also indicative by virtue of the properties of the motor and the winding gear. Property (f) is indicative, too: it depends only on the arrangement of the sensors in relation to an actuator attached to the lift car.

Optative properties are those that the controller is desired to bring about or maintain. Property (b) is optative. The lift controller must ensure that any request made by a passenger in the lift car is honoured at the first opportunity. Property (d) is also optative. People waiting at a floor rely on the direction indicator arrows to avoid getting into a lift that then departs in the wrong direction. (Incidentally, this property seems to cause developers a lot of trouble in the cases where the lift changes direction at the floor.) Property (g) is optative. The controller must manage the lights so that they indicate whether a request is outstanding. Property (e) is optative for most lifts; but a few lifts do have mechanical interlocks that ensure this property holds.

To develop the software to control a lift you must pay explicit attention to both classes of property. The purpose of the controller is to ensure that the lift domain has the optative properties: they are the REQUIREMENT. But to satisfy the requirement the controller must respect and exploit the indicative properties of the domain. For example, it must respect property (a) in scheduling the lift's journeys. It must exploit property (c) in despatching the lift, and property (f) in determining when the lift has arrived at a destination floor. If you don't know which properties are indicative and which are optative, then you don't know what you're trying to do and what environment you're trying to do it in.

A good way of dealing systematically with the distinction between indicative and optative properties is to separate them into different descriptions:

- *The Principle of Uniform Mood*
  Never mix indicative and optative moods in the same description.

If you observe this principle you will have no need for linguistic subtleties and confusions. Write each description as if it were purely indicative, so there are no distinctions of mood – no 'shall' and 'will' – within one description. Make the necessary distinctions of mood by putting each description in an appropriate place in the whole development structure.

David Parnas and Jan Madey take this approach. They describe their basic ideas in their paper *Functional Documentation for Computer Systems Engineering*. They make two descriptions of the domain that the system must control. Both descriptions are in the form of mathematical relations. One relation, *NAT*, captures the *natural* properties that the domain possesses regardless of the behaviour of the system. The other, *REQ*, captures the *required* properties with which the system must endow it. *NAT* is indicative; *REQ* is optative. A paper by Stuart Faulk and others describes how some of Parnas and Madey's ideas are incorporated into *The Core Method for Real-Time Requirements*.

Avoiding subtleties isn't the only reason to keep indicative and optative in separate descriptions. Another, equally compelling, reason is that the mood of a description changes during the project. The domain properties that are optative when the software is under development become indicative when the software is deployed. The machine interacts with the domain and – all being well – turns our wishes into facts.

A Multi-Frame Problem – 1

PROBLEM FRAMES are always simple. That's their role in life. They cut out all the nasty inconvenient complications that plague realistic problems, and leave you with something simple: a problem that you can understand, and an effective method for solving it.

When you're faced with a problem of realistic complexity you need to decompose it into a number of simple problems. That means decomposing it into problems you can solve – there's not much point in decomposing one problem you can't solve into several more problems that you still can't solve. And that means decomposing it into problems for which you have well-understood problem frames and methods.

Here's an example. Suppose you're developing an elementary CASE tool. The tool must provide operations for its users to create and manipulate CASE objects (in this CASE, just entity–relation diagrams). It must also provide information for the users' management, who want to monitor the progress of the project. They want to know which diagrams have been completed, how much work each CASE tool user has already done, how much work has been done on each CASE object, and other information of that kind. They also want to be able to restrict access to the tool, because they may be using it on high-security projects. Here's the CONTEXT DIAGRAM for the whole problem:

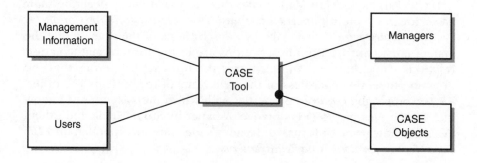

The heavy dot indicates that the CASE Objects domain is entirely contained in the CASE Tool domain: that is, the representation of the CASE objects is within the machine.

The whole problem can be decomposed into three simple problems that fit problem frames discussed in this book:

(1) The problem of editing entity–relation diagrams. The diagrams are to be stored inside the CASE Tool, and the Users must be able to edit them by invoking various operations such as *CreateDiagram*, *AddRelation*, *DeleteEntity*, *ChangeAttribute*, and so on.

(2) The problem of providing the management information. The Managers will put in requests for information, and the CASE Tool must respond by producing the Management Information as requested. The information will be about the Users and the CASE Objects.

(3) The problem of restricting access. Only people with security clearance will be allowed access to the CASE Tool. Different levels of clearance will permit different kinds of access – read-only, read-and-add, read-and-update, and so on. The interactions of Users and the CASE Tool must be controlled according to certain access rules based on passwords.

Why is this a good decomposition? Because each simple problem fits a recognizable problem frame. Problem 1, editing the CASE Objects, fits the WORKPIECES FRAME; Problem 2, providing the Management Information, fits the SIMPLE IS FRAME; and Problem 3, restricting access, fits the SIMPLE CONTROL FRAME. The basic assumption is that those problems are simple – that we know how to solve them. If you have a different collection of problem frames you might perhaps want to make a different decomposition.

The point is that you must decompose into problems that you recognize and know how to solve. This is just a slightly more systematic way of doing what you probably do already. Confronted with a complex problem you may say to yourself: 'This would be easy if there were no security problem'; or: 'Let's forget about the management information and just think about making an editor for entity–relation diagrams'; or: 'Let's imagine that the editor is already built, and all we have to do is to control access to it'.

To do this kind of decomposition successfully, you must bear these principles in mind:

● Each simple problem deals with only some parts and some aspects of the problem context.

● In different simple problems the same individuals – especially event individuals – may be differently classified and differently treated.

- In thinking about each simple problem you ignore the other simple problems. You assume that they are either irrelevant or already solved, whichever is more convenient.

- The machine in one simple problem may be a part of the application domain in another. So the machine you build to solve the whole problem may appear twice in one simple problem, in two different roles.

You can see how these principles work out for our three simple problems. Problem 1 fits the Workpieces Frame. Here's a FRAME DIAGRAM to show how:

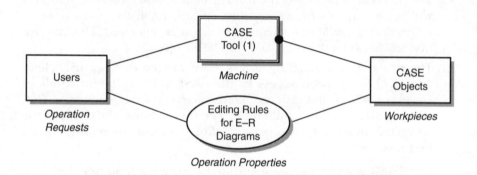

In this problem, the CASE Tool is the *Machine* to be built; the CASE Objects are the *Workpieces*; the *Operation Requests* come from the Users domain; and the required Operation Properties are the editing rules for entity–relation diagrams. We're ignoring the Managers and Management Information domains entirely. We're ignoring the individual Users, treating the Users domain just as the source of the unstructured stream of *Operation Requests*. And we are thinking of the CASE Tool only as an editing tool. That's why I have labelled it 'CASE Tool (1)'.

Problem 2 is the problem of providing the management information. It fits the Simple IS Frame. The solution task in a Simple IS Frame problem is to build a *System* to provide *Information Outputs* in response to *Information Requests*. The information is about a *Real World*, which must be dynamic and active. How the *Information Outputs* relate to the *Information Requests* and to the *Real World* is specified in the *Information Function*.

In our Problem 2, the *System* is the CASE Tool (in its role as a Management Information System). The *Real World*, about which information is to be provided, is the activities of the Users and the CASE Objects. The *Information Requests* are the requests made by the Managers for information about the Users and the CASE Objects. The *Information Outputs* are the Managment Information domain. And, finally, the *Information Function* is just the definition of the way the Management Information is to

be related to the requests for information and the events and states in the
the Users and CASE Objects domains – for example, the definition of what
the request 'List Users by Activity' should produce.

Here's how this frame fits the problem and its context:

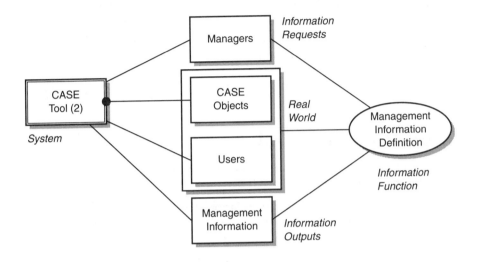

This time, we're interested in the Managers, but only as the originators
of a stream of *Information Requests*. We are imagining that the editor is
already built and working, and the Users are busy editing the CASE Objects.
Together the Objects and the Users form the *Real World* about which information is required. In that world we're interested only in occurrences of
certain important operations, such as opening or closing a diagram. And, of
course, we ignore the access control problem entirely.

Here's a frame diagram for Problem 3, the problem of controlling access
to the CASE Tool:

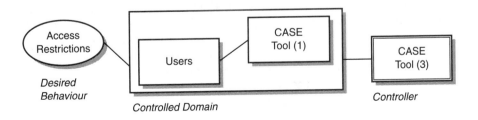

This problem fits the Simple Control Frame. The solution task in a Simple Control problem is to construct a *Controller* that will guarantee that a *Controlled Domain* observes a *Desired Behaviour*. Here the *Controlled Domain* is the Users and the CASE Tool (in its Problem 1 role as an editing tool). We're assuming that that problem is solved, and the Users are hard at work editing their diagrams. They're using the CASE Tool as an editor, so in this problem frame we don't think of the editor as a machine to be built: it's a part of the application domain. The *Desired Behaviour* is that only people who have the appropriate security clearance are permitted to use the editing tool. The *Controller*, which must impose this restriction, is the CASE Tool itself, this time in its Problem 3 role as a security guard.

A Multi-Frame Problem – 2

We decomposed our problem of developing an elementary CASE tool into these three simple problems:

(1) The problem of editing entity–relation diagrams. The diagrams are to be stored inside the CASE Tool, and the Users must be able to edit them by invoking various operations such as *CreateDiagram*, *AddRelation*, *DeleteEntity*, *ChangeAttribute*, and so on.

(2) The problem of providing the management information. The Managers will put in requests for information, and the CASE Tool must respond by producing the Management Information as requested. The information will be about the Users and the CASE Objects.

(3) The problem of restricting access. Only people with security clearance will be allowed access to the CASE Tool. Different levels of clearance will permit different kinds of access – read-only, read-and-add, read-and-update, and so on. The interactions of Users and the CASE Tool must be controlled according to certain access rules based on passwords.

This decomposition is different from a top-down functional decomposition into procedures or processes in two important ways. First, it is *heterogenous*: each of the simple problems needs a different problem frame. There's no rule that says you can't use the same problem frame more than once in decomposing a complex problem, but usually you need several different problem frames. Very few problems can be usefully decomposed into *homogeneous* structures in which all the parts are of the same kind. We usually impose such homogeneity on our *programs*, for good reasons. It's very convenient to program in a environment in which every part is a procedure, or every part is a process, or every part is a Smalltalk object, or every part is a recursive function. But the world, where *problems* are found, is scarcely ever considerate enough to exhibit the same homogeneity.

Second, the decomposition is not *hierarchical*. The three simple problems fit together in a *parallel* structure. They are concerned with overlapping parts of the whole requirement, and with overlapping subsets of the phenomena of the application domain. The simple problems are pinned together at the common phenomena that appear in the overlap.

Think, for example, about an event E in which a user U, whose password is P, opens a diagram D for updating. You can picture the way the simple problems are pinned together like this:

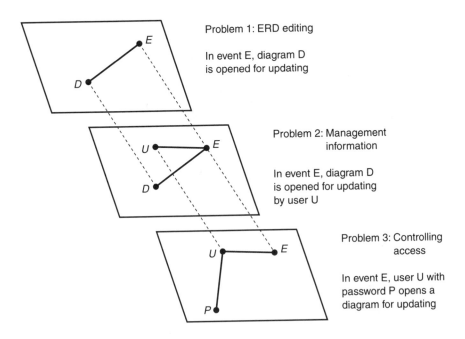

Problem 1: ERD editing

In event E, diagram D is opened for updating

Problem 2: Management information

In event E, diagram D is opened for updating by user U

Problem 3: Controlling access

In event E, user U with password P opens a diagram for updating

Problem 1 is about editing entity–relation diagrams. In this problem, event E is an *Operation Request*, and is associated with the *Workpiece* diagram D. User U and the password P don't figure at all here: they're not relevant to the editing problem.

Problem 2 is about providing management information. Because the managers want to know how much work each user has done, in this problem the event E is associated not only with diagram D but also with user U. Password P isn't relevant here either.

Problem 3 is about controlling access to the CASE Tool. The access restrictions don't distinguish between one diagram and another: all diagrams are at the same security level. So diagram D isn't relevant in this problem. But event E and user U are still relevant, and it's important that user U has password P.

Each simple problem makes sense on its own, and can be considered separately. You only have to consider them together at the points where they meet. At those points you must consider the different ways the common phenomena are treated in each different simple problem. The event *E* is treated very differently in the three problems:

- In Problem 1, event *E* is an autonomous *Operation Request*. The *Machine* – CASE Tool (1) – is required to respond by opening the diagram for updating.

- In Problem 2, the event and the response are both viewed as autonomous events of the *Real World*. The *System* – CASE Tool (2) – is required to update its internal model of the *Real World* to reflect the occurrence of this event.

- In Problem 3, the request is an autonomous event of the *Controlled Domain*, but the *Controller* – CASE Tool (3) – may be required to inhibit the response by preventing CASE Tool (1) from performing the requested operation.

This kind of parallel structure of problems is a powerful tool for simplifying complexity. Each of the three problems deals only with one coherent aspect of the complete development problem. There are many design choices for putting the three CASE Tool roles together. You don't have to consider those choices until you have thoroughly understood what problems the three roles are solving. That's what separation of concerns and problem decomposition are all about.

The Narrow Bridge

A map is useless if you can't align it properly on the terrain it describes. You take out the map, and look about you for the features it shows. That's the river over there, and that must be this bridge over the river right here. But where's the railway? Oh, we've got the wrong river. Turn the map round a bit. Here's the river, there's the bridge, and here's the railway. You can see that the railway goes into a tunnel just about there – oh yes, that's it, where my finger is pointing.

This process of aligning the map and the terrain is not too difficult, provided that two vital conditions are met. First, the terrain must have enough features and enough asymmetry in the terrain to make the alignment unambiguous. In practice, that's hardly ever a problem. The terrain always has enough features and enough asymmetry, unless you are in the middle of a desert. But the second condition is that the map must describe the terrain correctly. That won't always be true. The terrain may have changed since the map was made – this bridge has been demolished, that road has been diverted, and the river has dried up. Or the mapmakers may simply have made a mistake. The map may be wrong. Not very wrong, but wrong enough to leave you in doubt about how it corresponds to the terrain.

If the map doesn't describe the terrain correctly, you've got a problem. You can't rely on anything the map tells you. You know that something's wrong, but you don't know what. So everything the map tells you is under suspicion. The makers of the nineteenth-century British Ordnance Survey maps had a solution to this problem. They made the maps by the standard surveyor's method of triangulation. Each triangulation point used in the process of surveying was given a unique identifier. It was shown in the map by a black triangle and its identifier, and marked on the ground by a small stone pillar with the identifier inscribed on an inset brass plate. To align an Ordnance Survey map you need only find two triangulation points on the map, match them with the corresponding stone pillars on the ground, and the problem is solved. You don't have to look at the road and the river and the railway.

The problem of matching a description of a DOMAIN to the domain itself is rather like the problem of aligning a map. You need some triangulation points – reliably recognizable PHENOMENA by which you can align the description with the domain. The DESIGNATED phenomena of the domain play this role. They form the bridge between the description and the domain it describes. This bridge must be as narrow as possible. That means that you should use as few designated terms as possible in your descriptions, and they should be as unambiguously recognizable as the Ordnance Survey's triangulation pillars. For the other terms you need you don't make designations: you make DEFINITIONS, defining the new terms on the basis of the designated phenomena.

The narrow bridge lets you align the description easily. That's important, because in software development there may well be something wrong with the description. If every term used in the description is treated equally in a data dictionary or repository, it's impossible to say what is wrong when the map doesn't fit. When everything is a triangulation point, nothing is a triangulation point. You know that something in the description is false, but you don't know what it is. In short, you're lost.

Object-oriented Analysis

The ideas of object orientiation have their origins in programming. Here's what Ole-Johan Dahl wrote about objects in Simula 67:

> 'A procedure which is capable of giving rise to block instances which survive its call will be known as a class; and the instances will be known as *objects* of that class.'

Smalltalk drew on the ideas of Simula 67, elaborating them in some ways and simplifying them in others. Other object-oriented programming languages followed, including Eiffel and, of course, C++. In many application areas, especially those involving window interfaces, object-oriented programming has been spectacularly successful.

Inevitably, some people began to advocate an object-oriented approach to analysis and specification. What was succeeding so well in programming should surely succeed in the earlier stages of development. By adopting a uniform technology it should be possible to achieve a seamless progress in development, avoiding the dislocation that usually accompanied the transition to programming from analysis and specification.

Another reason offered was that objects would combine the virtues of data-oriented and process-oriented descriptions. A data-oriented point of view sees the world in terms of entities and relations and attributes; and a process-oriented point of view sees it in terms of behaviours built up from events and processes. Neither is enough on its own. Object orientation would combine the descriptive power of both, and throw in some extra benefits of its own – encapsulation and polymorphism and inheritance.

So object orientation in analysis and specification became cast in the role of a unifying phenomenology that accounts for everything we might see in the world. Everything is an object. The only PHENOMENA are the phenomena of objects. Objects completely subsume entities: like entities they are individuals; they have instance variables, which are something like entity attributes; and like entities they are organized in classes and subclasses. Objects can play the part of relations, too. If you have Course objects and Lecturer objects, you can relate them by Taught-By objects, which have references to Courses and Lecturers as values of their *taught* and *teacher* instance variables. In some versions of data modelling a relation can have attributes; in the same way, a Taught-By object could have an instance variable *popularity* to represent an attribute of the relation, in addition to the variables that represent the related entities.

Objects also subsume events and processes. An object has a repertoire of operations, usually called 'methods', which it performs in response to 'messages' sent by other objects. Sending and receiving a message can be regarded as an event. Like a sequential process, an object can have a behaviour that restricts the events it is willing to participate in at any particular point in its history.

Serious advocates of object orientation don't see objects as a combination of entities and events and other phenomena, but as the most natural phenomena of all in their own right. And they see them everywhere. Bertrand Meyer says in *Object-oriented Software Construction:*

> 'When software design is understood as operational modelling, object-oriented design is a natural approach: the world being modelled is made of objects – sensors, devices, airplanes, employees, paychecks, tax returns – and it is appropriate to organize the model

around computer representations of these objects. This is why object-oriented designers usually do not spend their time in academic discussions of methods to find objects: in the physical or abstract reality being modelled, the objects are just there for the picking! The software objects will simply reflect these external objects.'

But perhaps Meyer has got a bit carried away here. It's certainly true that objects are INDIVIDUALS, and that the world is full of individuals. Sensors, devices, airplanes, employees, paychecks and tax returns are all individuals, because you can say things like 'I mean *this* paycheck, not *that* paycheck'. Recognizing the importance of individuals in our view of the world has been a crucially important contribution of object-oriented programming languages. Before Simula 67 and Smalltalk, most commonly used programming languages – notably Fortran and COBOL – had no useful notion of individual at all.

But the idea of an *object* is a programming idea, and doesn't fit most of the individuals in the world very well. Airplanes, paychecks, and tax returns are certainly individuals. But they are not really *objects* in the usual object-orientation sense. When did you last send a message to a paycheck? What reply would you get back if you sent a message to an airplane? What methods does a tax return perform in response to messages it receives? Steve Cook and John Daniels, in *Designing Object Systems* – one of the best books about object-oriented development – ask: When the sun rises, does it send a message to each bird to tell it to start singing? They conclude rightly that it's a nonsensical question.

Well, you may say, messages and methods are often used just as a mechanism for getting at the properties and attributes of individuals. Surely we can disregard the details of the mechanism? Perhaps. But there are other, more serious, problems. Here are three restrictions that can cause difficulty in the style of object orientation most commonly practised in analysis and specification:

- Each object belongs to a fixed class, determined when the object is created. But the world is not like that: pupils become teachers, bills become laws, partnerships become corporations, doctors become lawyers, cotton mills become offices or hotels, and caterpillars become butterflies.

- Each object class inherits properties and behaviour from just one class at the next level up in the tree. That's single inheritance. But the logistics manager wants to classify the company equipment as production plant, office equipment, and distribution vehicles. The finance director classifies it as owned, rented, and leased. The two classifications can't coexist in the same single-inheritance hierarchy.

- Objects are reactive rather than active. If you don't send a message to an object, it won't do anything. But the world is full of individuals – like

people, and vessels in chemical plants and government departments –
that do things spontaneously.

All of these problems have programming solutions. There are more powerful object-oriented programming languages offering multiple inheritance,
delegation, dynamic object classification, concurrency, and objects that execute sequential processes throughout their lifetimes. Those languages may
be very good for writing programs. We are free to build the machine to our
own design. But the world outside the machine is simply too rich, too
capricious and too recalcitrantly multifarious to be captured in this way.

The Package Router Problem

The package router problem appears in Swartout and Balzer's paper *On
the Inevitable Intertwining of Specification and Implementation*. The
problem and its description are full of interest. Here is the problem
description as Swartout and Balzer give it, translated from the original
German version of Hommel:

'The package router is a system for distributing *packages* into destination bins. The packages arrive at a *source* station, which is connected
to the bins via a series of *pipes*. A single pipe leaves the source station.
The pipes are linked together by two-position *switches*. A switch
enables a package sliding down its input pipe to be directed to either
of its two output pipes. There is a unique path from the source station to any particular bin.

'Packages arriving at the source station are scanned by a reading
device which determines a destination bin for the package. The package is then allowed to slide down the pipe leaving the source station.
The package router must set its switches ahead of each package sliding through the pipes so that each package is routed to the bin
determined for it by the source station.

'After a package's destination has been determined, it is delayed for
a fixed time before being released into the first pipe. This is done to
prevent packages from following one another so closely that a switch
cannot be reset between successive packages when necessary.
However, if a package's destination is the same as that of the package
which preceded it through the source station, it is not delayed, since
there will be no need to reset switches between the two packages.

'There will generally be many packages sliding down the pipes at
once. The packages slide at different and unpredictable speeds, so it
is impossible to calculate when a given package will reach a particular
switch. However, the switches contain sensors strategically placed at
their entries and exits to detect the packages.

'The sensors are placed in such a way that it is safe to change a switch setting if and only if no packages are present between the entry sensor of a switch and either of its exit sensors. The pipes are bent at the sensor locations in such a way that the sensors are guaranteed to detect a separation between two packages, no matter how closely they follow one another.

'Due to the unpredictable sliding characteristics of the packages, it is possible, in spite of the source station delay, that packages will get so close together that it is not possible to reset a switch in time to properly route a package. *Misrouted* packages may be routed to any bin, but must not cause the misrouting of other packages. The bins too have sensors located at their entry, and upon arrival of a misrouted package at a wrong bin, the routing machine is to signal that package's intended destination bin and the bin it actually reached.'

The first matter of interest is the structuring of the PROBLEM CONTEXT. Which is the APPLICATION DOMAIN, and which is the MACHINE the software developers are to build? Swartout and Balzer complained that the problem description is 'contaminated with many implementation decisions'. They took this view because – as Balzer explained in another paper on *Operational Specification as the Basis for Rapid Prototyping* – they believe that the 'most abstract form' of the problem is this:

'At random times, a new package appears at a particular location called the source assigned to be routed to an arbitrary destination bin. Packages located at the source are moved to their destinations'.

They take exception to many parts of the mechanism – the sensors, the switches, the pipes, and the movement by gravity. They complain that a gantry crane or a conveyor belt might have been used instead. I think they are mistaken, and are confusing WHAT AND HOW. The mechanism is an integral feature of the application domain for the problem. It can't be dismissed as an artifact of a premature implementation decision. Their effort to find the 'most abstract form' of the problem is misconceived. A problem abstracted from its application domain is, simply, an entirely different problem.

Another interesting matter is the distinction between those parts of the problem description that are in the indicative MOOD and those that are in the optative mood. An indicative description describes the properties and behaviour of the world *as it is*: the properties and behaviour that the software developers may assume or rely on. An optative description describes the world as our customer *desires it to be*: the properties and behaviour that we as software developers must bring about or maintain by means of the machine we build.

These parts of the description are surely indicative – to be assumed or relied on:

'A single pipe leaves the source station.'
'The pipes are linked together by two-position *switches*.'
'The packages slide at different and unpredictable speeds ...'
'The switches contain sensors ... at their entries and exits to detect the packages.'

And surely these are optative – to be brought about by the machine we build:

'The package router must set its switches ahead of each package ...'
'*Misrouted* packages ... must not cause the misrouting of other packages.'
'... the routing machine is to signal that package's intended destination bin and the bin it actually reached.'

But these parts are much less clear:

'Packages arriving at the source station are scanned ...'
'The package is then allowed to slide down the pipe ...'
'After a package's destination has been determined, it is delayed for a fixed time ... '
'... if a package's destination is the same ... it is not delayed ...'
'... it is safe to change a switch if and only if ...'

Must the machine we build take some positive action to activate the scanner, or is scanning automatically activated by the package arrival? Must the computer allow the package to slide down the pipe by operating some kind of release mechanism? Is the fixed delay automatically introduced by the existing equipment, or is there some mechanism that we must activate to delay the release? If the writer of the problem description had separated indicative from optative we would not be in doubt.

Finally, there is some modest, but interesting, PROBLEM COMPLEXITY. This is definitely a MULTI-FRAME PROBLEM. Our first thought may be that the SIMPLE CONTROL FRAME will fit the problem easily. The mechanism of the package router, with its source stations, bins, pipes, sensors, switches, and sliding packages, provides the *Controlled Domain* principal part of the frame. The requirement to route the packages correctly by setting the switches, and to signal incorrectly routed packages, provides the *Desired Behaviour* principal part. But there is more to the problem than that.

There may be a further requirement to allow the configuration of pipes and bins to be changed. It would be unreasonable to expect to change it while the router is operating; but it would be perfectly reasonable to add new pipes and bins between one operating session and another. Evidently, a different problem frame is needed for this requirement. None of the frames discussed in this book seems to fit; another must be found or invented. Notice that the configuration of pipes and bins is a *static* part of the *Controlled Domain* in the simple control problem frame. But it will be *dynamic* in this new problem frame. The relevant DOMAIN CHARACTERISTICS depend partly on the problem frame.

Another modest complexity arises from the limited capabilities of the sensors. The sensors are capable of sensing the arrival of a package's leading edge, and, perhaps, the departure of its trailing edge. Presumably they are not capable of reading its destination. But when a package arrives at a switch, the controlling machine must set the switch according to the package's destination. And when a package arrives at a bin, the controlling machine must determine whether it has been misrouted and, if so, signal its intended and actual destinations.

This is a little information sub-problem that fits the SIMPLE IS FRAME. For this problem frame, the pipes and switches and bins and sensors, together with the sliding packages, furnish the *Real World* domain, about which *Information Outputs* are needed. Here the *Real World* – the pipes and bins and sensors and packages – is regarded as entirely autonomous, its behaviour being outside the control of the machine in the information system. The *Information Requests* arise whenever the arrival or departure of a package is sensed: the requested *Information Output* is always the destination of that package that was sensed just now.

The *System* to solve this little information sub-problem must, of course, maintain a MODEL of its *Real World* domain. For the system to work, the domain must have one crucial – indicative – property: it must be impossible for one package to overtake another in a pipe or switch. If the domain has this property, the packages in each pipe and switch form a FIFO queue. The identity, and hence the destination, of each package sensed can be read directly from the model.

Incidentally, did you notice that the source of the *Information Requests* is the *Controller* in the simple control frame sub-problem? In a complex problem the computer often plays different parts in different problem frames.

Partial Descriptions

To develop a system of any significance you must make many descriptions. Each one will be a *partial description*: that is, it will capture only a part of your total concerns; it will describe only a part of the whole universe of interest.

When programmers separate concerns into partial descriptions they call it *modularity*. The separation is at least as important in analysis as in programming – more important, really, because the subject matter to be described in requirements and specifications is so much more extensive and so much more varied. You have to do it right if your separations are to work properly. There are separations *in the large*, and separations *in the small*. There are also different *patterns* of separation – if you like, separations along different fault lines in the subject matter.

Whatever kind of separation you make, the resulting partial descriptions will be related by a logical *and*: description A is true, *and* description B is true. That means, of course, that description A and description B must not be mutually contradictory: if they are, then when they are taken together they amount to saying *P and not-P*, which is a description that can't ever be true.

You can picture the meaning of partial descriptions in a Venn diagram. The sets in the diagram are the sets of possible worlds of which the descriptions are true. If you have two descriptions, A and B, the diagram looks like this:

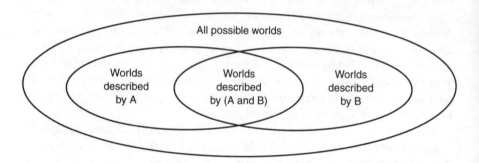

The outermost oval represents the set of all possible worlds. The smaller oval on the left represents the set containing just those worlds that are correctly described by description A, and the oval on the right represents just those that are correctly described by description B. The intersection of the two smaller ovals represents precisely the set of worlds that are correctly described by *A and B*. (If the descriptions A and B were mutually contradictory, they would not intersect, and there would be no possible world that is described by *A and B*. That's why it's not useful to make mutually contradictory descriptions.)

As each part of a development progresses, adding one partial description after another, the world that is being described is increasingly narrowed by each successive description. Eventually, when all the partial descriptions have been completed, the final result describes exactly the world of interest: no more and no less.

In analysis, a successful separation into partial descriptions must be based on separating out different parts and aspects of the problem. You must focus your attention on the APPLICATION DOMAIN, the REQUIREMENT, and the principal parts of the PROBLEM FRAMES that you identify as a result.

That's going to mean that the necessary separations will be different from problem to problem. Some methods prescribe problem-independent separations. For example, James Rumbaugh, in *Object-Oriented Modeling and Design*, recommends: a *functional model*, in the form of a dataflow diagram; an *object model*, in the form of a very elaborate data model; and a *dynamic model*, in the form of state diagrams. The recommendation is surprisingly close to the traditional separation of Structured Analysis. But because there's nothing about the problem in this formulation, you mustn't expect much help from it. It may be useful at some point to group your partial descriptions together under these headings, but you can't use them as a recipe for separation.

Phenomena

Phenomena are what *appear* to exist, or to be present, or to be the case, when you observe the world or some part of it in a domain. Philosophers contrast *phenomenology*, which is the study of phenomena, with *ontology*, which is about what really, truly, fundamentally, and objectively exists, independently of our perceptions and observations. Whether what 'appears to us to exist' is different from what 'really exists' is a deep question. But for many purposes we need not answer it. The physicist Neils Bohr wrote in his book *Atomic Theory*:

> 'In our description of nature the purpose is not to disclose the real essence of the phenomena but only to track down, so far as possible, relations between the manifold aspects of our experience.'

As software developers, we too, need not aim to disclose the real essence of the phenomena. We can deal with the phenomena as we experience them, as they appear to us and to our customers and the users of our systems.

But what does appear to us to exist? What phenomena does the world, or each particular domain, present to our observation? Each method supports, encourages, or enforces a specific way of seeing the world. A phenomenology, a way of seeing the world, is embodied in a language: the language is adapted to express what we see; and our seeing is conditioned by the concepts familiar from our language. To the users of a particular method or language, some kinds of phenomenon become almost invisible, or at least very hard to talk about; while others fill the field of view, and seem to be the only phenomena, or at least the most significant.

If you practise one of the usual styles of data modelling, you'll see *entities* and *relations* as the most significant phenomena. In a system to support the management of courses in a college, you might decide that the entities are the Courses, Subjects, Lecturers and Students; and the relations are Covered-By (a Subject is Covered-By a Course), Taught-By (a Course is Taught-By a Lecturer), Attends (a Student Attends a Course), and so on.

But if you're developing a system to control an automatic turnstile, you might adopt a view based on C A R Hoare's *Communicating Sequential Processes*. Then the world appears to you as an unfolding sequence of *events* involving *processes*. In your turnstile system the event types might be InsertTicket, UpdateTicket, ReturnTicket, Lock, Unlock, and Enter, and the process types might be Turnstile and Customer. The Turnstile is involved in all of the events, but Customer is involved only in InsertTicket, ReturnTicket, and Enter.

Obviously, both views have their uses in both systems. A pure phenomenology of entities and relations isn't enough for a full description of the world of courses and lecturers and students. You'll need events and processes there, too, because lecturers come and go, courses are modified, and students progress through their careers and eventually leave. And in the world of the automatic turnstile there are tickets and fares and destinations that demand something like an entity–relation view. Both views are necessary, and others also. Sometimes you will want to see the world as populated by *objects*, each object having an internal *state* and being capable of responding to *stimuli*. Or you might want to see the world as populated by *values*, related by *functions*.

Can all the phenomenological views we need be provided by one elaborate phenomenology that encompasses all the others? Some enthusiasts for OBJECT-ORIENTED ANALYSIS seem to think so. But they are focusing on programming, not on describing the world (they'll deny it, but don't believe them). It's reasonable to adopt a single phenomenology in programming languages. There are big advantages in coercing the machine you are building to an elegant uniformity. But the world outside the machine is not amenable to such coercion. It is too various to be described by one elaborate phenomenology: to do it justice you must have many at your disposal, and be able to use them freely. The question is then: how can the different phenomenologies be reconciled?

Instead of seeking one elaborate phenomenology, we can seek the simplest phenomenology: the lowest common denominator of all of them. It is rather like deciding to build RISC (Reduced Instruction Set Computer) machines instead of CISC (Complex Instruction Set Computer) machines. Just as a RISC machine can emulate the behavour of any CISC machine, building up the more complex instructions from its own simpler instructions, so you will be able to build up the more elaborate phenomena you will often need from the simple basic phenomena.

The basis of our RISC phenomenology is clearly explained by the disagreeable Mr Gradgrind of Charles Dickens' *Hard Times*. We will base all our phenomena on *facts*:

> 'Now, what I want is, Facts. Teach these boys and girls nothing but Facts. Facts alone are wanted in life. Plant nothing else, and root out everything else. You can only form the minds of reasoning animals upon Facts: nothing else will ever be of any service to them. This is

the principle on which I bring up my own children, and this is the
principle on which I bring up these children. Stick to Facts, sir!'

Here are some facts:

- Lucy loves John.
- Professor Jones wrote the book *Elementary Physics*.
- 6 is between 4 and 9.
- 23 is prime.
- Anna is a manager.
- Ted is a programmer.
- The battle of Hastings was won by William the Conqueror.
- 11 June 1999 is earlier than 10 June 2000.

A *fact* is a simple truth about the world: it is the smallest unit of observation, or the smallest phenomenon. Larger and more complex observations, and larger and more complex truths, can be broken down into facts. In this sense, 'All employees are people' is not a fact: it's a complex assertion about many facts.

It's important to distinguish facts, which are *phenomena* in the world, from *propositions*, which are *statements* of what may be facts. The sentence 'Anna is a manager' is a proposition. If indeed Anna is a manager, then the proposition is true – that is, it corresponds to a fact. If Anna is not a manager, then the proposition is false – that is, it does not correspond to a fact.

A fact involves INDIVIDUALS. The fact that Professor Jones wrote the book *Elementary Physics* is about two individuals: Professor Jones, and his book. The fact that 6 is between 4 and 9 is about three individuals: the numbers 6, 4 and 9. The fact that Anna is a manager is about one individual: Anna. The fact that the battle of Hastings was won by William the Conqueror is about two individuals: the battle and the king.

Anything can be an individual: a person, a number, an event, a date, a colour, an emotion. What you choose to treat as individuals will depend on how you choose to look at the world, and for what purpose. The only requirement is that you must be able to distinguish each individual from every other individual – to say 'I mean *this* one, not *that* one'. So the fact that Ted is a programmer is about one individual, not two: Ted is an individual, but 'a programmer' is not.

The idea of an *individual* is quite different from the idea of an *entity*. In the RISC phenomenology there is no built-in notion of entities. So there is no distinction between entities and attribute values. The fact 'Lucy's shoe size is 4' is symmetrically about the individual Lucy and the individual 4. It does not mean that 4 is the value of some attribute of Lucy any more than it means that Lucy is the value of some attribute of 4.

A phenomenology of facts is much simpler than the more elaborate phenomenologies of entities and relations, or of objects, or events. A convenient language for talking about facts is PREDICATE LOGIC. You can think of predicate logic as a kind of RISC assembly language for the world. Sometimes it's useful to translate other languages into it, when you want to explain exactly what they mean, or exactly how descriptions written in different languages fit together.

Poetry

Too many software descriptions are over-ambitious, like the young poet:

An over-ambitious young poet
said 'My poems don't scan, and I know it.'
When asked why it was
she confessed 'It's because
throwing more and more into the last line is so tempting
   that whenever I think of something, instead of saving it
   for another poem, I throw it.'

You can see the effects of this kind of over-ambition in some entity–relation diagramming notations. Here's a fragment of a diagram about the organization of a conference:

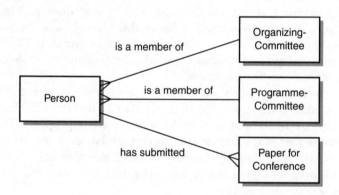

There is one organizing committee, and one programme committee, each with several members. People may submit as many papers as they wish, each paper being submitted by only one person.

But there are more rules, not shown in the diagram. No one may be a member of both committees; and no one who is a member of the programme committee may submit a paper. How can that be shown? You might be tempted to draw arcs on the diagram, like this:

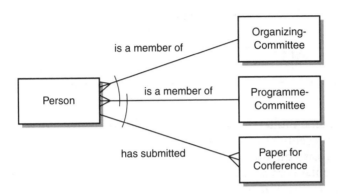

The upper arc says that no one can be a member of both committees; the lower arc says that no member of the programme committee can submit a paper. Then the rules are changed so that no one who is a member of *both* committees may submit a paper. What now? Ah, that's easy – you just draw one big arc through all three connections.

But you won't be able to keep it up. What if no one who is a member of *either* committee may submit a paper? Even in this tiny example, the difficulties begin to show themselves. It's impossible to define the arc notation so that it makes sense and fits in with the rest of the graphic notation. It has been thrown into the last line of the poem, and it spoils the scansion.

Ed Yourdon and Larry Constantine are two over-ambitious young poets who had the courage to confess. Here's the confession, in their book *Structured Design*:

> 'Such procedural detail is really beyond the structural model itself, but can make the structure chart easier to interpret. Generally, reference should be made to the flowcharts or other procedural documentation to obtain details of the procedural interrelationships between modules.'

They were confessing to the lack of scansion in their module hierarchy charts. Here's a basic module hierarchy chart showing what they call the structural model:

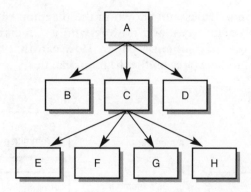

The structural model describes the program as a collection of procedure modules represented by the boxes. An arrow shows that the module at the tail of the arrow contains a call of the module at the head of the arrow. So module A contains calls of B, C, and D; and C contains calls of E, F, G, and H. A simple and useful piece of information, and clearly shown. The program text of the calling module may contain more than one call of a particular called module; but it certainly contains at least one.

Each time a calling module is executed, each call in its text may be executed zero or more times. But the structure chart gives no information about the order of execution of the modules. So here's something more that could be thrown in. This is the 'procedural detail' Yourdon and Constantine are talking about. It's expressed by adding diamonds and arrowed loops to the diagram, like this:

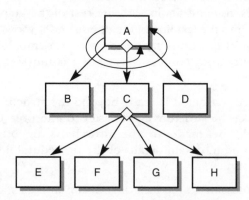

A diamond indicates that the called module is called conditionally, and a loop indicates that the enclosed calls are executed iteratively. The order of invocation is left to right. So the diamond and loops on the calls made by A show that the execution pattern in A is something like this:

```
A: while condition-1 do
      begin
         while condition-2 do
            begin B; if condition-3 then C end;
         D
      end
```

The diamond on the calls made by C might mean:

```
C: if condition-4 then
      begin E; F end
   else begin G; H end
```

but unfortunately it might also mean:

```
C: if condition-4 then E
   else begin F; G; H end
```

or even:

```
C: if condition-4 then E
   else      if condition-5 then F
             else      if condition-6 then G
                       else H;
```

You can see why 'such procedural detail is really beyond the structural model itself'. The complete set of invocation patterns in a module is, essentially, the set of all structured program skeletons. The set of patterns you can express in the notation of diamonds and arrowed loops is a small subset of this complete set. But which small subset one can hardly say. The notation is undefined, and doesn't fit at all with the underlying notation of boxes and arrows. Constantine and Yourdon were right to confess. The addition of the 'procedural detail' was a most unpoetic mistake.

Unfortunately, their good example has not been followed. The diagrams used in many object-oriented methods are horrendously complicated and ill-defined. But you don't have to use all the complications. Just remember: when you're thinking of throwing in something extra – however tempting – resist the temptation, and don't throw it. Save it for another poem.

Polya

The mathematician G Polya wrote an admirable book *How To Solve It*, in which he explains and amplifies ideas for solving mathematical problems. The ideas are wonderfully suggestive of ideas for solving software development problems. They come chiefly from the ancient Greeks: Polya's account is largely based on the work of Pappus, who lived in Alexandria about 1700 years ago. Pappus himself was drawing on the work of earlier Greeks, including Euclid.

The Greeks were the first people in the Western world to think systematically about how to solve problems. Many of the words we use to talk about problem solving – analysis, synthesis, method, system, theorem, heuristic – are derived from ancient Greek words. The word 'problem' itself is of Greek origin. It means something put forward, as a difficult question may be put forward to be answered.

The Greeks divided mathematical problems into two classes: problems to prove and problems to find. A problem to prove requires the solver to prove something. For example: prove that if the four sides of a quadrilateral are equal, then its diagonals bisect each other. A problem to find requires the solver to find or construct something. For example: given three lengths *a*, *b*, and *c*, construct a triangle whose sides are of those lengths.

Each kind of problem has its *principal parts* related in a characteristic PROBLEM FRAME or structure, and a *solution task* posed in terms of those parts. The principal parts of a problem to prove are the *hypothesis* and *conclusion*. The solution task is to demonstrate that the conclusion follows from the hypothesis – or, perhaps, that it does not. In the little example of the quadrilateral:

- the *hypothesis* is that the four sides of a quadrilateral are equal;
- the *conclusion* is that the two diagonals of the quadrilateral bisect each other.

The *solution task* is to demonstrate that the latter follows from the former.

In a problem to find, the principal parts are the *unknown*, the *data*, and the *condition*. The *solution task* is to find the unknown, which must be of the right kind and related to the data by the condition. In the little example of the triangle:

- the *unknown* is a triangle;
- the *data* is three lengths *a*, *b*, and *c*;
- the *condition* is that the three sides of the triangle are of the lengths given in the data.

The *solution task* is to find a triangle with sides of the required lengths.

The structure of principal parts, with the associated solution task, characterizes a problem class. Given a particular problem frame, with its named distinct principal parts of the problem, you can begin to talk about general METHODS for solving problems of the class that fit the frame. Polya gives many recommendations. For problems to prove his suggestions include:

- try to think of a familiar theorem having the same or a similar *conclusion*;

- ask whether the *conclusion* is more likely to be true or false, given the *hypothesis*;
- consider what other *conclusions* follow from the *hypothesis*.

For problems to find, he suggests:

- split the *condition* into parts;
- think of a familiar problem having a similar *unknown*;
- check that you are using all the *data*;
- check that you are using all the *condition*;
- think of a variation of the *unknown*, or of the *data*, or of both, so that the new *unknown* and the new *data* are nearer to each other.

All these recommendations are given in terms of the problems' principal parts. Without the problem frames and their named parts you couldn't talk about problem solving at all in such general terms. You couldn't devise or apply any kind of method, because you would have no language in which it could be expressed.

The classification into problems to prove and problems to find is not objective, and not always clear. A problem for which the original statement begins 'Prove that there is at least one integer such that ...' can be regarded as a problem to prove (with a null hypothesis), or as a problem to find (because if such an integer is found then its existence is proved). And a problem for which the original statement begins 'find an integer such that ...' might be solved by guessing the integer and proving that it has the required property.

This is not surprising. You don't fit a problem into a particular frame because you have previously classified it. Rather, you allocate it to a class, and choose a corresponding method, only after you have already fitted it comfortably into the associated problem frame. Checking the fit between a problem and a problem frame – identifying the principal parts and their relationships – is a primary activity in understanding any problem. Software development problems are no exception.

Predicate Logic

Classical logic is usually divided into propositional logic and predicate logic. Propositional logic is about combining propositions and reasoning about their combinations. True propositions correspond to facts in the world; false propositions don't. If you start with two propositions:

'Fred likes Easter'

and:

'Anne likes New Year'

you can make combinations like these:

'Fred likes Easter' ∧ 'Anne likes New Year' (∧ means *and*)

'Fred likes Easter' ∨ 'Anne likes New Year' (∨ means *or*)

¬ 'Fred likes Easter' (¬ means *not*)

'Fred likes Easter' → (¬ 'Anne likes New Year') (→ means *implies*)

'Fred likes Easter' ↔ 'Anne likes New Year' (↔ means *if and only if*)

∧ (*and*); ∨ (*or*); ¬ (*not*); → (*implies*); and ↔ (*if and only if*) are *logical connectives*. They mean just what you would think they do, except that you must be careful about two points. First, ∨ (*or*) is inclusive not exclusive. So P ∨ Q means that P is true or Q is true or both are true: that is, P and Q are not both false. Second, → (*implies*) doesn't carry any notion of causality. P → Q just means that once you know that P is true you can be sure that Q is also true: that is, P and *not*-Q are not both true.

Predicates are generalizations of facts. They let you go from particular propositions about individuals, such as 'Fred likes Easter', and 'Anne likes New Year', to generalizations such as 'Likes(*x,y*)'. You can get back to particular propositions from the generalization by substituting 'Fred' for the argument *x* and 'Easter' for the argument *y*, and so on.

The point of the generalization, of course, is that you can use it to make general statements – to say something in one breath about all the particular propositions about individuals that might be covered by the predicate. This is called *quantification*. There are two basic kinds of quantification. In *universal quantification* you use the symbol ∀ to say that something is true universally – that is, of all individuals. The symbol ∀ is just the 'A' of *all*. In *existential quantification* you use the symbol ∃ to say that at least one individual exists of which it is true, or the symbol ∃! to say that exactly one individual exists of which it is true.

Predicate logic extends propositional logic to express this kind of quantification. In natural language it's hard to make quantified statements precise. If you write 'Everyone likes a holiday', your readers may wonder exactly what you mean. Here are four possibilities:

(1) 'Everyone likes every holiday – that is, everyone is always glad to rest from work.'

(2) Or: 'There is at least one holiday such that everyone likes that particular holiday – for example, everybody likes New Year's Eve.'

(3) Or: 'For every person there is at least one holiday that that particular person likes – for example, Christine likes Easter and David likes Passover and Fred likes New Year's Eve (and Christmas).'

(4) Or: 'For every person there is exactly one holiday – one and only one – that that particular person likes – for example, Christine likes Easter (and only Easter) and David likes Passover (and only Passover) and Krishna likes Diwali (and only Diwali).'

In predicate logic you would be led to express yourself more clearly. Your choices are:

(1) $\forall x,y$ • $((\text{Person}(x) \wedge \text{Holiday}(y)) \rightarrow \text{Likes}(x,y))$
(For every possible choice of individuals x and y – not necessarily different – if x is a person and ($\wedge$) y is a holiday, then ($\rightarrow$) x likes y.)

(2) $\exists x$ • $(\text{Holiday}(x) \wedge (\forall y$ • $(\text{Person}(y) \rightarrow \text{Likes}(y,x))))$
(There is at least one individual x such that x is a holiday and that for every possible choice of individual y, if y is a person then y likes x.)

(3) $\forall x$ • $(\text{Person}(x) \rightarrow \exists y$ • $(\text{Holiday}(y) \wedge \text{Likes}(x,y)))$
(For every possible choice of individual x, if x is a person then there is at least one individual y such that y is a holiday and x likes y.)

(4) $\forall x$ • $(\text{Person}(x) \rightarrow \exists!\, y$ • $(\text{Holiday}(y) \wedge \text{Likes}(x,y)))$
(For every possible choice of individual x, if x is a person then there is exactly one individual y such that y is a holiday and x likes y.)

Existential and universal quantifiers take a little getting used to. They compel an unaccustomed precision of language in an area where natural language is especially ambiguous. If you really understand these examples about the people and the holidays, you have already understood a lot of what's needed to express yourself precisely in the language of predicate logic.

Predicate logic is very useful in software development. It can help to clarify what is meant by descriptions written in more elaborate languages. And it can provide a kind of common base language – a kind of machine language for the world. You don't want to write in machine language very often, but sometimes it's really useful.

Problem Complexity

Complexity has several meanings in software development. One meaning is the way the time needed for a computation increases with the problem size. If you increase the size of a look-up table from 10 to 1000 entries, a binary look-up will take only three times as long, but a linear look-up will take 100 times as long: a linear table look-up has greater *computational complexity* than a binary table look-up.

Thomas McCabe devised a measure of *cyclomatic complexity*, intended to capture the complexity of a program's control flow. A program with no branches is the least complex; a program with a loop is more complex; and a program with two crossed loops is more complex still. Cyclomatic complexity corresponds roughly to an intuitive idea of the number of different paths through the program.

Problem complexity is different: the kind of complexity that makes it hard to develop a system and achieve confidence in the results. A problem that is complex in this sense has many interacting and overlapping requirements. Every time you try to think about one part of it – for example, about dealing with one class of event – you find that in that one part alone there are many interrelated aspects competing for your attention. It's hard to see how to decompose the problem into anything simpler.

This kind of complexity is not absolute; it is relative to the knowledge and notations and methods at your disposal. Think, for example, about the complexity of writing a compiler. When Algol 60 was first designed, it was widely thought that compiling Algol 60 programs was a very complex problem. Some people even thought that it couldn't be done at all. Now, 35 years later, writing an Algol 60 compiler would be a reasonable project for a compiler-writing class in a computer science degree course. It's not that today's compiler writers are much cleverer than yesterday's: it's simply that they have access to a store of knowledge and technique that yesterday's compiler writers did not.

Often the key to mastering complexity lies in recognizing that a complex problem can be understood as a parallel structure of simpler problems. Complexity due to parallel simple structures doesn't yield to hierarchical decomposition. If you see someone juggling three balls in the air, you can't understand what they are doing by focusing just on one hand, or just on one short period of time. You have to see that they are actually doing three simple things at once. What's being done with each ball individually is simple: the complexity, and the astonishing skill, lies in doing the three things in parallel. The same kind of parallel structure gives rise to the complexity of musical canons and fugues. Douglas Hofstadter has a lot to say about this in his marvellous book *Gödel, Escher, Bach*.

There's an analogy closer to home. Look at this finite-state machine:

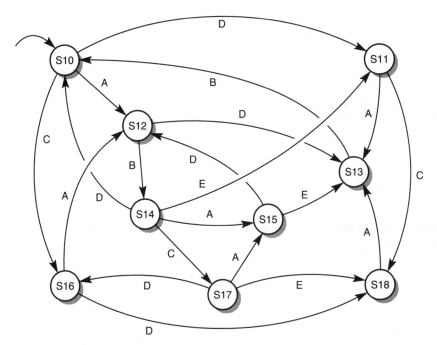

It describes a complex ordering constraint on five kinds of event: A, B, C, D and E. In the initial state, S10, B and E are disallowed; in state S17, B and C are disallowed; and so on. It's far from clear how to decompose this ordering. But in fact it's just the parallel composition of two simple orderings. Here they are:

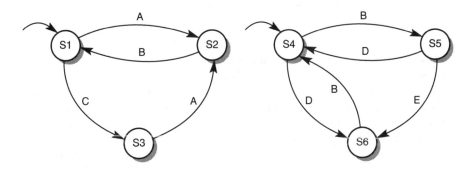

If you're facing the problem of describing the complex ordering constraint, you'll find it much easier to describe the two simple constraints and say that both are to be applied.

That's just like what you do when you recognize that a complex MULTI-FRAME PROBLEM is just a parallel composition of two simple problems. That's one of the ways in which PROBLEM FRAMES are important. They help you to recognize the simple problems that are being juggled to give you the complex problem you're facing.

The Problem Context

You're an engineer planning to build a bridge across a river. So you visit the site. Standing on one bank of the river, you look at the surrounding land, and at the river traffic. You feel how exposed the place is, and how hard the wind is blowing and how fast the river is running. You look at the bank and wonder what faults a geological survey will show up in the rocky terrain. You picture to yourself the bridge that you are going to build.

You are examining the *problem context*. A software development project is a project to build a MACHINE. The problem context is the part of the world in which the machine will be installed, in which the effects and benefits of the installed machine will be felt and evaluated. It's where a software developer goes on a site visit. You picture the problem context with the machine installed:

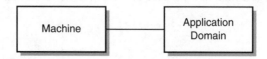

The APPLICATION DOMAIN is the particular part of the world in which your customer is interested, the part that is relevant to this particular problem. That can include people, the company's products, other computer systems, buildings, intangible things like graphics images or airline timetables or employment payscales, and absolutely anything else that will interact with the machine or furnish the subject matter of its computations.

The connecting line shows only that the machine and the application domain interact directly in some unspecified manner. If they did not, the machine could neither sense the application domain nor affect it in any way. The line doesn't show anything about the interactions except that they exist in the form of some SHARED PHENOMENA in which both the machine and the application domain participate. It doesn't show any structure of the interactions, or whether they are initiated by the machine or by the application domain, or the direction of any data transfer that may take place.

Initially, you need to think about the problem context – especially about the application domain – to help you to determine what the problem is about, and to begin to see what kind of a problem it is. To understand the problem you must understand the application domain. Exactly what parts of the world are in it? How are they interconnected? What are their significant properties that you must respect? What properties can you exploit? What interactions can they have with the machine?

The first step towards structuring and understanding the application domain and the problem context is to draw a CONTEXT DIAGRAM, dividing the application domain into broadly separable DOMAINS that can be individually studied. But this is only the very first step. The problem context is not the problem: it's only the background to the problem.

Think about this problem context. There is a river. On one side of the river there is a farmer, with a fox, a rabbit and a prize cabbage. There is a rowing boat, complete with oars, moored on that side of the river. On the other side of the river is a market. There is room in the boat for any two of the four: farmer, fox, rabbit, and cabbage. The fox is hungry, and so is the rabbit. Foxes like to eat rabbits, and rabbits like to eat cabbages. Are you ready to start solving the problem yet?

Of course not. I have sketched the context of the problem, but we have not yet identified the problem itself. Perhaps the problem is how to feed the fox? Or how the farmer can get the boat across the river without crossing it himself? Or how to send the cabbage to market without sending either the fox or the rabbit? The problem is, apparently, about a farmer, a fox, a rabbit, a cabbage, a river, a boat and a market. But we still have to say exactly what the problem is.

In other words: given the problem context, you still have to discover and describe the problem REQUIREMENT. In a software development problem you might set about doing that by designing the machine, describing its internal workings – perhaps in terms of data structures and processes and internal data flows among them. Then, as the work progresses, you could keep asking your customer: 'Will this machine solve your problem?'

But there's a better way. Instead of thinking about the machine at this stage, you could focus all your attention on the application domain. You could ask your customer not only what properties it has now, but what properties your customer would like you to bring about. This second way is much more direct, and makes for much better relationships with your customers. The problem in an accounts payable system is not to maintain a database, but to ensure that the suppliers are paid in accordance with their invoices and a prudent cash flow policy. The problem in an air traffic control system at an airport is not to process flows of data but to manage take-offs and landings so that runways are used efficiently while proper safety standards are observed by keeping planes sufficiently far apart in the sky and on the ground. The farmer's problem is not to execute some particular pattern of journeys, but to reach a situation in which the farmer, the fox, the rabbit, and the cabbage are all safe and sound at the market on the other side of the river.

The significance of the problem context, then, is that it contains both the machine and the application domain, just as the farmer's problem contains the boat and the oars and the river as well as the fox, the market, the cabbage and the rabbit. Building the machine will eventually provide the solution to the problem. But first you must concentrate your attention on the application domain to learn what the problem is about.

Problem Frames

I asked some friends – all software developers – to describe the problems they were currently working on. They said:

- 'I'm working on a system to control automatic ticket machines at a toll point on a highway.'

- 'I'm building a simple customer information system, with transactions to create and maintain and delete information, and queries to make the information available to telephone sales staff.'

- 'I'm doing a signal processing program, in which input signals have to be processed and converted and then output.'

- 'I'm working on a small interactive editor that will be part of a personal information manager.'

- 'I'm working on a system to manage calls to an emergency service.'

They're all working on software development, but the problems they are working on are all very different. The ticket machine system isn't at all like the editor, and neither of them is like the signal processor. The emergency service call management system may be a little like the customer information system, but it's nothing like signal processing at all.

To analyse software development problems, and to choose appropriate methods for solving them, you need to get a grip on the differences and similarities between different problems. You need to have a way of characterizing and classifying problems, of thinking about the particular nature of each problem right at the beginning, *before* you set about solving it. For example, you might start thinking about the editor problem by saying to yourself:

> 'There are *users*, working on *texts*. The texts are inside the computer, and the users works on them by invoking *actions*. The problem is to build the software so that each invoked action has the *appropriate effect* on the text being worked on'.

And you might approach the signal processing problem by saying to yourself:

> 'Let's see. There's an *incoming sequence* of signals and an *outgoing sequence* of signals. There's a specified *transform* between them, stipulating how the incoming signals must be processed to give the outgoing signals. The problem is to build the software so that it produces the right outgoing signals from the incoming signals it receives'.

What you're doing here is going over the domains of the PROBLEM CONTEXT and the REQUIREMENT in your mind, and thinking what you have to do to solve the problem. You're fitting the problem into a *problem frame*, a structure consisting of *principal parts* and a *solution task*. The principal parts of the editor problem are the *users*, the *texts*, the *actions* and the *appropriate effects*. The principal parts of the signal processing problem are the *incoming sequence* and *outgoing sequence*, and the specified *transform* that relates them.

A problem frame is a generalization of a class of problem. If there are many other problems that fit the same frame as the problem you're dealing with, then you can hope to apply the method and techniques that worked for those other problems to the problem you're trying to solve right now. That's the whole point of development methods. Because problem frames are general they won't use the same names for their principal parts that you're using for the parts of your particular problem. Your editor problem has *users*, *texts*, *actions* and *effects*. It probably fits the WORKPIECES FRAME, which has *Operation Requests*, *Workpieces*, and *Operation Properties*, in addition to the *Machine* to be built. You have to establish the equivalences between the parts of your particular problem and the parts of the general frame:

- Your *texts* are the *Workpieces*.
- Your *action invocations* are the *Operation Requests*.
- Your *effects* are the *Operation Properties*.
- Your editor is the *Machine*.
- Your *users* don't fit in anywhere (except as the anonymous originators of the *Operation Requests*).

Does your problem fit the frame well enough? That depends. A problem frame isn't just a list of names of principal parts. It also stipulates that the principal parts must be connected in certain ways, and must have certain characteristics. For example, the *Workpieces* must be intangible and inert. You couldn't fit the ticket machine system into this problem frame by making the ticket machines the *Workpieces*, because the ticket machines are not at all intangible. And you couldn't fit the emergency service system into the frame by making the emergency calls the *Workpieces*, because the calls are not inert. Is it all right to leave out your *users*? If the users play no part in the problem except to produce the *action invocations*, then it's all right. Otherwise, it's not. We'll come back to this point later.

The reward for finding a problem frame that fits your problem really well is that the frame brings with it a method that will be really effective for solving the problem. That's the essential value of a problem frame. If the frame fits, then the method will work. There's a bit of wishful thinking here. Not very many problem frames have yet been explicitly described, and even fewer have sound and effective methods to go with them. Some frames are described in this book: the SIMPLE IS FRAME; the SIMPLE CONTROL FRAME; the JSP FRAME; CONNECTION FRAMES; and the WORKPIECES FRAME.

You can add to your repertoire of problem frames. Examine a method that you think has real value, and try to work out what its problem frame is. When you read a book about a method, pay particularly careful attention to the description – often just hints – of the associated problem frame. Here, for example, is Carroll Morgan, introducing his program refinement method in *Programming from Specifications*:

> 'Any program takes a computer from an initial state to a final state. ... We suppose that the data on which the computer is to operate (the input) are placed in the initial state; the results of the computation (the output) are found subsequently, in the final state. ...
>
> 'The specification ... precondition describes the initial states; its postcondition describes the final states; and it ... lists the variables whose values may change.'

The problem is assumed to concern a computer with input and output data values in initial and final states. The principal parts of Morgan's problem frame are: the initial states of the computer as described by the *precondition*; the final states as described by the *postcondition*; and a *variable list* restricting what the program may change. The solution task is to devise a behaviour of the computer – an executable program – that will take it from any state satisfying the precondition to a state satisfying the postcondition, without changing the value of any variable that is not in the list.

A very different problem frame underlies Ivar Jacobson's *Use Case Driven Approach* to object-oriented development. Here's what he says:

> 'Since the whole system development starts from what the user wishes to be able to do with the system, we build the system from the user's point of view....
>
> 'The use case model specifies the functionality the system has to offer from a user's perspective and we define what should take place inside the system. This model uses **actors** to represent roles the users can play, and **use cases** to represent what the users should be able to do with the system.'

The principal parts of Jacobson's problem frame include the *users* and the roles they can play; the *system* itself; and the *use cases*, which are essentially scenarios based on the various types of transactions that the users can initiate. The solution task is to build the system so that it executes the use cases on demand.

At first sight you may wonder whether all problem frames can't just be reduced to inputs and outputs, or to transitions from one state to another. The difference between one problem frame and another may seem to be artificial, rather subtle and perhaps even unimportant. But it is not so. A good method relies on a close fit between the frame and the problem. It exploits the definitions of the principal parts in stipulating what descriptions should be made; the problem structure in stipulating how the descriptions should fit together; and the expected characteristics of each principal part in stipulating languages for its description. To get a real benefit from a good method you must be sure that your problem fits its frame closely.

Suppose, for example, that you are developing a system for controlling the toll ticket machines. Could you use Carroll Morgan's refinement problem frame? No. The machines to be controlled must run continuously: shutting them down is a disaster, not a goal. So although you may perhaps be able to identify an initial state and a *precondition*, you certainly couldn't point to any desired final state, and hence to any *postcondition*. One of the principal parts is missing, so the problem frame is inappropriate: the method that assumes it must be inappropriate too. You have a problem frame MISFIT. If you go ahead anyway, you will run into serious trouble: when the method tells you to do something with the *postcondition*, you won't know what to do. The method will be hindering you, not helping.

There's a general rule about problem frames. All useful problem frames are unrealistically simple. If you look carefully at the frames I have outlined in this book you'll find that they are purged of all the complications that make realistic problems difficult. A problem frame characterizes a class of problem by stripping away everything except the essential elements. In this way they are very reminiscent of the classroom. Have you ever been on a course about abstract data types? First, the teacher presents and discusses one or two standard examples. Here is the abstract data type stack. And here is the abstract data type bag. Now here's a class exercise: specify the abstract data type queue. Now specify double-ended queue. The problems are all simple: not in the sense that you don't have to think hard and work hard to solve them properly; but in the sense that they're stripped down to their essentials. They don't have awkward and irrelevant complications. You can focus on applying the method you're learning, knowing that it will be effective unless something really surprising turns up.

Realistic problems are not that simple. They have all kinds of awkward complications. Perhaps you can't just ignore the *users* in your editor problem: perhaps you must allow different *users* to establish different editing preferences and styles. That's a complication you must deal with. But such complications are just due to the interplay of several simple problems wrapped up in the one realistic problem. They are MULTI-FRAME PROBLEMS. You deal with a realistic problem by analysis, by decomposition, by breaking it into a number of simple problems – that is, problems for which you have well-understood problem frames.

Problem Sensitivity

Here's an important methodological principle:

- *The Principle of Problem Sensitivity*
  A method for solving problems must be closely expressed in terms of the problems it can help you to solve.

The principle is clear enough. If a method doesn't talk about the problem, how can it help you to solve it?

Now look at this paragraph:

> 'The method used in designing the program is to break the specified problem down into a number of sub-problems expressed in English. The same idea is then used to break down each sub-problem into further sub-problems. The method is applied successively until each of the sub-problems can be readily and easily expressed in the programming language. This technique is called *programming by stepwise refinement*.'

This is the very antithesis of problem sensitivity. Any problem whatever can be regarded as 'the specified problem'; any problem whatever can be 'expressed in English', and 'broken into a number of sub-problems'. There is no sensitivity at all here to the problem being solved. Because there is no sensitivity to the problem, there can be no real guidance for the developer. The 'method' is empty.

Some methods are not problem-sensitive because they are expressed in terms of the solution rather than the problem. Such a method is, if you like, solution-sensitive. It tells you how to build a solution of a particular type. That can be very useful – once you are sure you need a solution of that type, and you know which solution of that type you need. Methods based on programming languages tend to be of this kind.

Some solution-sensitive methods tell you how to evaluate the solution – once you have found it. A method of program design based on applying the criteria of module *cohesion* and inter-module *coupling* would be a solution-sensitive method. One list of coupling measures, in order from worst to best, is: content coupling; common coupling; external coupling; control coupling; stamp coupling; data coupling. The best, data coupling, is found when one module calls another and all data is passed between them as arguments of the call, and all arguments are data elements and not control elements or data structures. One of the worst, common coupling, is found when two modules refer to a shared global data structure (COMMON data in Fortran).

The lack of problem sensitivity is clear. Nothing is said about the problem features that might make a worse form of coupling necessary. There are no heuristics of the form 'if your problem has feature X you will find stamp coupling unavoidable'. So the best you can do with the criteria is to measure your design not against the problem being solved, but against some absolute standard. 'Scoring the coupling measures from worst to best on a scale from 1 to 6, the average coupling between all module pairs in your program should not be less than 4.5'.

Breaking the principle of problem sensitivity does not necessarily make a method completely useless. Many methods on offer break the principle, and most of them – though not all – do have some value. But it's a strictly limited value. You're really relying on your instinct and experience, not on explicit help from the method. A problem-sensitive method could give you some solid guidance on how to tackle your problem. That would be worth much more.

Procrustes

Procrustes, also known as Damastes or Polypemon, was a legendary innkeeper at Eleusis in ancient Greece. His guest bedroom – he had only one – was equipped with a bed of a certain size, which unfortunately was hardly ever the right size for his guests. Procrustes' solution to this difficulty was bold. He ushered the guest into the room, and to ensure a comfortable night's rest he adjusted the guest to the bed: shorter guests were stretched on a rack, and taller guests were chopped to fit.

Procrustes must have been an early advocate of a software development method. Don't think I'm criticizing. Procrustes was a very hospitable person, and method advocates, too, like to be able to accommodate all comers. They are always unwilling to turn people away, to say: Sorry, we have nothing suitable for you – why not try the inn further along the road? They would much rather say: Of course your problem will fit my method – just squeeze it a little here, and stretch it a little there. It's also only fair to say that some guests fit in pretty well when they arrive, but they stay so long that they outgrow the accommodation. Being an innkeeper is a hard job, like being an enthusiast for a development method.

Eventually, Procrustes was killed by Theseus, the legendary king of Athens. It's interesting that Theseus also slew the Minotaur. The Minotaur was a bull-like beast that lived in the infinitely complex maze of the Labyrinth and liked to eat young Athenians. King Minos demanded a tribute of ten young Athenians every year, and threw them into the maze. They could not master its complexity, and were eaten by the Minotaur. Theseus

mastered the complexities of the Labyrinth by following a red thread given
to him by Ariadne. So the same hero slew both Procrustes *and* the
Minotaur. There's a lesson in that, I'm sure.

Raw Materials

Real engineers – who practise established disciplines such as civil, aeronautical, electrical, electronic, automobile and chemical engineering –
understand the choice and use of raw materials. They don't build paper
bridges or lead aeroplanes or stone motor cars. They choose an appropriate raw material for each part in everything they make. The engine block of
a motor car is made of iron or aluminium, the windows of glass, and the
body of sheet steel. Often the distinctions are fine. The glass of the wind-
screen is different from the glass of the headlight lenses, and both are
different from the glass of the headlight bulbs. An iron engine block must
be made from cast iron, not from wrought iron. The exact properties of
each material are discovered by study or experiment, and the right material
is chosen, or even specially developed, for each part.

Software engineers must be no less careful about raw materials. We
create our products by constructing, manipulating, composing and assem-
bling descriptions. Not all of these descriptions appear as components of
the finished program texts: some are used only in analysis, requirements or
specifications, in testing or verifying, in explaining or justifying. But all
must be constructed from properly chosen raw materials, and those raw
materials are languages. You must understand the properties of the languages you use, and choose an appropriate language for each description.

You must also respect the limitations of your materials. For physical
materials that means being careful not to overstress them, and not using
them in environments that can break down their structures and so weaken
them. The raw materials of software don't have quite that kind of limitation. But when you're using a language, you and the language together do
have a somewhat similar limitation, imposed by the limits of your understanding and the quality of the language definition. Respecting limitations
then means observing this principle of language use:

● *The Skater's Principle of Language Use*
  Stay in the middle, where the ice is thicker.

Don't use a language feature unless its definition and your knowledge are
both rock-solid.

To develop software successfully you have to use, and know a lot about,
a wide range of descriptive languages. It's hard to put this advice into practice unless you're quite a polymath, or you use subcontractors. When you

subcontract a part of your product you're also subcontracting the need for knowledge of the materials of which it's made. The car designer subcontracts the tyres. So car designers don't need to know about the properties of rubber and nylon or steel cords. In software development we have a tradition of doing everything ourselves. True, it's normal to use a bought-in operating system and DBMS and GUI and comms package. But, as Bill Scherlis of Carnegie Mellon University has pointed out, we don't usually use subcontractors. There are thousands of subcontractors for a product like a Boeing 747. How many were there on your last software project?

There are also problems of composition and compatibility. Established engineers have paid a lot of attention to techniques for putting together parts made in different materials. They use nuts and bolts, rivets, pins and spring clips; they weld, press, glue, solder, braze and shrink parts together. In software engineering there are remarkably few techniques for combining different languages, and many software development environments – especially those that support development in functional, object-oriented, or logic programming languages – effectively prevent you from using more than the one language that is supported.

Restricting the use of materials in this way is a mark of a primitive technology. The most primitive artifacts are made just of stone, or just of wood and stone, or just of wood and iron. Carry out a little test on your technology level – it's easier than evaluating your process maturity.

First, make a list of all the languages that you use in all your development activities. Be honest: don't list all the languages you have ever heard of; include only languages that you have used for real work at least once. Your list might include one or two programming languages along with languages like Dataflow Diagrams, State–Transition Diagrams and Decision Tables.

Now, ask yourself which of the languages on your list you would choose to say these things, and how easily you could say them:

- The lift car can't move from the nth to the $n+2$th floor without passing the $n+1$th floor.

- No class has more than one teacher unless it has more than ten pupils.

- The pipes and switches of the package routing machine form a binary tree.

- If you lift the receiver when the phone is ringing that's an *answer-call* event; if it's not ringing it's a *request-service* event.

- The system is required to prevent two trains from occupying the same track segment at the same time.

- An ancestor of a person P is a natural parent of P or a natural parent of an ancestor of P.

- When the button is pressed, the machine should turn the lamp on within 250 milliseconds.

- The vending machine can prevent a coin-insertion event, but only the customer can cause it.
- A student who passes the examination becomes a graduate.
- An account can be closed only by the person who opened it.

Did you find it all easy? I didn't.

Refutable Descriptions

To refute an assertion is to demonstrate that it is wrong. Not just to claim that it is wrong; not just to put forward a different, competing assertion; but to demonstrate clearly that it does not fit the facts.

Respectable scientific theories are refutable. A scientist who puts forward a theory runs the risk that another scientist will point to some known fact, or perform an experiment, demonstrating that the theory is wrong. This exposure to the risk of refutation is the great strength of the established natural sciences. A theory that is not refutable will not be taken seriously.

Respectable software development depends on refutability in a similar way. A domain description of the system's environment, or application domain, claims to describe how things are; a specification or requirement claims to describe how things ought to be when the system is installed and operating. Both of them must be refutable. The domain description must run the risk that someone will say: 'That's not true – here's a counter-example'. And the requirement description must run two risks: that your customer will say: 'No, that's not the effect I require'; or, later: 'Yes, that was the effect I required, but the system isn't achieving it – just look at what it did here'.

To attain refutability you need, above all, explicit DESIGNATIONS. You write a designation for each basic kind of phenomenon, describing how to recognize it in the domain, and giving it a name that you can use in your descriptions. Your choice of phenomena and designations is severely constrained: the phenomena must be reliably and unambiguously recognizable. That's very important, because it means that you're cutting out a major cause of ambiguity. You're not giving yourself the chance to weasel out of a refutation by saying things like 'Well, it all depends on what you mean by a *payment*'.

Then you write your description – several descriptions, usually – asserting relationships among the designated phenomena. You are running the risk of refutation because your readers can use the designations to pin down what you are saying well enough to find counter-examples if any exist. 'Look,' they may say, 'this is definitely a *motor vehicle* according to your designation, isn't it? And these are definitely *road wheels* according to your designation, aren't they? Well, your description says that all *motor vehicles* have an even number of *road wheels*, but this one has three. So your description is wrong.' You have to admit it. They are right, and your description is wrong. You should be proud and pleased. Your description is precise enough to be refutable.

Explicit designations are more important than they may seem at first sight. If you skip the designations, or leave them implicit, you run the risk of drifting off into vagueness or abstraction. Look at this description of the arrangement of the tracks for a railway traffic control system.

> 'A *plain segment* of track is a continuous stretch of single track with its sole entry point at the *entry* of the segment, and the sole exit point at the *exit* of the segment. A *fork switch* is a configuration with one *entry* and two *exits*; and a *join switch* is a configuration with two *entries* and one *exit*. *Plain segments*, *fork switches*, and *join switches* are all subtypes of the type *track unit*.
>
> 'A *rail network* consists of an assemblage of *track units* such that each *exit* of each *unit* is connected to an *entry* of a different *unit*, and vice versa. Two *units* with a connected *entry* and *exit* are said to be *adjacent*.'

Almost certainly, this is not a refutable description. It's quite precise, in a mathematical kind of way, but it's not refutable because it is not tied clearly to the phenomena of the reality it claims to describe. Do *entry* and *exit* refer to the direction of train travel? If so, what about single-line working in which trains travel in both directions – at different times – over a single track? What about crossovers, where two tracks cross without either being accessible from the other? What about the turntables that are found in some marshalling yards, that allow an engine or carriage to be rotated through 360 degrees so that it can be moved to any of several lines radiating from the turntable? Does the description say that there is no single-line working, no crossovers, and no turntables?

You can get another perspective on the same defect in this description by asking whether its contents – 'A *plain segment* of track is a continuous stretch ...', 'A *fork switch* is a configuration with one *entry* and two *exits*...', 'A *rail network* consists of an assemblage ...', and so on – are actually DEFINITIONS rather than assertions. They may well be. But a document consisting entirely of definitions says nothing whatsoever about any part of the real world at all. It is certainly not a refutable description.

Reification

To reify something is to convert it mentally into a thing. But such mental conversions are dangerous, and liable to introduce spurious INDIVIDUALS into your application domain descriptions: individuals that have no significance or recognizability in the domain. This is especially true of individuals that are aggregates or structures of other individuals. Some formal specification languages, such as Z and VDM, rely heavily on the use of aggregate and structured objects, such as sets and mappings. For example, in a Z specification of a telephone system, you might see something like this:

[PHONE ...]

    ...

    busy: $\mathbb{P}$ PHONE

PHONE is a primitive type: that is, it is the set of all individual phones. 'busy' is declared to be a subset of all phones, with the intended meaning that a phone is a member of this set if it is busy and not otherwise. In this description, 'busy' appears to be a domain individual that is a set of phones in the same way as a football team might be a domain individual that is a set of players. But the appearance is misleading. The only sensible interpretation of the Z specification is that 'busy' is a predicate that may be true of an individual phone: the set 'busy' is a spurious individual, an artifact of the way the specification has been written.

You can distinguish a spurious individual like the 'busy' set from a legitimate individual like the football team by considering what facts might be true of them. The football team may have a home ground, a goal average, a place in the football league, a manager, an owner, a supporters' club. It is an individual in its own right, participating in facts independently of the players that are its members. The 'busy' set of phones, by contrast, cannot participate independently in facts in this way: it is not really a domain individual at all.

Whether an individual is a recognizable domain individual or not is, of course, a matter of phenomenology: of your point of view, of what appears to you to be the case. There is no reason in principle why the set of busy phones should not be a legitimate domain individual: it just happens to be the case that in any plausible telephone system it is not. Consider a different example: the hand held by a player at some point in a card game. The hand is a set of cards. Perhaps the hand consists of the Jacks, Queens and Kings of Hearts and Spades. Then, if pairs of the same denomination are significant according to the rules of the game, the hand also consists of three pairs: a pair of Jacks, a pair of Queens, and a pair of Kings. A pair of Aces, no doubt, would be higher than any of them. And if runs are also significant, the hand also consists of two runs: the Jack, Queen and King of Hearts and the Jack, Queen and King of Spades. The hand, the pairs, and the runs are all legitimate and recognizable domain individuals. The busy set is not.

Requirements

The traditional practice in software development has been to ignore the APPLICATION DOMAIN and focus attention on the machine. That is why some writers have tried to explain the distinction between WHAT AND HOW as a distinction between the *outside* and the *inside* of the machine; or between a *logical* description of the machine and a *physical* description of the machine; or between the *essential* system and the *implemented* system – that is, between the machine as it would be if we had perfect technology and the machine as it will be in the actual implementation.

Not surprisingly, when we focus attention on the machine in this way we find that our customers are not very good at deciding on their *requirements*. They don't know about computers, so they can't choose the machine they need. Traditionally, we software developers have thought of our customers as bears of very little brain. 'They don't know what they want', we said to each other smugly. But in truth we achieved this superior perspective only by virtue of our own limitations and failures. We were the bears of very little brain.

Requirements are about the phenomena of the application domain, not about the machine. To describe them exactly, we describe the required relationships among the phenomena of the problem context. A lift passenger who wants to travel from the third to the seventh floor presses the Up button at the third floor. The light beside the button must then be lit, if it was not lit before. The lift must arrive reasonably soon, travelling in an upwards direction. The direction of travel is indicated by an arrow illuminated when the lift arrives. The doors must open, and stay open long enough for the passenger to enter the lift. The doors must never be open except when the lift is stationary at a floor. There's nothing here about the machine that will control the lift.

But the machine can ensure that these requirements are satisfied because it shares some phenomena with the application domain: they have some events or states in common. When a shared event happens, it happens in both; a shared state, with its changes of value, is visible in both. For example, pressing the lift button is an event common to the application domain and the machine that controls the lift. To the passenger the event is 'Hit the Up button on the third floor'. The machine may see it as 'input signal on line 3U'. But they are both participating in the same event. Another shared event is the activation of the lift winding motor. The event 'turn winding motor on' in the problem context is the same event as 'output signal on line M+' in the machine.

Examples of shared states in the lift control problem are the settings of the sensor switches that detect the presence of the lift at a floor, and the positions of the doors. Suppose that the machine has a Direct Memory Access connection to the sensor switches in the lift shaft. Then the state that appears in the problem context as 'switch 3 is closed' appears in the machine as 'Floor_Sensor_State[3] = 1', or something similar. These are two ways of talking about the same state of the world, seen from the two different points of view of the controlling machine and the mechanical switches installed in the lift shaft at each floor.

But not all the phenenomena of the problem context are shared with the machine. For example, the movement of the lift when it is travelling between floors is not shared. The machine has no direct indication of the lift travel until it reaches the next sensor. Nor are the entry and exit of each passenger shared events. The machine has no way of knowing that the passenger who pushed the request button to travel to floor 4 actually got out at floor 2.

In general, that opens up a gap between the customer's requirements and what the machine can achieve directly, because the customer's requirements aren't limited to the phenomena shared with the machine. Think of it like this:

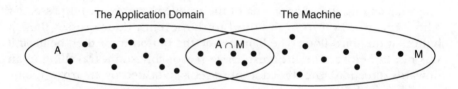

The Application Domain   The Machine

A is the set of all phenomena of the application domain. M is the set of all phenomena of the machine. A ∩ M is the set of all shared phenomena, which belong both to A and to M. The requirement is described in terms of A, so it may involve phenomena that are not shared with the machine. The programs will, eventually, be written in terms of M.

Think of the traditional progression from requirements to programs as a way of bridging the gap between them. Call the requirement R. From the requirement, expressed in terms of A, you derive a SPECIFICATION S, expressed in terms of A ∩ M. Then you derive the programs P from the specification. To justify an eventual claim that the program satisfies the requirement, you need to reason like this:

- First, if the computer behaves as described by the programs P, then the specification S must be satisfied.

- Second, if the specification S is satisfied, then the requirement R must be satisfied.

To convince yourself that the programs satisfy the specification you must make use of the underlying properties of the computer, as expressed in the hardware description and the semantics of the programming language. Let's call these properties of the computer C. Your argument will be that if the computer has the underlying properties C, then by adding the properties that it takes on because of your program P, it will have the properties S – that is, it will satisfy the specification. Or, more formally:

$C, P \vdash S$

If C is true and P is true, then it follows logically that S is true. If you've ever written a program, you must have reasoned like that many times. 'This instruction here has the effect of adding 1 to x', you say. That's C. 'x starts at 0, and the instruction is executed for each character in the string'. That's P. 'So the final value of x must be the number of characters in the string, which is what we want'. That's S.

The second step is very similar. You must make use of the underlying properties of the application domain. Let's call those properties D. Your argument will be that if the domain has the underlying properties D, then by adding the properties S that it takes on because of your programs, it will also have the properties R – that is, it will satisfy the specification. Or, more formally:

$D, S \vdash R$

If D is true and S is true, then it follows logically that R is true. The properties in D are the properties that the application domain possesses independently of anything the machine may do or fail to do. In the lift control problem, the requirement R is expressed in terms of the movements of the lift in response to passengers' requests. The specification S will be expressed in terms of states of the sensor switches, button pressings, and settings and activations of the winding motor, because these are the phenomena shared with the machine. D contains properties like these:

- the lift is constrained to move in the shaft so that it never goes from one floor to another without passing all the intermediate floors;
- if the winding motor polarity is set to *up* and the motor is activated, then the lift starts to rise;
- if the lift arrives at a floor travelling upwards, the floor sensor switch is set on when the lift is nine inches below the home position at the floor;
- the lift doors take 2250 msecs to reach the fully closed from the fully open state.

Without properties like these, it would be completely impossible for the machine to make the lift behave as you want it to. That's why it's essential to understand the properties of the application domain – especially for safety-critical systems. In one well-known incident an aeroplane overshot the runway on landing. The pilot had tried, correctly, to engage reverse thrust, but the system would not permit it. The reason was that the runway was wet, and the wheels were aquaplaning instead of turning. Reverse thrust could be engaged only if pulses from the wheel sensors showed that the wheels were turning. Here are the phenomena we're concerned with:

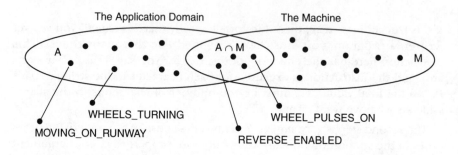

The requirement *R* was:
    REVERSE_ENABLED if and only if MOVING_ON_RUNWAY.

The developers thought that the domain properties *D* included both:

    WHEEL_PULSES_ON if and only if WHEELS_TURNING; and
    WHEELS_TURNING if and only if MOVING_ON_RUNWAY.

So they derived the specification *S*:

    REVERSE_ENABLED if and only if WHEEL_PULSES_ON.

Unfortunately, they had not understood the domain properties correctly.

    WHEEL_PULSES_ON if and only if WHEELS_TURNING

was indeed a domain property. But

    WHEELS_TURNING if and only if MOVING_ON_RUNWAY

was not. When the wheels are aquaplaning while landing on a wet runway, MOVING_ON_RUNWAY is true, but WHEELS_TURNING is false. The error – fortunately not catastrophic in this case – was in the step from requirement to specification.

Restaurants

It's surprisingly easy to think that you understand a description that you're reading – or have just written – when in fact you don't really understand it at all. Using a formal language doesn't guarantee clarity and understanding. Restaurant menus are interesting examples of description, full of possibilities of confusion. They're usually written in a formal – or, at least, very stylized – language, but the interplay of customers, serving staff and cooks invites some subtle misunderstandings. The restaurant customers, like software development customers, don't always get what they expect.

Some years ago I went with a group of people on a program design course to a traditional New York diner for lunch. The menu looked something like this:

Melon . French Onion Soup .
Soup of the Day . Marinated Herring

- - o - -

Broiled Flounder with Butter...$4.25
Broiled Half Spring Chicken...$4.50
Calves Liver Greek Style..$3.95
Spanish Omelette...$3.25
Eggplant Parmigiana...$3.75
Spaghetti with Tomato Sauce...$3.00

- - o - -

Apple Pie a la Mode . Blueberry Pie
Rice Pudding

Looking at the menu, you can probably guess what it means. Software developers get a lot of practice at guessing what descriptions mean. The menu is a sequence of three parts: a starter, a main dish and a dessert, in that order. Each part of the sequence is a selection, in which one element is to be chosen. The convention is that only the main dishes are priced: you can choose any starter and any dessert, and they are included in the price of the main dish.

The waiter came and took orders for our starters and main dishes. When we had eaten them, he returned to take our dessert orders. 'What do you want?' he asked me. 'No dessert, thank you,' I said. 'Apple pie, blueberry pie, or rice pudding?' said the waiter. 'No, thank you,' I said, 'I don't want anything.' 'You paid for it,' said the waiter; 'and you can have apple pie, blueberry pie, or rice pudding.' 'No, really,' I said, 'I don't want anything at all.' 'I gotta bring it,' said the waiter; 'you want a doggy bag?' 'No doggy bag,' said I; 'you can bring something if you like, but I won't eat it – I'll just leave it on the table.' 'Blueberry pie,' said the waiter. He brought the blueberry pie, and I left it on the table uneaten.

We went back to our program design course for the afternoon sessions, but we spent the first session talking about the waiter and the diner menu. Joe said the question was whether the menu described *safety* properties or *liveness* properties. If a safety property holds at a certain point, that means that something definitely will not happen at that point. If a liveness property holds, it means that something definitely will happen. The waiter, said Joe, thought that the menu described a liveness property – that after the main dish one of the listed desserts definitely had to happen. In fact, said Joe, the waiter was wrong: it described a safety property – that after the main dish nothing other than the listed desserts (such as chocolate cheese cake) could happen.

Lucy said that Joe's explanation didn't work. If I could pass up the dessert then surely I must be able to pass up the starter. If Joe was right, and the menu described a safety property for each course, then one safety property would be that at the very beginning of the meal nothing could happen except melon, soup of the day, French onion soup, or marinated herring. But that would stop me passing up the starter: broiled flounder with butter wouldn't be one of the things that can happen at the very beginning. Lucy said that the right explanation was that a selection always had an implicit null part: in any selection you could choose *nothing* if that was what you wanted. A selection was like an IF statement without an ELSE clause, in Pascal or C or COBOL.

Elaine said that she didn't agree about the null part. If a selection had a null part it should be shown explicitly. COBOL was a lousy language. And anyway, the main dish selection didn't have a null part: you certainly couldn't choose to have a starter, no main dish, and a dessert, and pay nothing.

Fred said that the problem was a confusion about what the menu entries denoted. The menu described a time-ordered sequence of three selections of events. There were no implicit null parts in the selections. The question was: exactly what events was it talking about? The waiter thought the events were the bringing of food to the table: 'Melon' meant 'The waiter brings melon to the table', and so on. That was the cause of the waiter's mistake. Actually, 'Melon' meant 'The waiter *offers* to bring melon to the table', and so on.

Bill said that Fred's general idea was right, but his suggestion about the *offer* events had to be wrong. It would mean that the waiter should offer the customer only one dish in each course, when in fact all the dishes in each course were being offered, and the customer had to choose.

Anne had the last word. She said these difficulties only arose because the menu was a SPECIFICATION. They didn't arise with programs, and the course was supposed to be about designing programs, not about writing specifications. And, anyway, it was time for the coffee break.

Rough Sketches

One important kind of description is a rough sketch. A rough sketch is a tentative description of something that is in process of being understood or invented. It records vague, half-formed ideas, at a stage when you want to say 'well, perhaps something roughly like this might be right', without devoting much time or effort to saying exactly what you have in mind. You have a rough idea, and sketch it quickly before it escapes. Too much precision would be harmful, not helpful, here: it would inhibit the flow of ideas.

The defining characteristic of a rough sketch is its *vagueness*. This vagueness is inevitable when development focuses initially, as it too often does, on describing the system to be built – that is, the MACHINE – to the exclusion of almost everything else. For, after all, the system to be built is, by definition, not yet built. It exists only in your imagination. You can describe it only by picturing it in your mind's eye, and writing down an account of what you see through that notoriously clouded organ. First you describe the dimly perceived outlines; then you fill in a little more detail; and then a little more; and, eventually, the picture is complete.

It is very much a matter of artistry. The developer, like ancient bards whose epic poems were not written down but recited from memory, must choose structures that will be readily remembered, that will help the audience not to lose the thread of the story. Just as no episode in a bardic poem should last for more than two hundred lines, so no description in a bardic software development should be more than one page long, or have more than six parts. Doug Ross, the originator of SADT, likening SADT descriptions to storytelling, says:

> 'No matter how these principles are addressed, they always end up with hierarchic decomposition as being the heart of good storytelling.
>
> '... Usually a story establishes several such levels of telling, and weaves back and forth between them as the need arises, to convey understanding, staying clear of excesses in either detail (boredom) or abstraction (confusion).
>
> '... Everything worth saying about anything worth saying something about must be expressed in six or fewer pieces.'

The hierarchic approach to description inevitably begins and ends in vagueness and uncertainty, because what is being described at each stage is, as yet, only vaguely perceived. At every level, except possibly the very lowest, the description is expressed in undefined natural language terms, whose meanings are expected to emerge more clearly from descriptions yet to come. As you go from level to level, these natural language meanings, and the structures built around them, provide successively more detailed pictures until finally – if the concluding levels are absolutely precise – everything is clear. Only when the whole description is complete does it becomes possible to go back to the earlier levels and see what they must mean if the whole description is to make sense.

The rough sketch, sadly, is often the cuckoo in the software development nest, pushing out every other kind of description. Some software developers are so accustomed to vagueness and uncertainty that they no longer notice its pervasive presence. They don't expect anything to be precise – except perhaps the program texts – and they speak of the roughest sketch as a *formal* description.

This is a great pity. Rough sketches do have a proper place in software development, but it is a limited place. They belong only in the preliminary skirmishing of each development stage. There may be rough sketches of requirements, rough sketches of system architecture, rough sketches of the system's environment, and rough sketches of programs. But in each case you must soon progress beyond them to precise descriptions. Keep your rough sketches for the light they shed on your development path, or your motivation. Or rework them into precise descriptions. Or discard them, just as builders' scaffolding is discarded once the building is complete. But don't mistake them for precise documentation. That's something quite different.

If you let them usurp the role of precise description you are doing yourself a great disservice. Always be on your guard against the danger of producing a rough sketch when something quite different is needed. If more than 25% of your descriptions are rough sketches, then either your project is trivial and unimportant, or you're not doing it right.

Scope of Description

A description describes some part of the application domain or of the machine you are building. The scope of a description is what it's about, what Phenomena of the described domain it's concerned with. To be exact about the scope of a description, you use a set of explicit Designations to spell out which phenomena you're talking about and how you're referring to them. The designations connect the description to the domain. Like this:

Setting the scope for a description is rather like putting on a pair of tinted spectacles. Through the spectacles you can see only the phenomena of the selected colours: everything else is hidden from view. In terms of designations, this means that you can see only certain classes of facts about individuals. Suppose that the domain is a company. And suppose that this is the designation set:

x is a company employee in time interval y	$\approx \text{Comp}(x,y)$
x is a time interval in the life of the company	$\approx \text{Intl}(x)$
x is the manager of y in interval z	$\approx \text{Superior}(x,y,z)$

Then the description can talk about the relationships among these phenomena, *but no others*. For example, it may say:

(a) Comp(X,Y) is not true unless Intl(Y) is true; and

(b) Superior(X,Y,Z) is not true unless both Comp(X,Z) and Comp(Y,Z) are true; and:

(c) Superior(X1,Y,Z) and Superior(X2,Y,Z) are not both true unless X1 and X2 are the same individual; and

(d) In any interval Z there is exactly one individual Y for which Super(X,Y,Z) is false for every X.

The assertions (b), (c), and (d) say that the manager and the managed are both employees at the time of the relationship; that no one has more than one manager at once; and that at any time there is one and only one top boss who doesn't have a manager.

The scope of the description is strictly limited to the designated phenomena. It can't say anything at all about employee pay, or holidays, or the allocation of offices, or working hours: they are outside its scope. But it can be extended, without altering its scope, to say more about the phenomena that are already in scope. For example, you could add a definition and another assertion:

(e) Dominates(x,y,z) $\triangleq$ Superior(x,y,z) or there is some individual w for which both Superior(x,w,z) and Dominates(w,y,z) are true.

(f) There are no individuals X and Z for which Dominates(X,X,Z) is true.

Together, (e) and (f) say that you can't be your own boss, either directly or indirectly.

One way of thinking about description scope is by analogy with parameterized program procedures. A procedure has formal parameters, which are replaced by actual parameter values when the procedure is called. A description, looked at in isolation, also has formal parameters. They are the terms by which it refers to the phenomena whose relationships it describes. If the description above is named D1, then its declaration is:

description D1 (Comp(x,y), Intl(x), Superior(x,y,z));

Applying a description is like invoking a procedure. If you write the call with keyword notation for the actual parameters, it looks like this:

D1 (Comp(x,y) = 'x is a company employee in time interval y',
      Intl(x) = 'x is a time interval in the life of the company',
      Superior(x,y,z) = 'x is the manager of y in interval z');

Just as a parameterized procedure can be invoked to work on different data, so a description can be applied to different phenomena. Without changing the company description D1 in any way, you can apply it to a domain of tennis tournaments. Appropriate designations might be:

x is a competitor in the tournament y	$\approx$ Comp(x,y)
x is an international knock-out tennis tournament	$\approx$ Intl(x)
x beats y in tournament z	$\approx$ Superior(x,y,z)

If you write this application like a procedure call with keyword notation for the actual parameters, it looks like this:

D1 (Comp(x,y) = 'x is a competitor in the tournament y',
      Intl(x) = 'x is an international knock-out tennis tournament',
      Superior(x,y,z) = 'x beats y in tournament z');

Everything the description says is still true (yes, really!). It's just true of an entirely different domain, with entirely different designations. Same description, different scope.

Shared Phenomena

You can think of the PHENOMENA of the world as facts about INDIVIDUALS. An individual may be a person, or an event, or a number, or a character string, or a song, or anything else of which you can say 'I mean *this* one, not *that* one'. You can think about all of the world that way. But you don't want to think about the whole world at once. If you're developing a system with a graphical user interface and a database, you don't want to think about the database while you are thinking about scrolling and menus and mouse clicks. In a banking system you don't want to think about how the ATMs work while you are thinking about how the bank deals with unpaid cheques. So you structure the problem context into DOMAINS to let you consider each domain separately.

This structuring into domains is a division into sets of individuals. Each domain is a set of individuals, and the facts in that domain are the facts that you choose to observe about the domain's individuals. But each domain must share some individuals and some facts with at least one other domain. If it did not, it would be isolated in a world of its own, and could not be a part of a larger system. For the structuring to work well, the collection of phenomena that are private to each domain must be richer and more interesting than the phenomena that it shares with other domains. But there must always be shared phenomena. A central reason for introducing the MACHINE domain into the problem context is precisely for it to share phenomena with domains that would otherwise be isolated. In the banking system, there are no phenomena common to the ATM and the account balances. But by connecting the Machine to both of them you connect them indirectly to each other.

A very common kind of shared phenomenon is a shared event. Shared events are at the heart of Hoare's CSP. At the beginning of his book, *Communicating Sequential Processes*, he gives a very nice example: the interaction of a customer with a vending machine. The vending machine is a domain (Hoare would say that it is a process) in which several kinds of individual events can occur. For example:

coin events, in which a coin is inserted into the machine's coin slot;
choc events, in which the machine dispenses a chocolate bar;
clunk events, in which the machine makes a clunking noise;
refill events, in which the machine is refilled with chocolate bars.

The customer is also a domain, in which these events can occur:

coin events, in which the customer inserts a coin;
choc events, in which the customer receives a chocolate bar;
curse events, in which the customer says a naughty word;
arrive events, in which the customer arrives at the machine;
leave events, in which the customer leaves the machine.

The *coin* and *choc* events, of course, are the shared phenomena. This means that each individual *coin* event, and each individual *choc* event, is an event in both domains. The *clunk* and *refill* events are private to the machine; and the *curse* and *arrive* and *leave* events are private to the customer. Here's a CONTEXT DIAGRAM annotated to show the events explicitly:

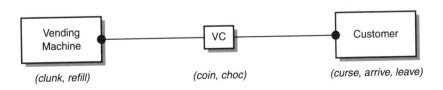

(clunk, refill)   (coin, choc)   (curse, arrive, leave)

The behaviours of the two domains will be separately described – that's the whole point of separating the domains – but they will be pinned together at the shared events. Each domain will contribute its own behaviour to the composite behaviour of the two together. The machine will only perform a *clunk* event after a *coin* event has occurred and before it performs a *choc* event. The customer can't perform a *coin* event without first performing an *arrive* event. So in the composite behaviour a *clunk* event can occur only after an *arrive* event and before the next *choc* event.

In this simple example, the two domain descriptions use the same terms – *coin* and *choc* – to denote the common phenomena. But in a practical development the two domain descriptions would probably be made by different people and at different times. Almost certainly they wouldn't use the same terminology. Even if they use the same words, they'll probably mean something quite different by them. That's a well-known difficulty in systems analysis. Words like *customer, supplier, employee, product,* have different meanings in different departments of the same organization.

These different meanings are not the result of perversity or stupidity: they simply reflect the different views appropriate to the different domains. In our tiny example of the vending machine and the customer, suppose that the customer is not completely honest. He has a supply of the required coins, which are Ruritanian dinars; but he also has some Utopian thalers, which are worth much less than Ruritanian dinars but are roughly the same size and weight. Sometimes he is tempted to cheat. So instead of the single class of *coin* events he had before, he now has:

pay events, in which he inserts a Ruritanian dinar; and
cheat events, in which he inserts a Utopian thaler.

The machine's designers know that customers may act dishonestly. They have equipped the machine with a more sophisticated coin-accepting mechanism, and instead of the single class of *coin* events the machine now has:

OK_coin events, in which an acceptable coin is inserted; and
bad_coin events, in which an unacceptable coin is inserted.

Of course, the accepting mechanism is imperfect. Sometimes it fails to reject a Utopian thaler, and sometimes it refuses to accept a Ruritanian dinar. Now the analysis of the shared phenomena is a little more complicated:

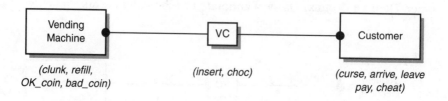

The shared phenomena are *choc* and *insert* events. Every *pay* and every *cheat* event is an *insert* event; and every *OK_coin* and every *bad_coin* event is an *insert* event. The distinction between *pay* and *cheat* events isn't directly observable in the Vending Machine domain: that's why the customer can sometimes cheat successfully. And the distinction between *OK_coin* and *bad_coin* events isn't directly observable in the Customer domain: that's why the customer is sometimes surprised by the rejection of a perfectly good Ruritanian dinar. The two domains have very different views of the same set of *insert* events.

For any class of shared events you have to consider questions of control. Which of the sharing domains determines what events will occur? One very common pattern of control is that a shared event occurs only if one domain *takes the initiative*, and the other *does not prevent* the occurrence. An insert event can't occur unless the customer takes the initiative and puts the coin in the slot. But it also can't occur if the vending machine prevents it – for example, by barring the slot. This pattern is asymmetric between the sharing domains. In CSP the pattern is symmetric. There is no notion of *initiative* on the part of a CSP process; instead, the process may be *ready to engage in* one or more events. At any time, the event that happens next is any event all of whose sharing processes are ready to engage in it.

It's important to recognize that control distinctions are quite different from the distinction between input and output. An input event may be like an interrupt, initiated by the source of the data; or like the execution of a read operation, initiated by the recipient of the data. And similarly an output event may be initiated by either the source or the recipient of the data. A machine running a simple Pascal program initiates both its input and its output events. For an inert domain, by contrast, such as a database, all input and output events are initiated by the other domains that share them.

Simple Control Frame

In the simplest kind of control system problem, there is a tangible *domain*, external to the *machine*, to be *controlled*. This domain is connected to the machine directly, by SHARED PHENOMENA. The machine interacts with the controlled domain, using the shared phenomena both to sense the state of the domain and to affect its state by causing shared events. The purpose of the machine is to bring about some desired behaviour of the controlled domain.

Here is the FRAME DIAGRAM:

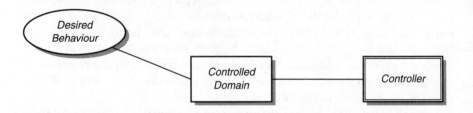

The *Controlled Domain* principal part is *dynamic* and both *active* and *reactive*. That is, some events and state changes occur spontaneously, without external stimulus; and there are also events that are externally controlled and cause the domain to respond by events and predictable internal change. Explicitly describing this behaviour of the *Controlled Domain* will be a necessary part of any appropriate method.

The *Controller* is the machine to be built. It is directly connected to the domain: effectively, there is no unreliability, no noise and no significant time delay in the connection. That makes it easy for the machine to control the domain in a simple, deterministic way. This absence of a CONNECTION DOMAIN from the problem frame is a typical example of the simplification that characterizes problem frames. In a realistic problem you would probably need to deal with the difficulties arising from an imperfect connection domain. That would be a PROBLEM COMPLEXITY, and you would need another problem frame in addition to this one.

The *Desired Behaviour* is, essentially, the REQUIREMENT. It describes the desired relationships among the phenomena of the controlled domain that the machine is required to bring about.

Although the *Controlled Domain* is shown as a single principal part, it may comprise two or more tangible domains in the problem context. For example, in a problem to develop a program sequencer for a washing machine, the CONTEXT DIAGRAM may look like this:

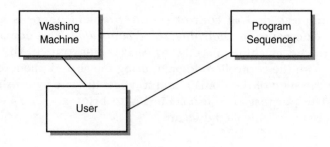

The washing machine and its user are separate domains. They share some phenomena – for example, the user puts clothes to be washed into the washing machine, and puts in soap, and opens and closes the door. Each one also shares some phenomena with the program sequencer. When the user adjusts the programme settings, the adjustment events are shared with the sequencer. The sequencer can switch on the washing machine motor, and change its speed of rotation; it can also switch the pump on and off, and sense the presence of water in the tub.

When the problem frame is fitted to the problem context, it will be appropriate to treat both the Washing Machine domain and the User domain as parts of the *Controlled Domain* principal part:

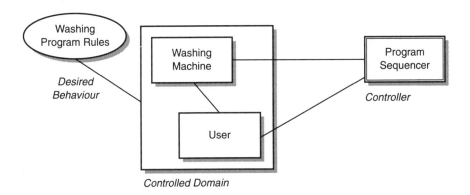

From the point of view of the developer of the washing machine sequencer, the user appears only as a source of spontaneous activity in the controlled domain. It is not possible for the sequencer to cause any activity on the part of the user; the user is a purely active part of the controlled domain, and not reactive. The washing machine itself is essentially reactive: everything that happens in the washing machine happens in response to something done by the sequencer or by the user.

Any method that claims to deal adequately with this kind of problem must provide for two distinct descriptions of the *Controlled Domain*, one in each of two distinct MOODS. One of these is a description in the *indicative* mood, which describes the given properties and behaviour that the domain has regardless of the behaviour of the machine. For example, if the pump is switched on when the tub is full of water, then after 125 seconds the tub will have emptied; and if the hot water inlet valve is opened then the tub will fill with hot water in not less than 90 seconds.

The other description that the method must provide is a description in the *optative* mood, which describes the desired properties and behaviour of the domain. Essentially, this is a description of the requirement, the principal part that we have called *Desired Behaviour*. For example, if the programme setting is 'Hot Rinse and Spin', then the washing machine should go through a particular sequence of events, filling the tub with hot water and then emptying the tub and spinning for 60 seconds.

These two descriptions are necessary because the *Controller* relies on the given properties and behaviour – as described in the indicative description – in its efforts to bring about the desired properties and behaviour of the requirement. To achieve the requirement 'fill the tub' it opens the hot water inlet valve; to empty the tub it switches on the pump. The indicative description fills the gap between the domain requirements and the machine SPECIFICATION.

Simple IS Frame

In its simplest form, an information system provides information, in response to requests, about some real-world domain of interest. Here's the FRAME DIAGRAM:

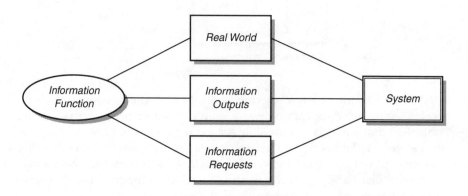

The double rectangle surrounding the *System* principal part shows that it is the machine you have to build. (That's what people often mean by *system*, even when they tell you they mean something else.)

The *Real World* principal part is a domain directly connected, by SHARED PHENOMENA, to the *System*. The *Information Outputs* and *Information Requests* are also directly connected to the *System*.

The *Information Function* principal part is the REQUIREMENT in this frame. It is a required relationship among the *Real World*, the *Information Outputs*, and the *Information Requests*. The outputs are to be related to the real world in the obvious way: the information contained in the outputs must be an accurate reflection of the state of the world. The outputs must also be related to the requests, because they are produced in response to requests and because their content is partly determined by the requests – for example, when a request asks for information about a particular individual or class of individuals, or a range of dates.

Most methods for solving problems that fit the Simple IS frame rely on the technique of making a MODEL of the *Real World* and embodying that model in the *System*. In effect, the system becomes a simulation of the real world, and derives its information directly from its model, and only indirectly from the real world itself. This kind of modelling technique is at the core of the JSD method, described in my book *System Development*.

The *Real World* may be a *static* domain: for example, the system may provide information about the texts of Shakespeare's plays. Or it may be *dynamic*: for example, the activities of a currently operating business. The differences between a problem with a purely static real world and a problem with a dynamic real world are considerable. In particular, they need different kinds of model, and different methods would be appropriate: JSD focuses only on problems with a dynamic *Real World*. You might well say that there are really two problem frames not one – a Simple Static IS frame, and a Simple Dynamic IS frame. Here I'm talking about the Simple Dynamic IS frame.

The *Information Requests* principal part is always an *active dynamic* domain, in which requests occur spontaneously and autonomously. The requests domain has no internal state or structure: it is regarded simply as the source of a stream of information requests, ordered in time but otherwise unstructured.

The problem frame, as always, is a simplification. There may be many kinds of complication in a realistic problem. Sometimes it will be necessary to control access to the system. That would mean applying the Simple Control frame in addition to the Simple IS frame, treating the information requests as the domain to be controlled. This multiplicity of roles for a single domain of the problem context is typical of MULTI-FRAME PROBLEMS. Or it might be necessary to report on the usage of the system in response to requests from the computer services manager. That would mean applying a second instance of the Simple IS frame to the problem. In this second instance *(2)*, the computer services manager's requests would be the *Information Requests (2)* principal part, and the original information requests would be a component of the *Real World (2)*. If it's also necessary to report on the machine resources used to respond to requests, then the *System* of the original Simple IS problem would also be a component of the *Real World (2)*.

The *Real World* is dynamic and also *active*. Some of the information outputs may be required when certain conditions arise in the real world, rather than in response to requests. For example, bank account statements may be produced monthly, or exception reports may be produced when unusually large transactions occur. A dynamic real world is always regarded, in this problem frame, as *autonomous*. That means that the events and state changes in the real world are internally caused. The system merely tracks and reports on them, but does not initiate them or affect the real world in any significant way. This is a crucial difference between this problem frame and the Simple Control frame, in which the chief purpose of the machine is to exert control over the world.

Suppose, for example, that you're using this Simple IS problem frame to develop a simple information system about some bank accounts. And suppose that some of the *Information Outputs* are reports on account balances. Then it may well be that account holders will sometimes react to reports showing overdrawn balances by paying money into their accounts, to avoid interest charges. So to that extent the system does affect the *Real World*. The effects may even be quite consciously intended: information, after all, is usually intended to be acted on. But – and this is the crucial point – consideration of the effects is completely outside this problem frame. A method based on this frame, such as the JSD method, provides no place to describe the effects you want the *System* to have on the *Real World*.

This restriction – ignoring the effects of the *System* on the *Real World* – is typical of the simplifications inherent in a problem frame. That's the whole point about problem frames. They may occasionally capture a whole real problem, but most often, in a realistic development, one problem frame captures only a sub-problem. To solve the whole real problem you have to put several problem frames together. That's the nature of problem complexity.

One more simplification in this frame is the stipulation that the *System* is directly connected, by shared phenomena, to the *Real World*. In practice this often not the case at all. Often the system is connected to the real world only indirectly, through a CONNECTION DOMAIN that introduces all kinds of distortion and error into the connection. To deal properly with it you would need to use a CONNECTION FRAME, with its own principal parts and its own solution. JSD, like many methods, has a partial recognition of this complexity. It recognizes the need for an *input subsystem*, and the need to deal systematically with the difficulties that arise from erroneous input, when the *System* can embody only a very imperfect model of the *Real World*. The *input subsystem* of JSD is just another, partial, view of a multi-frame problem.

Software

Ken Orr – of the Warnier–Orr method – tells a delightful story about Barry Boehm and the intangibility of software. Barry was working, many years ago, on the avionics software – written in Fortran – in a project to develop a new aeroplane. The weight of the plane was critical, and the project director had appointed a weights manager, whose job was to ensure that the total weight of the plane's components did not exceed the design limit. The weights manager came to Barry to ask how much the software would weigh. 'Nothing,' said Barry. 'That's ridiculous,' said the weights manager; 'the software is costing a million dollars and doesn't weigh anything? I don't believe it.' But Barry insisted. The manager went away. Next day he returned, triumphantly holding the punched-card deck of a Fortran program that he had picked up in the computer room. 'Look,' he said; 'here's some software, and it does weigh something.' Barry held one of the cards up to the light. 'See those holes?' he asked the manager. 'Those holes are the only part of the software that actually goes into the plane.'

This is the paradox at the heart of any software development task. The product is intangible: it doesn't weigh anything. Yet we like to think of ourselves as engineers. One justification for that view is that we do, in a sense, create physical machines. Our central artifact, and the end product of our work, is a tangible MACHINE that controls an aeroplane or a chemical plant or a motor car, or helps to administer a library, or switches telephone calls, or manipulates documents, or transforms visual images. As a software engineer you need only make a DESCRIPTION of the required machine, and magically it becomes available. You exploit the programmability of the general purpose computer: it accepts your description, and behaves as if it were itself the required machine.

Describing the required machine, of course, is usually not a simple task. The machines we build in software are complex: few of them can be described by simply writing down their descriptions directly in a programming language. We have to work hard to master this complexity, organizing and structuring our descriptions of the machine to maximize clarity and minimize unnecessary interaction.

Nor is it enough to describe only the machine. You may need to describe the problem. And you may need to describe other DOMAINS that interact with the machine – its operators, the aeroplane or chemical plant it is controlling, the telephones whose calls it switches, the texts it searches and manipulates. In most systems of any size or importance these other concerns demand explicit description in their own right, to clarify what the machine must do, to help you to solve the problem, and to satisfy your customers that their problem has been understood and solved.

Organizing, structuring and making descriptions is the central activity of software development. So software development is engineering in a second sense: it is the engineering of complex structures of descriptions. An engineer confronted with the problem of bridging a river designs and builds a structure of parts, using concrete and metal as the raw materials. A software developer confronted with the problem of creating a system designs and builds a structure of descriptions, using languages and notations as the raw materials. A software development METHOD stipulates what descriptions to make to solve the problem, in what order, by what operations, in what languages.

Like parts in other engineering disciplines, a description can be of good quality or bad quality. It can be made of appropriate or inappropriate material. It can be too big or too small. It can be doing too much or too little. It can be hard or easy to manipulate. It can be hard or easy to assemble with other descriptions. The technology and engineering of descriptions is an important subject in its own right. It's what software development is about.

Software Engineering

Some chemists and biologists suffer from 'physics envy'. They wish their own subjects had the character and reputation and achievements of physics. In the same way, a lot of software scientists suffer from 'engineering envy'. Naur and Randell's report on the first NATO Software Engineering conference puts it clearly:

> 'In late 1967 the [NATO Science Committee] Study Group recommended the holding of a working conference on Software Engineering. The phrase "software engineering" was deliberately chosen as being provocative, in implying the need for software manufacture to be based on the types of theoretical foundations and practical disciplines that are traditional in the established branches of engineering'.

But envy, as so often, is not a good basis for improvement. Envy clouds the vision of the envious, so that they cannot see why they are deprived of what they desire. 'It's all your fault,' says Tweedledum, 'because you won't measure things. You can't be a real engineer if you don't measure and calculate things.' 'No, it's all your fault,' says Tweedledee, 'because you don't do experiments. There's no real engineering without experiments – you know, wind tunnels and so on.' The bitterness of deprivation leads to recrimination instead of action, and to the wringing of hands instead of the analysis of differences.

The most prominent difference is that the traditional, established branches of engineering are all highly specialized. Chemical engineers don't build electricity generating plants. The automobile engineers at GM or Toyota would not accept a commission to specify a replacement for the Brooklyn Bridge. The aeronautical engineers who designed the Airbus would not undertake the design and construction of the Channel Tunnel.

In fact, the established disciplines are so specialized and so different as to have almost nothing in common. How can we hope to be like all of them when they are so unlike each other? Software engineers would be analogous to 'physical engineers', imaginary polymaths who understand how to specify, design, and build any useful physical object whatsoever, in any material, to serve any purpose. But, of course, those imaginary 'physical engineers' and their imaginary discipline do not exist. In software development, as in the established kinds of engineering, the real successes have been achieved by its specialized branches, such as the construction of compilers and operating systems. Compiler engineering makes more sense where software engineering makes rather less.

The significance of specialization in an engineering discipline has been ignored or misunderstood by some proponents of formal methods. They admonish software developers to focus on *calculation*. After all, structural engineers calculate stresses; automobile engineers calculate torque and acceleration; electrical engineers calculate voltage and current and resistance and capacitance. Clearly, software engineers should calculate too. 'Here is Z,' they say. 'Now you can *calculate* the precondition of an operation. Now you can *calculate* the correctness of a refinement.' These, they claim, are the 'theoretical foundations' that software engineering needs.

Well, they've got a point. It would be silly to tolerate vagueness, uncertainty and confusion where you could have precision and exact calculation instead. But they've missed a much bigger and much more important point. Engineers in the established branches of engineering make their calculations only within very well-defined and narrow contexts. Calculation isn't used for the big decisions: the big decisions are already in place when the work begins. Automobile engineers don't design a new car from first principles. They don't calculate whether to use a steam engine, whether to use tracks, or articulated legs, or four wheels, or eight, or whether the driver should face sideways or forwards.

They already know the answers to these questions. They use a collection of standard designs, evolved over many decades of experience. Each new design is just a small perturbation from the standard. To combine the chassis and body in one unit, or to set the engine transversely, was a radical departure. Only the most brilliant and daring designers would try it for the first time. For practising automobile engineers the design space to be explored is very narrow. Their engineering calculations are done on familiar components, with familiar characteristics, in a familiar design configuration.

In most areas of software development – except, of course, the few existing specializations – there are no such established standard designs. That's what some of the enthusiasts for object-oriented development want to put right. They have been inspired by the work of Christopher Alexander, the software methodologists' favourite architect. About 30 years ago, Alexander wrote a fine book, *Notes on the Synthesis of Form*, that was much read by the structured revolutionaries of the 1970s. Now his slightly more recent architectural book, *A Pattern Language*, written in 1977, has inspired the idea of patterns in software development.

You can read about one approach of this kind in *Design Patterns: Elements of Reusable Object-Oriented Software*, by Erich Gamma and others. Of course, these are patterns in design: that is, patterns in solutions. Ralph Johnson, one of the authors of the book, says:

> 'Alexander focuses as much on the problem to be solved and the various forces on the problem as he does on the solution to the problem. We have a tendency to focus on the solution...'

Engineers in the established branches don't focus on the problem to be solved, either. That is, they don't focus on the generalized or abstract problem – 'design a vehicle', or 'design a bridge' – because each branch deals only with problems of a relatively small and well-defined class. The design solutions are already well classified, and with them the problems that they solve. But in a lot of software development it's not like that. A new bespoke system, tailored to the needs of a particular organization or a particular environment, will be different from every other software system. Not because it's a different solution to the same problem, but because it's a solution to a different problem. In non-specialized software development we need a way of getting to grips with problems – of classifying and analysing them. That's why PROBLEM FRAMES are so important.

Span of Description

Last month I telephoned a mail-order company, and was greeted by the recorded message:

> 'Thank you for your call. We value it highly. It will be answered in the order in which it was received.'

There's something wrong here, isn't there? It's a *span* error. The span of a description is the part of the world it's concerned with. The span of the recorded message was evidently meant to be just one call – the call I was making. But the last sentence tries to talk – nonsensically – about 'the order in which *it* was received'. The notion of ordering had wandered in from another description of a larger span:

'*All* calls are answered in the order in which *they* are received.'

When you fix the SCOPE OF DESCRIPTION, you are, as it were, putting on a pair of tinted spectacles through which you can only see certain kinds of domain phenomenon. You focus on the whole domain, but your vision is very selective. When you fix the span, you usually focus your attention more narrowly. Instead of seeing the whole domain, you want to see only a segment of it. One way to think about it is that you're still seeing the same kinds of phenomenon, the same kinds of fact about individuals; but you're seeing fewer individuals. For example, you're only talking about one telephone call instead of all of them.

Scope and span are quite closely related. Individuals are accessible only through the facts in which they play a role. An individual who doesn't appear in any fact is invisible. Therefore if you filter out certain kinds of fact, you also filter out the individuals who appear only in those facts. So the way to express a reduced span is often to define new terms that denote a narrower collection of facts. Then you can use those terms for scoping your description and giving it a reduced span.

Here's an example. If you start with a designated predicate for all citizens of all countries:

$$x \text{ is a citizen of country } y \qquad \approx \text{CountryCitizen}(x,y)$$

and you want to restrict your span to just one country, Ruritania, you can define a new term:

$$\text{Citizen}(x) \triangleq \text{CountryCitizen}(x,\text{Ruritania})$$

Now you can use the term $\text{Citizen}(x)$, instead of $\text{CountryCitizen}(x,y)$, to give you the reduced span. In the Z formal notation you can go the other way by using a technique called *promotion*. You can promote a description originally written to describe only Ruritanian citizens to a context in which it can be applied to citizens of all countries. The technique is nicely explained in John Wordsworth's book *Software Development with Z*.

Choosing the right span for a description is very important. You choose the span of a description so that what you want to say fits exactly into that span. A smaller span would not allow you to say everything you want to, and a larger span would force you to say too much.

The correct span is not always obvious. Suppose that you want to describe the rules for right-justifying text in a little program design problem. The lines of text have already been arranged so that they are small enough to fit into the fixed line width. Now the need is to insert spaces so that the lines will appear right-justified in the output. What span do you need? One character? One word? One line? One paragraph? One page? One chapter? The whole book?

The right choice will depend on the justification rules. You can see at once that one character or one word is not enough: the rules apply to lines. But is one line enough? It could be – provided that no distinctions are to be made between one line and another: each line to be right-justified is to be treated in exactly the same way.

This won't often be true. In fact, it won't ever be true in an English language text. The last line of each ordinary paragraph is not right-justified; and there may be whole subparagraphs, containing mathematical formulae or poetry, that are to be excluded from the right-justification.

Even among the lines to be justified, treatment may vary. The extra spaces added in right-justification can't be added perfectly evenly. If the larger interword gaps are always at the right, or at the left, or at the outside of each line, the resulting text will look thinner where the larger gaps are concentrated. The result may be 'rivers': the paragraphs look as if they have rivers of white space meandering from top to bottom. To avoid rivers, different lines are differently justified – perhaps by adding the extra spaces to the rightmost and leftmost gaps in alternate lines.

These considerations will make a larger span necessary. But which? If you must treat alternate lines differently, what exactly do you mean by 'alternate'? Alternating within each page? Then the span must be one page. Alternating within each paragraph? Then the span must be one paragraph.

At first sight, you may think that this enlarged span is unnecessary. If the lines are numbered, or marked 'odd' and 'even', you can use the marking when you consider each line individually. Then you can consider just one line at a time. That's true. But how will you mark the lines? In effect, the marking technique splits the description of right-justification into two parts. One part has the full span needed for the requirement. This part defines the numbering or marking, in the form of a predicate such as IsOddLine(l). The other part has a span of one line only, but relies on the predicate IsOddLine(l) to determine whether the line should have its extra spaces to the left or to the right.

A span that is too small doesn't allow you to say everything you want to. A span that is too large is damaging because it forces you to say too much. Saying too much in a description makes the description less context-independent than it need be. That can make it much less reusable. It can also frustrate a proper separation of concerns. Here is the smallest possible example of what I mean, in the form of two Z schemas:

```
┌─ Accounts ──────────────────┐        ┌─ Open ───────────────────┐
│  Active: ℙ ACCT             │        │  Δ Accounts              │
│  ...                        │        │  a? : ACCT               │
│                             │        ├──────────────────────────┤
├─────────────────────────────┤        │  a? ∉ Active ∧           │
│                             │        │     Active' = Active ∪ {a?}│
│  ...                        │        └──────────────────────────┘
│                             │
└─────────────────────────────┘
```

The schema on the left describes the state of an accounts system. One component of the state is named *Active*: it is a set of accounts.

The schema on the right uses the schema on the left in describing the operation type *Open*. The *Open* operation changes the state of the accounts system: the notation *ΔAccounts* means that the *Open* operation is associated with an old value of *Accounts* (the set *Active*) and a new value of *Accounts* (the set *Active′*). A parameter *a?* is supplied with the *Open* operation, identifying the account to be opened. The part of the *Open* schema below the line says that the account *a?* is not already active – it is not in the old set *Active* – and that the new account set *Active′* is equal to the old set with the addition of *a?*, the opened account.

The span of the description of *Open* is too large, because it talks about the whole set *Active*, and thus about all of the accounts, instead of only the account *a?* that is being opened. That may not seem very damaging. But it is. Quite unnecessarily, it tells us that the new value of the *Active* set must be exactly the old set plus the one new account. So an *Open* event in which one account is opened cannot also be an event in which another account is opened or closed. That's a completely pointless restriction. We were, after all, only wanting to say that opening an account makes that account active. The other accounts should not have been in the span of the description.

Specifications

The terminology of software development is mostly in a chaos that correctly reflects the chaotic state of the field. Usage of the word *specification* is no exception. Alan Davis, in his book *Software Requirements*, defines a specification simply as:

> 'A document; for example, a *requirements specification* is a document containing *requirements*; a design specification is a document containing the *design*; a test specification is a document containing the *testing* process'.

Carlo Ghezzi, in *Fundamentals of Software Engineering*, is more exact:

'In general, we can view a specification as the statement of an agreement between a producer of a service and a consumer of the service, or an implementer and a user'.

I like to use the term in a much more restricted way. It's one of a trio of terms: requirements; specifications; and programs. Look at this picture:

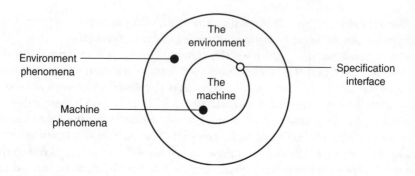

The machine interacts with its environment. Think of that as its physical environment, although in fact I mean something a little wider than that. The interaction consists of the sharing of some phenomena – events and states – between the machine and the environment. The event in which I depress the X key on the keyboard is the same event as the event in which the machine receives an X input. The state in which the machine is emitting a continuous beep is the same state as the state in which I am hearing a continuous beep. These shared events and states form the interface between the machine and the environment. This is the specification interface: specifications are all about – and only about – the shared phenomena – the shared events and states – at this interface.

Requirements are all about – and only about – the environment phenomena: that is, the phenomena shown in the outer ring in the picture. The customer for the system is interested in the environment, not in the machine. The customer wants the chemical plant to run properly, or the aeroplane to land safely, or the paychecks to be correctly calculated and printed. Some of the customer's interests may perhaps accidentally concern shared phenomena at the specification interface. But that would be accidental as far as requirements are concerned.

Programs, on the other hand, are all about – and only about – the machine phenomena: that is, the phenomena shown in the inner ring in the picture. Programs are about the behaviour of the machine. Programmers – *qua* programmers – are interested in the machine's behaviour. Some of these interests will almost certainly concern shared phenomena at the specification interface, but usually this interest is motivated only by a desire to know more about the machine's behaviour.

If you take this view of programs, specifications, and requirements, you can see that every specification is, in a formal sense, both a requirement and a program. It's a requirement because it's about – and only about – the environment phenomena. And it's a program because it's about – and only about – the machine phenomena. That's why specifications, in this sense, form a bridge between requirements and programs.

Specifications are difficult things. Although they are requirements of a kind, they may not seem to make obvious sense in the environment. That's because they have been derived from customers' requirements by a number of reasoning steps. They represent the answer to the question: What behaviour at the specification interface would produce *these effects*, which are required in the environment at large? Looking only at the answer you may find it quite hard to imagine what *these effects*, described in the question, must have been. Why should the machine be required to produce these particular outputs in response to these particular inputs? And although specifications are programs of a kind, unlike ordinary programs they may be impossible to execute. They represent the answer to the question: What behaviour at the specification interface must the program produce? But looking only at the specification you may find it quite hard to see what internal behaviour of the machine would produce that external behaviour. Programming isn't always trivial.

Specifications are often difficult to understand for other reasons. One reason is that writers of specifications – especially those who are strongly drawn to a mathematical view of their work – want to make their specifications as abstract as they can. A concrete specification – the opposite of abstract – is thought likely to be tainted with IMPLEMENTATION BIAS, with irrelevant detail of the machine. But the shared phenomena at the specification interface are irreducibly concrete: they are events and physical states that involve both the real world outside the computer and the computer itself. A specification cannot be completely abstract because its ultimate subject matter is concrete. If you rely on too much abstraction in the wrong places your specification will be about an abstract problem, not about the real problem that your customer expects you to solve.

Another difficulty is that because a specification lies at the boundary between the machine and its environment there is scope for confusion about what exactly it describes. The confusion is compounded by the fact that the machine often embodies a MODEL of at least part of the environment: so a description of part of the environment may be simultaneously a description of part of the machine.

But why should this confusion matter? Isn't the specification a description of a boundary or interface? Doesn't it therefore serve equally well to describe either side of the interface?

No, it doesn't. The boundary or interface looks the same from both sides only if you ignore some vital considerations. Have you ever seen one of those weathervanes in the shape of a wooden figure turning a crank which causes a propeller to rotate? It's a joke, of course. It looks as if the figure is turning the crank, and the crank is turning the propeller. But in fact the wind is turning the propeller, the propeller is turning the crank, and the crank is moving the figure.

You can be left in exactly the same kind of doubt by a specification. Specifications – especially formal specifications – are often written in languages that abstract away all considerations of causality and control. When you read a specification like that, you are left with a view of the interaction between the machine and the application domain rather like your view of the weathervane figure. You could call it the 'idiot observer' view. Everything is carefully observed and noted. Nothing is understood. Not what you need in a specification, really.

Top-down

By the standards of computing, hierarchical top-down development has a long history. As early as 1951, Wilkes, Wheeler and Gill wrote a book, *The Preparation of Programs for an Electronic Digital Computer*, in which they gave serious attention to methods for constructing programs out of subroutines. But the idea did not become widely known until the 1960s.

Here is what Dijkstra wrote in 1965, in *Programming Considered as a Human Activity*, one of the seminal texts of the top-down culture:

'The technique of mastering complexity has been known since ancient times: *Divide et impera* (Divide and rule).

'... I assume the programmer's genius matches the difficulty of his problem and assume that he has arrived at a suitable subdivision of the task. He then proceeds in the usual manner in the following stages:

- he makes the complete specification of the individual parts
- he satisfies himself that the total problem is solved provided he had at his disposal program parts meeting the various specifications
- he constructs the individual parts, satisfying the specifications, but independent of one another and the further context in which they will be used.

'Obviously, the construction of such an individual part may again be a task of such a complexity, that inside this part of the job, a further subdivision is required.'

The result is a HIERARCHICAL STRUCTURE of parts, with the original problem as the sole part at the top level, and the ultimate solution parts at the lowest levels. The approach is *top-down* because the hierarchy is obtained by successive subdivision from the top. An alternative approach is *bottom-up*: it too assumes hierarchical structure, but works by successive aggregation from a repertoire of lowest-level parts.

Another name for the top-down approach is stepwise refinement. Top-down program development and stepwise refinement went hand in hand with *structured programming*. Structured programming replaced the tangled chaos of `goto` statements and labels with tidily nested structures of sequence, selection, and iteration, and so extended the benefits of hierarchical structure from the level of procedure invocations down to the level of the executable code within procedures.

In the programming world of the 1960s, and for a long time afterwards, this seemed an unassailable doctrine. A program was a single sequential process – concurrency and parallelism were exotic or unknown – so a single hierarchy seemed an obviously appropriate structure. The design question – What hierarchy is needed? What subdivision? – was clearly quite intractable, and should be left to the 'individual genius' of the programmer. And what was so beneficial to programming should obviously be imported into the wider territory of analysis and specification: Structured Analysis proudly announced that it, too, adhered to top-down principles.

But all was not well, even in the programming heartland. After the suitable subdivision of the task that Dijkstra assumed, each of the stages that followed was to be based on *complete specification of the individual parts*. Suppose that you have a problem 'Do a Transaction', and you have subdivided it like this:

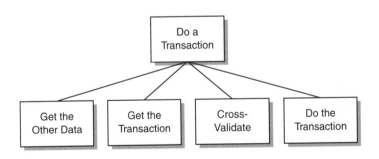

You can't be confident that this will solve your problem unless you know – and that means know *exactly* – what 'Get the Other Data', 'Get the Transaction', 'Cross-Validate', and 'Do the Transaction' mean. (Don't ask me what they mean: I took the picture from a book about Structured Design.) So, according to Dijkstra, you must write a complete specification of each of them. You use the specifications to check that the parts will solve your problem, and also, later on, to check that each one has been constructed correctly.

But the proposal was psychologically unrealistic. Programmers are always unwilling to defer the gratification of writing and executing code, and even more unwilling to defer it in favour of mere documentation.

Dijkstra himself could certainly not be accused of succumbing to the temptation to execute program code. Eleven years later he wrote proudly in his preface to A *Discipline of Programming*: 'None of the programs in this monograph, needless to say, has been tested on a machine'. Yet even he soon abandoned the idea of complete specification of each part. For example, in *Notes on Structured Programming*, written in 1968, he shows a high-level description of a program to print the first thousand prime numbers:

```
begin variable "table p";
        "fill table p with first thousand prime numbers";
        "print table p"
end
```

The texts "fill table *p* with first thousand prime numbers" and "print table *p*" are certainly not complete specifications of those parts. (It could be said that the idea of complete specifications of parts returned, in the form of preconditions and postconditions, in his later work and that of his followers.)

As a result, the top-down idea took hold in the form in which we know it today. Successive subdivision sounded attractive: it seemed to satisfy a natural desire to limit the scope of our thoughts at any one time. So successive subdivision was eagerly adopted. But *complete specification* sounded arduous, and even positively frightening. So it was quickly forgotten. The subdivision into parts, which, according to Dijkstra, should be based on the specifications of those parts, was expected to serve as its own foundation. At each level the subdivision itself implicitly specifies its parts: they must be whatever will make sense of the subdivision. At the bottom level the program code provides one final level of certainty, but not in the form of a specification. In short, there were no specifications of the parts. Top-down became a philosophy of procrastination, of forever deferring the burden of exactness to the next level.

Outside the programming heartland there were even more serious difficulties. It was one thing to impose a single hierarchical structure on a sequential program of the programmer's own devising; it was quite another to impose it on a given, inconveniently ill-structured, real-world domain. If, in an insurance application, you say 'The insurance business has two top-level processes: one dealing with claims, and one dealing with premiums', you may be making a serious mistake. Have you forgotten the need to deal with a no-claims bonus, in which the premium is reduced for a policy on which there was no claim in the previous year? Which process does this fit into? What about the activity of finding new business? What about maintaining the information about the policies and policyholders? When you recognize the existence of these activities, are you compelled to abandon your subdivision into two processes? Or can you adjust the subdivision to take account of them? Or is no adjustment needed? Without Dijkstra's complete specifications of the parts the discussion must wander in a fog of uncertainty.

There are two basic difficulties with top-down. The first is that for inventing or designing new things to be built – data flows in a process network, or procedure hierarchies in a program – top-down enforces the riskiest possible ordering of decisions. The largest decision is the subdivision of the whole problem: it is the largest in scale, and the largest in its consequences. Yet this decision is taken first, when nothing is yet known and everything remains to be discovered: if it is wrong, most or even all of the work that follows will be wrong or useless. Even worse, if the decision is wrong you won't find out until you reach the bottom level, or until you write the code. This is one reason, among others, why Fred Brooks says in *The Mythical Man-Month:* 'plan to throw one away: you will, anyhow'. The moral is that to succeed in top-down development, you must already have solved the problem before the solution process is begun.

The second difficulty is that the real world – even quite a small part of the real world – hardly ever has a single hierarchical structure. Instead, there are many parallel and overlapping structures. A few of the overlapping structures may be hierarchical, but more will be more like chains or networks or rings. If you force such complex structures into a single hierarchy you are sure to get distorted descriptions in which many things are in the wrong places and many things are omitted. Even something so simple as the structure of a two-dimensional spreadsheet cannot be properly described in a single hierarchy. If your top-level subdivision is into rows you can't do justice to the columns; if you favour the columns first you can give no good account of the rows.

In short, my advice to those about to work top-down is like Mr Punch's advice to those about to marry: Don't.

Tree Diagrams

Tree diagrams are very useful in program design. They can be used to describe ordered collections of events or other elements in terms of the familiar trio of 'structured' component types: *sequence, selection,* and *iteration*. Here is a tree diagram:

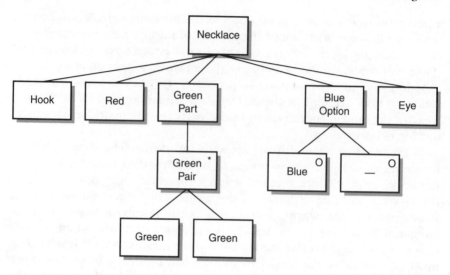

A Necklace begins with a Hook. Then there is a Red bead. Then there are zero or more pairs of Green beads. Then there may, or may not, be a Blue bead. The necklace ends with an Eye.

Elementary components have no parts: Hook, Red, Green, Blue, and Eye are elementary. '—' is the *null* elementary component, representing *nothing*. The type of each non-elementary component is shown by markings on its parts. A selection component has parts marked with an 'o' in their upper right corner: Blue Option is a selection of Blue or *null*. An iteration component has just one part, marked with an '*' in its upper right corner: Green Part is an iteration of Green Pair. A sequence component has unmarked parts: Necklace and Green Pair are sequences.

An important advantage of tree diagrams is that they make it easy to see relationships among components, both within one structure and between different structures. The JSP program design method exploits this property. In JSP program design you begin by describing the structures of the input and output data streams of your program. Then you look for corresponding components. For example, an output stream component corresponds to an input stream component if it is produced from the data contained in that component. You mark the correspondences between the structures, and build the program structure by fitting together corresponding components of the data structures. Here's a little illustration:

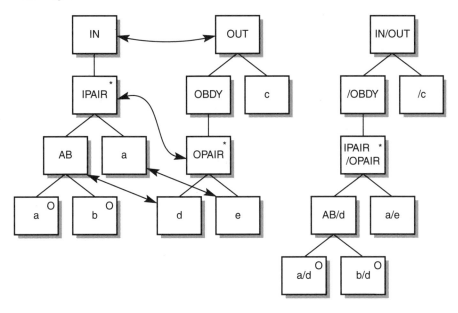

You can see from the diagram how the program structure, IN/OUT, is derived from the structures of two data streams, IN and OUT. The lines with arrows indicate correspondences between components of IN and components of OUT. For example, the component AB of IN corresponds to the elementary component d of OUT. The form of the diagram makes it easy to see these correspondences and their context of structural similarities and relationships.

Finite-state machines offer an alternative to tree diagrams. Our Necklace could have been described by a finite-state machine:

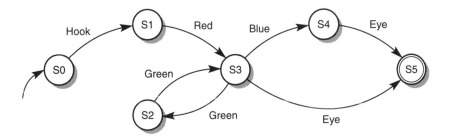

The unlabelled arrow entering S0 shows that S0 is the starting state. The double circle on S5 shows that S5 is a finishing state: that is, the Necklace is complete when S5 has been reached.

Both finite-state machines and tree diagrams describe strings: collections of elements, occurring in some order. Both notations are capable of describing exactly the same strings: in fact, you can derive a tree diagram from any finite-state machine, and vice versa. So why should you ever prefer one notation to the other?

One reason is that there's more to talk about than just the order of elements. A finite-state machine also lets you name states: S0, S1, and so on; states are resting places in the journey from the beginning to the end of the string. Tree diagrams don't let you name states very easily, but they do let you name substrings (which finite-state machines don't): Green Part, Green Pair, Blue Option, and so on. For the necklace, you're more likely to want to talk about substrings than states. Describing the movements of the gear-shift lever of a car, you would be more interested in states.

Both notations are graphical, revealing certain relationships clearly to the eye. But the relationships they reveal are different. The finite-state machine shows directly what can come next at each point: after state S3, a Blue or a Green or an Eye can come next. That's harder to see in the tree diagram. But the tree diagram makes it easier to see relationships among different strings and substrings. That's why they are used in the JSP program design method.

Another reason to choose one of the notations is that some strings are much more easily described in one notation than the other. Here's a description of a journey on the Ruritanian circle line. The line runs in one direction round the circle, continually serving the country's three stations:

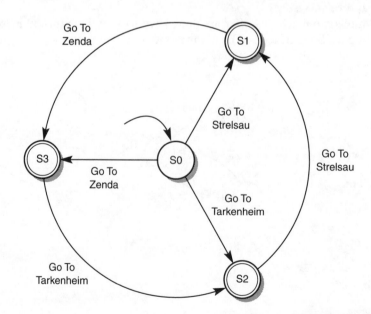

Ruritanian train journeys are not nearly so conveniently described in standard tree diagrams. Try it. On the other hand, look at this tree diagram describing the behaviour of a worried guest at a sumptuous banquet:

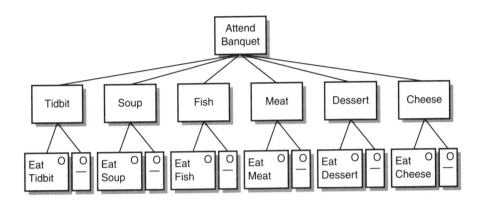

A description of this behaviour would make a very cumbersome finite-state machine (if you don't allow *null* transitions). Cameron, Campbell and Ward discuss and illustrate some of these points in their paper *Comparing Software Development Methods*.

You can extend the tree diagram notation in various ways. For example, you can use it for recursive structures. Here is a Palindromic Necklace. Between the Hook and Eye, it looks the same from both ends:

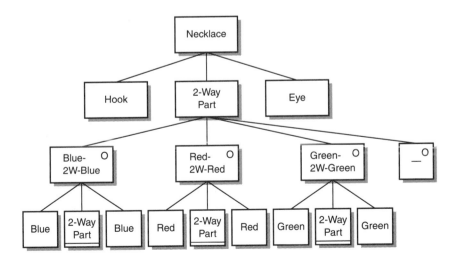

The double line on the three 2-Way Part boxes at the bottom level indicates that they are recursive references to the 2-Way Part component higher up in the tree.

Less ambitiously, you can introduce a variant of the '*' of iteration. '*' denotes *zero* or more occurrences of the iteration's part. Often '+' is used to indicate *one* or more occurrences. You can also introduce special notations for *prefix, suffix,* and *infix* substrings of a string. A prefix may finish early; a suffix may begin late; and an infix may do both. Look at these structures:

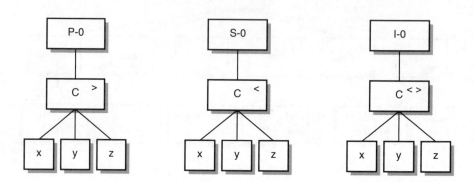

P-0 is a prefix of C. So it can be *null*, or (x), or (x,y), or (x,y,z). S-0 is a suffix. So it can be (x,y,z), or (y,z), or (z), or *null*. I-0 is an infix. So it can be *null*, or (x), or (y), or (z), or (x,y), or (y,z), or (x,y,z).

You can represent a *non-empty* prefix, suffix, or infix like this:

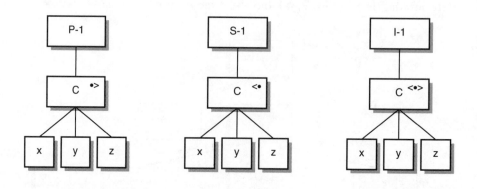

A non-empty substring has at least one element. So P-1 can be x, or (x,y), or (x,y,z), and so on. The Ruritanian train journey is easy now. It's just:

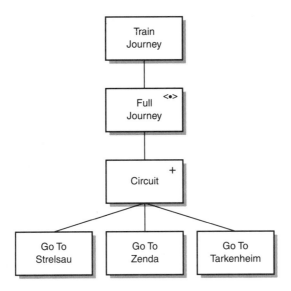

Trip-lets

A trip-let ('*trip*le-*let*ter') is a wooden block shaped so that the shadows it casts in three orthogonal directions are three letters. Hang a 'BGE' trip-let in the north-east corner of a room, and shine three lights from above, from the south and from the west. Shadows of the letters B and G will appear on the walls, and E on the floor. The shadows look like this:

The trip-let is an invention of Douglas Hofstadter: a picture of two trip-lets, GEB and EGB, appears on the cover of the first edition of his book *Gödel, Escher, Bach*. Hofstadter explains that he sees the trip-lets as symbols of 'the unity of Gödel, Escher, and Bach'. He also explains how he fashioned the trip-lets from four-inch redwood cubes.

A trip-let is a tantalizing thing. You can see the shadows it casts; but what does the wooden block itself look like? Can you draw a three-dimensional sketch of a BGE trip-let? Are trip-lets real, or are they impossible objects that can be drawn but not made, like some of M C Escher's creations? If trip-lets are real, can a trip-let be cut as just one piece of wood? If it must be more than one piece, can the pieces be held together without spoiling the shadows? Must the shadows be cast in orthogonal directions, or could there be diagonal trip-lets? Can any three letters form a trip-let, or are some combinations impossible? What about 'III'? Or 'OOO'? Or 'OIO'? Can the Greek letter Ξ be one of the characters? Does the font of the letters matter? Must all the letters in a trip-let be the same height?

The machines we build are like trip-lets. We want to give a machine certain properties: we want it to conform to a number of different descriptions, to cast certain shadows when viewed from one angle and others when viewed from other angles. Somehow these properties, these descriptions, must be fitted together to give the finished artifact – if possible. That, in essence, is software COMPOSITION.

What and How

Everyone agrees that a software development should be structured in some way – that there should be a separation of concerns. That just means that you should not try to think about everything at once. Even a developer working alone should find some way of dividing the development work into separate tasks producing separate descriptions. That's what methods are for. Although people disagree about the merits of different methods, almost everyone agrees on the value of one particular separation of concerns. You should separate the *what* from the *how*.

Those two small words – *what* and *how* – are an obligatory topic of discussion in any software engineering book. Here are some typical statements:

> 'We distinguish the work of analysis (defining "what" the system will do) from the work of design (defining "how" it will do it), recognizing that analysts often do design and designers often do analysis.'

and:

> 'Some analysts prefer to think of the logical–physical distinction as the difference between *what* is accomplished and *how* it is accomplished.'

and:

> 'If one wishes to have something constructed, it is necessary to provide a description of its required properties. The term "specification" can be used for such a description.

'... the specification should describe only the external view of a system (*what* it does) and omit the description of the realization (*how* it works).'

and:

'The gross division of system development into the two stages of specification and implementation is widely accepted. We first determine the "what", and then determine the "how".'

I won't tell you who wrote each of these extracts. I suspect that the authors are not particularly proud of them – at least, I know that's true of my own contribution to the collection. That's why their whole discussion of the *what* and *how* distinction is always short, and there's never an index entry for it. When you read one of these discussions you are left with a dissatisfied feeling that there is a distinction to be made, but it's not clear exactly what the distinction should be. Just labelling it – *what* is labelled with the words 'analysis', 'logical', 'external', 'specification' and 'requirements', while *how* is labelled with 'design', 'physical', 'realization' and 'implementation' – is not very helpful. If the distinction is useful it should be properly explained.

In fact the distinction between *what* and *how* in software development is very simple. A little thought experiment will clarify it. Think about motor cars, and ask yourself the question: *what* does a motor car do? Your answer, of course, must be untainted by any description of *how* it does it. And ask your friends the same question. If your mind has not been warped by prolonged exposure to the confusions of software development methods, your answer is probably something like this: 'A car transports people and their baggage along roads from place to place'; or 'A car moves on any reasonably flat and firm surface wherever its driver directs it to go'.

These are good answers. Why? Because they do not talk directly about the car itself: instead they talk about the domain of its application and use – the real world, the problem domain – where the effects and benefits of the car are to be observed, interpreted, assessed and enjoyed. People, baggage, roads, drivers, and flat and firm surfaces are not parts or properties of cars: they belong to the APPLICATION DOMAIN in which cars are used.

This is hardly a novel idea, and hardly surprising. After all, when you talk about *what* a system does you are really talking about its purpose. And the purpose of an inanimate thing, even a thing so complex as a computer system, must be sought outside it: only human beings, and perhaps animals, have their own internal purposes. The purpose of a computer system is to bring about, or change, or maintain, relationships in its application domain. The purpose of a payroll system is to bring about a relationship between work and pay. And the purpose of an airline reservation system is to bring about a relationship among passengers, tickets, seats, and flights. That's *what* those systems do.

So if you want to talk about *what* a computer system does you must talk about the domain of its application and use, and not about the computer system itself. To talk about *what* a payroll system does you must talk about the employees, their work, their promotions within the organization, their periods of holiday and sickness, their agreed rates of pay, and their tax liabilities and payments. To talk about *what* an airline reservation system does you must talk about the flights, the airports, the passengers, the seats in the planes, the booking agents, the tickets, the boarding passes and the fare schedules. If you're talking about the processes and the data streams inside the computer, or if you're talking about the structure and states of the database, you're not talking about the *what*: you're talking about the *how*.

Workpieces Frame

One important way of using a computer is as a production tool. Just as you can make metal parts by turning them on a lathe, so you can make texts and graphic images by working on them in a computer. The texts or images are the *workpieces* – the products you are working on. You work on them by *requesting* the machine to carry out certain *operations*, such as inserting and deleting words in a text, or repaginating the whole text, or adding a graphic component to a picture, or scaling and rotating a graphic. You want the operations to have certain *properties*. These include their basic effects – for example, inserting a word places it in the text at the point indicated by the cursor. They also include constraints, especially constraints specifying what must not be changed by an operation. For example, scaling a graphic must change the absolute size of the graphic but preserve the orientation and aspect ratio; and inserting a word into a text must not alter the existing words.

Here is the generic problem FRAME DIAGRAM:

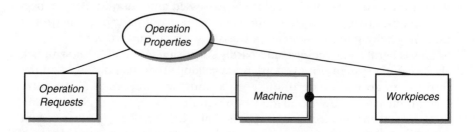

The principal parts of the problem frame are the W*orkpieces*, the *Machine*, which is to be built, the *Operation Requests*, and the *Operation Properties*. The connection between the operation requests and the machine is direct, by SHARED PHENOMENA. The workpieces are entirely contained in the machine: that is, there are no phenomena involving the workpieces that do not also involve the machine. The operation properties relate the operation requests to the workpieces.

The operation requests are a *one-dimensional active dynamic* domain: requests occur in some time ordering without external stimulus. The workpieces form an *inert dynamic* domain: that is, the workpieces can change, but only in response to externally controlled events. Left to their own devices, the workpieces will do nothing. It is also assumed that the individual workpieces are independent of one another: an operation is an operation on just one workpiece.

This problem frame fits closely the problem of constructing a very simple Editor. The CONTEXT DIAGRAM for the problem may be like this:

Because this is a modern editor, the texts it deals with are thought of as Text Objects. The Editor has Users, of course. No doubt there are several users, who work mostly on different text objects and have different working styles and different preferences for layout, for fonts, and for other aspects of the graphic presentation of their objects.

Fitting the frame to the problem is direct and immediate:

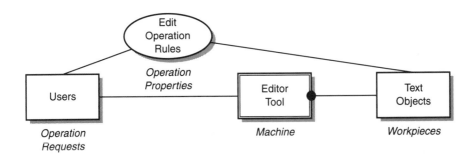

The Text Objects domain is the *Workpieces* principal part; the Editor is, of course, the *Machine*; and the Users domain is the *Operation Requests* principal part. As demanded by the problem frame, the Users domain is dynamic and active, the Text Objects domain is dynamic and inert, and these two domains are indeed related by a requirement. The requirement may be called the Edit Operation Rules: it is the *Operation Properties* principal part.

The *Workpieces* principal part accounts for only some aspects of the Text Objects domain. The Text Objects, perhaps, are interrelated in various ways; but the workpieces in the problem frame are seen as independent of one another, rather than forming a single structured whole. In the same way, the *Operations Requests* principal part accounts for only some aspects of the Users domain. Most importantly, the operation requests are seen simply as a time-ordered sequence of operations, structured only with respect to the individual workpieces they affect. The association of each operation with the user who requests it, and the resulting structures of operations with respect to their originating users, are ignored.

Ignoring these aspects is typical of a problem frame. A problem frame is, by design, the characterization of a certain kind of problem, simplified to the point where you really know how to solve it. To take full account of all the properties of the text objects and users in a realistic editor, you would have to use an additional problem frame. You would be dealing with a MULTI-FRAME PROBLEM.

There are several other complexities that are typically found in association with the workpieces frame. There may be requirements to report on the use of the tool, or to control its use. These complexities would lead you to use other problem frames in conjunction with the workpieces frame: perhaps the Simple IS frame, or the Simple Control frame.

One interesting kind of complexity is particularly closely associated with the workpieces frame. The workpieces must usually be viewed from several different perspectives. A text, for example, must be viewed as a single long character string for purposes of a search-and-replace operation: the paragraphing and the division into lines and pages are not relevant to that operation. But, at the same time, when the search-and-replace succeeds, the character string changes, and the division into lines and pages may change too. So the lines-and-pages view must coexist and cooperate with the single character string view. There's an interesting exploration of this kind of complexity in the paper *Structuring Z Specifications with Views* by Daniel Jackson.

One way to think of the two views is as two distinct instances of the workpieces frame. They have the same *Machine*, and they share many of the same *Operation Requests*. But they have different *Workpieces*, and different *Operation Properties*. The frame instances are pinned together by shared phenomena. The characters in the character string *are* the characters in the lines and pages; and the operation in which a word is deleted *is* an operation in which a line's content and length are changed. That's typical of problem complexity.

BIBLIOGRAPHY

1 Bibliographic notes

1.1 Acknowledgements: Mark Twain

The Mark Twain quotation about his father, which appears in the Acknowledgements, was hard to track down. Enlightenment was eventually provided by Sarah Rosenblum, the kind and energetic reference librarian at the Millburn Public Library in Millburn, New Jersey. The quotation appears in P M Zall's *Mark Twain Laughing*. Zall took it from a *Readers' Digest* article of September 1937, but it may well be apocryphal. Ralph Keyes, in *Nice Guys Finish Seventh*, says that the Library of Congress queried many Twain scholars about its authenticity, but none could confirm it. Many quotations are spuriously attributed to Mark Twain, as to Abraham Lincoln.

1.2 Dekker

A good account of the mutual exclusion problem, and of concurrency in general, is the article by Andrews and Schneider in *Computing Surveys*. The program proposed as Version 4 is discussed in the article *Myths about the mutual exclusion problem*, by G L Peterson.

1.3 Machines

There are some wonderful books about computers and their precursor machines. Three of them are: *The Origins of Digital Computers*, a collection of papers (including some by Charles Babbage and Ada Lovelace) edited by Brian Randell; *A History of Computing in the Twentieth Century*, a collection of specially contributed papers edited by Metropolis, Howlett, and Rota; and *Landmarks in Digital Computing*, a beautifully illustrated little book by Peggy Kidwell and Paul Ceruzzi. All three are strongly recommended.

1.4 Predicate logic

If you want to study predicate logic properly – and to use it for precise reasoning as well as precise description – there are many good sources. Guttenplan's *Introduction to Formal Logic* is an easy way in if you're nervous. *Logic for Computer Science*, by Steve Reeves and Michael Clarke, is more demanding but very good. There is a good presentation in Jim Woodcock and Martin Loomes's book on *Software Engineering*

Mathematics. Carroll Morgan's book *Programming from Specifications* will convince you that you should learn to calculate as easily and accurately in logic as you can in arithmetic.

1.5 Brunel and Stephenson
If you're interested in Brunel and Stephenson, the engineers mentioned in ASPECTS OF SOFTWARE DEVELOPMENT, you could consult the two biographies by L T C Rolt. There is a lot of interesting material about Brunel and his many projects – he built ships as well as railways – in John Pudney's beautifully illustrated book. A more technical assessment of Brunel's works can be found in the book edited by Alfred Pugsley.

1.6 Formal methods
David Gries' book expounds a formal method of program development, based on the ideas advocated by Dijkstra. If you want to learn about formal methods in requirements and specification, you can't do better than to start with Jeannette Wing's paper, *A Specifier's Introduction to Formal Methods*. Two leading formal methods are VDM and Z. VDM is excellently described in Cliff Jones's book *Systematic Software Development Using VDM*. Two accessible books on Z are Ian Hayes' book *Specification Case Studies* and John Wordsworth's *Software Development with Z*. Both VDM and Z are based on the idea of operations on an explicit system state. Another formal method, Larch, is also concerned with operations, but drops the idea of an explicit system state. Larch is described in the paper by Guttag, Horning and Wing in *IEEE Software* of September 1985.

2 References

References are given in order by the first author's surname.

Harold Abelson and Gerald Jay Sussman with Julie Sussman (1985). *Structure and Interpretation of Computer Programs*. MIT Press.

R L Ackoff (1962). *Scientific Method: Optimizing Applied Research Decisions*. Wiley.

Christopher Alexander (1971). *Notes on the Synthesis of Form*. Harvard University Press.

Christopher Alexander, Sora Ishikawa and Murray Silverstein (1977). *A Pattern Language*. Oxford University Press, New York.

Gregory R Andrews and Fred B Schneider (1983). Concepts and notations for concurrent programming. *ACM Computing Surveys*, Vol. 15 No. 1, pp. 3–43, March.

Alfred Jules Ayer (1936). *Language, Truth and Logic*. Victor Gollancz. 2nd edition 1946.

Charles Babbage (1837). *On the Mathematical Powers of the Calculating Engine*. Unpublished manuscript (reprinted in Brian Randell's book).

Robert M Balzer, Neil M Goldman and David S Wile (1982). Operational specification as the basis for prototyping. *ACM Sigsoft SE Notes,* Vol. 7 No. 5, pp. 3–16, December.

Barry W Boehm (1988). A spiral model of software development and enhancement. *IEEE Computer,* Vol. 21 No. 5, pp. 61–72, May.

Niels Bohr (1934). *Atomic Theory and the Description of Nature.* Cambridge University Press.

Frederick P Brooks, Jr (1975). *The Mythical Man-Month: Essays on Software Engineering.* Addison-Wesley.

J R Cameron, A Campbell and P T Ward (1991). Comparing software development methods: example. *Information and Software Technology,* Vol. 33 No. 6, pp. 386–402, July.

Lewis Carroll (1865). *Alice's Adventures in Wonderland.* Macmillan. (Martin Gardner's edition provides a wonderful commentary.)

Lewis Carroll (1871). *Through the Looking-Glass, and What Alice Found There.* Macmillan. (Martin Gardner's edition provides a wonderful commentary.)

Steve Cook and John Daniels (1994). *Designing Object Systems.* Prentice-Hall.

O-J Dahl, E W Dijkstra and C A R Hoare (1972). *Structured Programming.* Academic Press.

Alan M Davis (1990). *Software Requirements Analysis and Specification.* Prentice-Hall International.

Tom DeMarco (1978). *Structured Analysis and System Specification.* Yourdon Press.

Tom DeMarco (1982). *Controlling Software Projects: Management, Measurement and Estimation.* Yourdon Press.

Pierre-Arnoul de Marneffe (1973). *Holon programming: a Survey.* Université de Liège, Service Informatique.

Charles Dickens (1854). *Hard Times.* Bradbury & Evans, London, reprinted 1985 in Penguin Classics, Penguin Books.

E W Dijkstra (1965). Programming considered as a human activity. In *Information Processing 65: Proceedings of IFIP Congress* pp. 213–17, North-Holland.

E W Dijkstra (1968). Cooperating sequential processes. In *Programming Languages,* F Genuys (ed.), Academic Press.

Edsger W Dijkstra (1976). *A Discipline of Programming.* Prentice-Hall.

M C Escher (1972). *The Graphic Work of M C Escher Introduced and Explained by the Artist,* translated from the Dutch by John E Brigham. Pan/Ballantine.

Stuart Faulk, John Brackett, Paul Ward, and James Kirby, Jr (1992). The Core method for real-time requirements. *IEEE Software,* Vol. 9 No. 5, pp. 22–33, September.

Peter Freeman and Anthony I Wasserman (1983). *Tutorial on Software Design Techniques,* 4th Edition. IEEE Computer Society Press.

John Gall (1977). *Systemantics: How Systems Work And Especially How They Fail.* Quadrangle / The New York Times Book Company Inc.

Erich Gamma, Richard Helm, Ralph Johnson, and John Vlissides (1994). *Design Patterns: Elements of Reusable Object-Oriented Software.* Addison-Wesley.

Chris Gane and Trish Sarson (1979). *Structured Systems Analysis: Tools and Techniques.* Prentice-Hall.

Martin Gardner (1970). *The Annotated Alice: Alice's Adventures in Wonderland and Through the Looking-Glass by Lewis Carroll, Illustrated by John Tenniel; With an Introduction and Notes by Martin Gardner.* Penguin Books, revised edition.

Carlo Ghezzi, Mehdi Jayazeri and Dino Mandrioli (1991). *Fundamentals of Software Engineering.* Prentice-Hall International Editions.

David Gries (1981). *The Science of Programming.* Springer-Verlag.

J V Guttag, J J Horning and J M Wing (1985). The Larch family of specification languages. *IEEE Software,* Vol. 2 No. 5, pp. 24–6, September.

Samuel Guttenplan (1986). *The Languages of Logic: An Introduction to Formal Logic.* Basil Blackwell.

Ian Hayes (ed.) (1987). *Specification Case Studies.* Prentice-Hall International.

C A R Hoare (1985). *Communicating Sequential Processes.* Prentice-Hall International.

Douglas R Hofstadter (1979). *Gödel, Escher, Bach: an Eternal Golden Braid.* Basic Books.

W S Humphrey (1989). *Managing the Software Process.* Addison-Wesley.

Daniel Jackson (1992). *Aspect: A Formal Specification Language for Detecting Bugs.* PhD Thesis, MIT.

Daniel Jackson (1994). *Structuring Z Specifications with Views.* Technical Report CMU-CS-94-126, School of Computer Science, Carnegie Mellon University, March.

M A Jackson (1975). *Principles of Program Design.* Academic Press.

M A Jackson (1983). *System Development.* Prentice-Hall International.

M A Jackson (1991). Description is our business. Keynote address at VDM'91. in *Proceedings of VDM'91* Vol. 1, pp. 1–8, LNCS 551, Springer Verlag.

Michael Jackson and Pamela Zave (1993). Domain descriptions. In *Proceedings of Requirements Engineering 93,* pp. 56–64, IEEE CS Press.

Ivar Jacobson, Magnus Christerson, Patrik Jonsson and Gunnar Övergaard (1992). *Object-Oriented Software Engineering: A Use Case Driven Approach.* Addison-Wesley.

Ralph E Johnson (1992). Documenting frameworks using patterns. In *OOPSLA '92 Proceedings, ACM SIGPLAN Notices,* Vol. 27 No. 10, pp. 63–76, October.

Ralph E Johnson (1994). Why a conference on pattern languages? *ACM Sigsoft SE Notes,* Vol. 19 No. 1, pp. 50–2, January.

Cliff Jones (1990). *Systematic Software Development Using VDM.* Prentice-Hall International, 2nd Edition.

William Kent (1978). *Data and Reality: Basic Assumptions in Data Processing Reconsidered*. North-Holland.

Ralph Keyes (1989). *Nice Guys Finish Seventh*. Harper Collins.

Peggy A Kidwell and Paul E Ceruzzi (1994). *Landmarks in Digital Computing*. Smithsonian Institution Press.

Donald E Knuth (1974). Structured programming with **go to** statements. *ACM Computing Surveys*, Vol. 6 No. 4, pp. 261–301, December.

Philip Kraft (1977). *Programmers and Managers: The Routinization of Computer Programming in the United States*. Springer-Verlag.

Nancy G Leveson and Clark S Turner (1993). An investigation of the Therac-25 accidents. *IEEE Computer*, Vol. 26 No. 7, pp. 18–41, July.

T J McCabe (1976). A complexity measure. *IEEE Transactions on Software Engineering*, Vol. 2 No. 4, pp. 308–20, December.

Thomas J McCabe and Charles W Butler (1989). Design complexity measurement and testing. *Communications of the ACM*, Vol. 32 No. 12, pp. 1415–25, December.

Steve McMenamin and John Palmer (1984). *Essential Systems Analysis*. Prentice-Hall.

David A Marca and Clement L McGowan (1988). *SADT: Structured Analysis and Design Technique*. McGraw-Hill.

Peter Mataga and Pamela Zave (1995). Multiparadigm specification of an AT&T switching system. In *Applications of Formal Methods*, Michael G Hinchey and Jonathan P Bowen (eds), Prentice-Hall International.

N Metropolis, J Howlett, Gian-Carlo Rota (eds) (1980). *A History of Computing in the Twentieth Century*. Academic Press.

Bertrand Meyer (1988). *Object-oriented Software Construction*. Prentice-Hall.

Marvin Minsky (1972). *Computation: Finite and Infinite Machines*. Prentice-Hall International.

Carroll Morgan (1990). *Programming from Specifications*. Prentice-Hall.

E Mumford and M Weir (1979). *Computer Systems in Work Design – The ETHICS Method*. Associated Business Press, London.

Peter Naur and Brian Randell (eds) (1969). *Software Engineering: Report on a conference sponsored by the NATO Science Commitee*, Garmisch, Germany, 7–11th October 1968. NATO, January.

Kristen Nygaard (1992). How many choices do we make? How many are difficult? In *Software Development and Reality Construction*, C Floyd *et al.* (eds), Springer-Verlag.

D L Parnas and J Madey (1991). *Functional Documentation for Computer Systems Engineering (Version 2)*. CRL Report 237, McMaster University, Hamilton, Ontario, Canada.

G L Peterson (1981). Myths about the mutual exclusion problem. *Information Processing Letters*, Vol. 12 No. 3, pp. 115–16, June.

G Polya (1957). *How To Solve It*. Princeton University Press, 2nd Edition.

Karl Popper (1959). *The Logic of Scientific Discovery*. Basic Books/ Hutchinson.

John Pudney (1974). *Brunel and his World*. Thames and Hudson.

Alfred Pugsley (ed.) (1980). *The Works of Isambard Kingdom Brunel*. Cambridge University Press.

Brian Randell (ed.) (1975). *The Origins of Digital Computers: Selected Papers*. Springer-Verlag, 2nd edition.

Steve Reeves and Michael Clarke (1990). *Logic for Computer Science*. Addison-Wesley.

L T C Rolt (1988). *George and Robert Stephenson: the Railway Revolution*. Penguin Books.

L T C Rolt (1970). *Isambard Kingdom Brunel*. Penguin Books.

Douglas T Ross (1977). Structured Analysis (SA): A language for communicating ideas. *IEEE Software Engineering Transactions*, Vol. 3 No. 1, pp. 16–37, January. (Reprinted in the Freeman and Wasserman Tutorial.)

James Rumbaugh, Michael Blaha, William Premerlani, Frederick Eddy and William Lorensen (1991). *Object-Oriented Modeling and Design*. Prentice-Hall International.

Bertrand Russell (1905). On denoting. *Mind*, Vol. 14 (reprinted in *Readings in Philosophical Analysis*, Herbert Feigl and Wilfrid Sellars (eds), pp. 103–15; Appleton-Century-Crofts, 1949.)

Bertrand Russell (1959). *My Philosophical Development*. George Allen and Unwin.

Sally Shlaer and Stephen J Mellor (1988). *Object-Oriented Systems Analysis: Modeling the World in Data*. Prentice-Hall.

Sally Shlaer and Stephen J Mellor (1992). *Object Lifecycles: Modeling the World in States*. Prentice-Hall.

W P Stevens, G J Myers, and L L Constantine (1974). Structured design. *IBM Systems Journal*, Vol. 13 No. 2, pp. 115–39. (This paper is reprinted in the Freeman and Wasserman Tutorial.)

William Swartout and Robert Balzer (1982). On the inevitable intertwining of specification and implementation. *Communications of the ACM*, Vol. 25 No. 7, pp. 438–40, July.

John von Neumann and Oskar Morgenstern (1944). *Theory of Games and Economic Behaviour*. Princeton University Press.

Peter Wegner (1987). The object-oriented classification paradigm. In *Research Directions in Object-Oriented Programming*, Bruce Shriver and Peter Wegner (eds), MIT Press.

Gerald M Weinberg (1971). *The Psychology of Computer Programming*. Van Nostrand Reinhold.

Hermann Weyl (1941). *The Mathematical Way of Thinking*. In *Bicentennial Conference*, E. A. Speiser *et al.* (eds), University of Pennsylvania Press.

Dick Whiddett (1987). *Concurrent Programming for Software Engineers*. Ellis-Horwood.

M V Wilkes, D J Wheeler and S Gill (1951). *The Preparation of Programs for an Electronic Digital Computer, with Special Reference to the EDSAC and the use of a Library of Subroutines*. Addison-Wesley.

Jeannette M Wing (1990). A Specifier's Introduction to Formal Methods. *IEEE Software*, Vol. 23 No. 9, pp. 8–24, September.

Jim Woodcock and Martin Loomes (1988). *Software Engineering Mathematics: Formal Methods Demystified*. Pitman.

J B Wordsworth (1992). *Software Development with Z: A Practical Approach to Formal Methods in Software Engineering*. Addison-Wesley.

Edward Yourdon and Larry L Constantine (1979). *Structured Design: Fundamentals of a Discipline of Computer Program and Systems Design*. Prentice-Hall.

Edward Yourdon (1989). *Modern Structured Analysis*. Prentice-Hall International.

P M Zall (ed.) (1985). *Mark Twain Laughing: Humorous Anecdotes about S L Clemens*. University of Tennessee Press.

Pamela Zave and Michael Jackson (1993). Conjunction as composition. *ACM Transactions on Software Engineering and Methodology*, Vol. 2 No. 4, pp. 379–411, October.

INDEX